OCT 3 0 2012

THE CAMBRIDGE COMPANION TO
AMERICAN CRIME

From the execution sermons of the Colonial e
Wire and *The Sopranos*, crime writing has play
culture. Its ability to register fear, desire and an
with a wide audience. These new essays, written ιѳι students as well as readers of
crime fiction, demonstrate the very best in contemporary scholarship and challenge long-established notions of the development of the detective novel. Each
chapter covers a sub-genre, from "true crime" to hard-boiled novels, illustrating
the ways in which "popular" and "high" literary genres influence and shape each
other. With a chronology and guide to further reading, the Companion is a
helpful guide for students of American literature and readers of crime fiction.

A complete list of books in the series is at the back of this book.

OCT 3 0 2012

THE CAMBRIDGE
COMPANION TO
AMERICAN CRIME
FICTION

EDITED BY
CATHERINE ROSS NICKERSON

GLENVIEW PUBLIC LIBRARY
1930 Glenview Road
Glenview, IL 60025

CAMBRIDGE
UNIVERSITY PRESS

CAMBRIDGE UNIVERSITY PRESS
Cambridge, New York, Melbourne, Madrid, Cape Town, Singapore,
São Paulo, Delhi, Dubai, Tokyo

Cambridge University Press
The Edinburgh Building, Cambridge CB2 8RU, UK

Published in the United States of America by Cambridge University Press, New York

www.cambridge.org
Information on this title: www.cambridge.org/9780521199377

© Cambridge University Press 2010

This publication is in copyright. Subject to statutory exception
and to the provisions of relevant collective licensing agreements,
no reproduction of any part may take place without the written
permission of Cambridge University Press.

First published 2010

Printed in the United Kingdom at the University Press, Cambridge

A catalogue record for this publication is available from the British Library

Library of Congress Cataloguing in Publication data
The Cambridge companion to American crime fiction / edited by Catherine Ross Nickerson.
p.   cm. – (Cambridge companions to literature)
ISBN 978-0-521-19937-7 (hardback)   1. Detective and mystery stories, American – History
and criticism.   I. Nickerson, Catherine Ross.   II. Title.
III. Series.
PS374.D4C35   2010
813'.087209–dc22
2010000334

ISBN 978-0-521-19937-7 Hardback
ISBN 978-0-521-13606-8 Paperback

Cambridge University Press has no responsibility for the persistence or
accuracy of URLs for external or third-party internet websites referred to in
this publication, and does not guarantee that any content on such websites is,
or will remain, accurate or appropriate.

CONTENTS

NOTES ON CONTRIBUTORS

LAURA BROWDER is Professor of English at Virginia Commonwealth University. She is the author of *Her Best Shot: Women and Guns in America* (2006), *Slippery Characters: Ethnic Impersonators and American Identities* (2000) and *Rousing the Nation: Radical Culture in Depression America* (1998). She is the writer/co-producer of the documentary *Gone to Texas: The Lives of Forrest Carter* and co-author of *When Janey Comes Marching Home: Portraits of Women Combat Veterans* (2010).

SARA CROSBY is Assistant Professor of American Literature at Ohio State University at Marion, and is a past NEH Fellow at the American Antiquarian Society. She writes and teaches in the areas of early American literature, crime writing, feminist theory and popular culture studies. She is currently at work on a book about female poisoners and popular authorship in nineteenth-century American print culture.

FRED L. GARDAPHE is Professor of English and Director of the John D. Calandra Italian American Institute at Queens College of the City University of New York. He is the author of several books on Italian American culture, including *From Wiseguys to Wise Men: The Gangster and Italian American Masculinities* (2006) and *Leaving Little Italy: Essaying Italian American Culture* (2004).

MARGARET KINSMAN is Senior Lecturer in English Studies at London South Bank University. Her research and teaching interests include women writers and crime and mystery fiction. She is Executive Editor of *Clues: A Journal of Detection*, published by McFarland. She has contributed essays on crime and mystery to publications such as the *St. James Guide to Crime and Mystery Writers*, the *Oxford Companion to Crime and Mystery Writing*, the *Dictionary of Literary Biography*, the *Scribner Mystery and Suspense Writers*, *Diversity and Detective Fiction* (ed. Kathleen Gregory Klein) and *Women Times Three: Writers, Detectives, Readers* (ed. Kathleen Gregory Klein). She is a member of the UK Crime Writers Association, and is currently a member of the judges' panel for the CWA Gold Dagger Award.

SEAN McCANN is Professor of English at Wesleyan University. He is the author of *Gumshoe America: Hard-Boiled Crime Fiction and the Rise and Fall of New Deal Liberalism* (2000) and *A Pinnacle of Feeling: American Literature and Presidential Government* (2008).

EDDY VON MUELLER is a lecturer in Film Studies at Emory University. He is extensively published in the popular press as a media critic and commentator, and has authored scholarly articles on the American film industry in the first decades of the twentieth century, and the work of Akira Kurosawa. He is currently completing a book on the impact of animation aesthetics and technology on contemporary cinema.

ILANA NASH is an assistant professor of English and Gender and Women's Studies at Western Michigan University, where she teaches in the areas of youth literature and popular culture. She is the author of *American Sweethearts: Teenage Girls in Twentieth Century Popular Culture* (2006). She is founder and manager of the Girls' Studies Internet Discussion List.

CATHERINE ROSS NICKERSON is Associate Professor in the Institute of the Liberal Arts at Emory University. She is the author of *The Web of Iniquity: Early Detective Fiction by American Women* (1998) and the editor of a volume of reprinted novels by Anna Katharine Green, *Lost Man's Lane and that Affair Next Door*, and another by Metta Victor, *The Dead Letter and the Figure Eight* (2003).

ANDREW PEPPER is a lecturer in English and American literature at Queen's University Belfast. He is the author of *The Contemporary American Crime Novel: Race, Ethnicity Gender, Class* (2000). He is also writing a series of detective novels set in London in the mid nineteenth century, *The Last Days of Newgate* (2006), *The Revenge of Captain Paine* (2007) and *Kill-Devil and Water* (2008).

STEPHEN RACHMAN is Associate Professor of English at Michigan State University. He is the editor of *The Hasheesh Eater* by Fitz-Hugh Ludlow (2006), a co-author of *Cholera, Chloroform, and the Science of Medicine: A Life of John Snow* (2003), and co-editor of *The American Face of Edgar Allan Poe* (1995). He is at work on a book project titled "Memento Morbi: Lam Qua's Paintings, Peter Parker's Patients." He is president of the Poe Studies Association.

MAUREEN T. REDDY is Professor and Chair of English at Rhode Island College. Her books include *Traces, Codes and Clues: Reading Race in Crime Fiction* (2002), *Crossing the Color Line: Race, Parenting, and Culture* (1994), and *Sisters in Crime: Feminism and the Crime Novel* (1988). Her current research focuses on race in Irish popular culture, including crime fiction.

DAVID SEED is a professor in American Literature at the University of Liverpool and has been elected Fellow of the English Association. He is author of *American*

Science Fiction and the Cold War (2002) and editor of *A Companion to Science Fiction* (2008). He edits the Science Fiction Texts and Studies Series for Liverpool University Press.

SUSAN ELIZABETH SWEENEY is Associate Professor of English at the College of the Holy Cross. She co-edited the collection *Detecting Texts: The Metaphysical Detective Story from Poe to Postmodernism* (1998) and has written many articles on the detective genre, most recently "The Magnifying Glass: Spectacular Distance in Poe's 'The Man of the Crowd' and Beyond" (*Poe Studies*, 2003). She is vice president of the Poe Studies Association, past president of the Vladimir Nabokov Society, and co-editor of the Vladimir Nabokov Electronic Forum.

AMERICAN CRIME FICTION: A CHRONOLOGY

This chronology is not offered as an exhaustive documentation of the history of this large and varied genre. Texts and events listed here correspond to the content of the chapters in this volume.

1674	Samuel Danforth, *The Cry of Sodom Enquired Into*
1789	William Hill Brown, *The Power of Sympathy*
1821	James Fenimore Cooper, *The Spy*
1833	Benjamin Day founds the *New York Sun*
1841	Edgar Allan Poe, "The Murders in the Rue Morgue"
1866	Metta Fuller Victor, *The Dead Letter*
1878	Anna Katharine Green, *The Leavenworth Case*
1908	Mary Roberts Rinehart, *The Circular Staircase*
1910	Thomas Duke, *Celebrated Criminal Cases of America*
1914–18	First World War
1919–33	Prohibition Era
1919	The "Red Summer" of race riots throughout the USA
	Baseball's World Series "Black Sox" scandal
1923	Carroll John Daly, "Three Gun Terry"
1925	Earl Derr Biggers, *The House Without A Key*
1926	Joseph T. Shaw begins editorship of *Black Mask*
1927	S. S. Van Dine, *The Benson Murder Case*
	Franklin Dixon, *The Tower Treasure* (Hardy Boys)

1929	Wall Street Crash, beginning of the Great Depression
	Dashiell Hammett, *Red Harvest*
	Mignon Eberhart, *The Patient in Room 18*
1930	Carolyn Keene, *The Secret of the Old Clock* (Nancy Drew)
	Little Caesar (film)
1934	James M. Cain, *The Postman Always Rings Twice*
	Leslie Ford, *The Strangled Witness*
1938	Mabel Seeley, *The Listening House*
1939	Raymond Chandler, *The Big Sleep*
1941–45	US involvement in the Second World War
1945–c.1990	The Cold War
1945	Lawrence Treat, *V as in Victim*
1949	Patricia Highsmith, *Strangers on a Train*
1950–51	Kefauver Congressional Hearings on organized crime
1952	Jim Thompson, *The Killer Inside Me*
1954	Evan Hunter, *Blackboard Jungle*
1955–68	*Dragnet* (television series)
1956	Ed McBain, *Cop Hater*
1959	Richard Condon, *The Manchurian Candidate*
1961	Construction of the Berlin Wall
1962	US publication of Jorge Luis Borges, *Ficciones*
1964	Amanda Cross, *In the Last Analysis*
1965	Truman Capote, *In Cold Blood*
1969	Mario Puzo, *The Godfather*
1970	Tony Hillerman, *The Blessing Way*
1971–78	*Columbo* (television series)
1972	Ishmael Reed, *Mumbo Jumbo*

1975	Mary Higgins Clark, *Where Are the Children?*
1977	Marcia Muller, *Edwin of the Iron Shoes*
1980	Robert Ludlum, *The Bourne Identity*
	Ann Rule, *The Stranger Beside Me*
1981–87	*Hill Street Blues* (television series)
1982	Sara Paretsky, *Indemnity Only*
1982	Sue Grafton, *A is for Alibi*
1983	Joe McGinniss, *Fatal Vision*
1985	Paul Auster, *City of Glass*
1989	Destruction of the Berlin Wall
1990	Walter Mosley, *Devil in a Blue Dress*
	Patricia Cornwell, *Postmortem*
	Goodfellas (film)
1992	Barbara Neely, *Blanche on the Lam*
1993–2005	*NYPD Blue* (television series)
1995	S. J. Rozan, *China Trade*
1997	Don DeLillo, *Underworld*
1999–2007	*The Sopranos* (television series)
2000	*Memento* (film)
2001	Attacks of September 11
2002–08	*The Wire* (television series)
	The Shield (television series)
2006	Alex Berenson, *The Faithful Spy*

I

CATHERINE ROSS NICKERSON

Introduction: The satisfactions of murder

When coroners and medical examiners decide that the corpse before them is the victim of homicide, they announce their findings with a ringing locution: "by a person or persons unknown." And while the identity of the killer may truly be a cipher in the real world, within the confines of a detective novel, the perpetrator is known to us. He or she is hiding in plain sight among the array of characters in the book. What we do not know is who it is, which other characters are involved, why they did what they did, and how they pulled it off. Resolving all these questions – questions whose answers are somewhere in the text – becomes, for readers, a mental itch that we cannot scratch. We just *have* to know the answers. Looking for clues in a detective story is like searching for a mislaid housekey; we soon become more fixated on the fact that we cannot find it than on the necessity of the thing itself. When the author of a detective story hooks us in this way, our inflamed curiosity drives us to read with fierce attention and all due speed.

The enormous popularity of mystery and crime writing can be attributed largely to the way it structures our reading experience. There is a serious problem (a dead body, a missing child, stolen money) and there is a serious and talented person who takes up its investigation. We readers can be participants in the puzzle-solving, or we can be mere observers, but in any case we know that there will be a solution to the mystery by the end. (Certain postmodern texts play with these expectations, as Susan Elizabeth Sweeney's chapter in this volume points out.) A mystery story makes a very clear pact with its reader: "*If you will endure confusion, obfuscation and false leads, I will reveal all in the end. Read me, and you will be enlightened.*"

So important is this pact that, in the early decades of the twentieth century, several different writers wrote essays outlining the regulations of "fair play" for authors of detective fiction. In one of the most famous, "Twenty Rules for Writing Detective Stories," S. S. Van Dine laid down laws such as, "if the reader, after learning of the explanation for the crime, should reread the book, he [should] see that the solution had, in a sense, been staring him in the face – that all the clues really pointed to the culprit" (rule fifteen). Most of the rules express concern for the reader, especially for wasting a reader's time. Van Dine insists that "no lesser crime than murder will suffice. Three hundred pages is far too much bother for a crime other than murder" (rule seven) and that the death must "never turn out to be an accident or a suicide. To end an odyssey of sleuthing with such an anti-climax is to hoodwink the trusting and kind-hearted reader" (rule eighteen).[1] Disdain for the whole enterprise of detective fiction bubbles up through his witty lines. Dorothy Sayers likewise belittled the genre, famously asserting that detective fiction could never attain "the loftiest levels of literary achievement" since it was merely "literature of escape" and not "literature of expression."[2]

Sayers's assertion was just as famously rebutted by Raymond Chandler in his essay "The Simple Art of Murder." Usually appreciated as a manifesto of the hard-boiled school and a tribute to Dashiell Hammett, the essay also makes the case that good detective fiction can be as rich and significant as any kind of writing. In the hands of a "realist in murder" a detective story *is* a literature of expression, giving "an effect of movement, intrigue, cross-purposes, and the gradual elucidation of character." It is also a literature of social critique, one that exposes "a world where a judge with a cellar full of bootleg liquor can send a man to jail for having a pint in his pocket, where the mayor of your town may have condoned murder as an instrument of money-making." Chandler instructs: "It is not a fragrant world, but it is the world you live in."[3]

One of the most often quoted passages from "The Simple Art of Murder" is this: "Hammett gave murder back to the kind of people that commit it for reasons, not just to provide a corpse; and with the means at hand, not hand-wrought dueling pistols, curare, and tropical fish." Scholars like those in this volume might thank Chandler for doing something similar: giving us reasons, and "the reasons for the reasons," to take detective fiction seriously.[4] It is only fairly recently that the multiple genres of crime writing have been taken up as subjects of academic study; before that, they were entirely in the hands of connoisseurs and collectors, with their endless taxonomies, lists and value judgments. What Chandler opened up was a new way of looking at crime narratives, or rather looking *through* them, as lenses on the culture and history of the United States.

The collection of essays assembled here gives a sense of the long trajectory of crime writing in America, from Sara Crosby's essay on the earliest forms, the execution sermon and the penny press, to Eddy Von Mueller's study of the police procedural and its proliferation on television. The advent of the fictional detective is described in Stephen Rachman's essay on Edgar Allan Poe, and essays by myself, Sean McCann, Margaret Kinsman, and Maureen

T. Reddy trace the development of the detective from the early work of women writers, to the ascendancy of the hard-boiled style, to the increasing diversity of writers over the course of the twentieth century. Andrew Pepper delineates the mutual influences of roman noir and hard-boiled fiction, and Ilana Nash examines the place of crime writing in the youth culture of the early and middle twentieth century. David Seed surveys the spy novel from its origins to the present day, Fred L. Gardaphe outlines the development of a literature and a mythology about the mafia, and Laura Browder traces the origins and history of the true crime book. Finally, Susan Elizabeth Sweeney examines the influence of the mystery story on the shapes and subjects of postmodern fiction.

While there is a great deal of information here about the history of each sub-genre, there is also attention to the way crime fiction documents the social structures and manners of any moment. Crime fiction is famous for its specialized slang and patois; McCann, Pepper, Reddy and Sweeney examine what that language might actually be expressing, as does Mueller in his discussion of "copspeak." We can learn much about the dress and domestic duties of women in the late nineteenth century from the women writers in my essay, but what is ultimately more interesting is what their work reveals about a gap that opened between generations of women during the transition from the Victorian era to the Modern. Crosby shows the link between the rise of a literature about sinners and changing aspirations for national identity.

When we study detective fiction, we can think broadly and deeply about American history and culture. When we are looking at stories about deviants in conflict with the agents of law and order, we are looking straight into the workings of society. The villains and heroes of popular literature are very instructive; they tell us about what we fear and who we would conjure up to contain what threatens us. They reveal our racial and religious prejudices and our gender biases. The literary figure of the detective, for example, developed in response to the emergence of actual detectives in the middle of the nineteenth century, a period shaped by the tumultuous forces of urbanization, social stratification, geographical mobility and changing gender roles. And fictional detectives have continued to develop in response to the needs of their audience, from the erudite consultant to the police we see in early American detective stories to the morally ambiguous hard-boiled private eyes of the middle of the twentieth century to the industrious and unstoppable feminist detectives of the last three decades. Cold War spy thrillers arose, in part, out of misgivings that perhaps the "American century" was not going as well as it might. Gangsters of the early film era expressed a fear of social anomie, while the mafia stories that arose in the 1960s have served as a discourse on our fear of powerful conspiracies and entrenched subcultures, an America dis-united.

Crime fiction also allows us to look straight into the workings of narrative itself. Because mystery stories in general and detective fiction in particular are about gathering up the necessary clues and weaving them into a coherent narrative, they are interesting to consult on questions of narrative authority. All narratives claim to be presenting events as they happened in the past; detective fiction simply raises the stakes for authors, characters and readers. The story that the detective reconstructs and presents has to be wholly convincing and beautifully shaped. American crime fiction has long appealed to "highbrow" writers from many nations and writing traditions; they find the tropes of mystery, conspiracy, fragmentation and investigation to be well matched to the interrogation of received wisdom and surface truths that is at the heart of the modern and postmodern modes. Crime narrative can also be a place to examine the ethics of storytelling, especially in the true crime subgenre.

It is evident from the intellectual energy displayed in the following chapters that these scholars find the study of crime writing to be exciting and richly rewarding. It is my hope that the work presented here will inspire others to explore the satisfactions of the field.

NOTES

A generous grant from the Woodruff Research Fund of Emory College made possible the dedicated editorial assistance of Kira Walsh and Haipeng Zhou. Megan Friddle was also a tireless assistant in the editing process; all three went far above and beyond the call of duty, and I am deeply grateful to them.

1. S. S. Van Dine [pseud. for Willard Huntington Wright], "Twenty Rules for Writing Detective Stories," *American Magazine*, 106 (September, 1928): 129–31. See also Carolyn Wells's textbook, *The Technique of the Mystery Story* (Springfield, MA: Home Correspondence School, 1913).
2. Quoted in Raymond Chandler, "The Simple Art of Murder" (1944; repr. in *The Simple Art of Murder*, New York: Ballantine, 1972), p. 13.
3. *Ibid.*, pp. 19, 20.
4. *Ibid.*, pp. 16, 5.

2

SARA CROSBY

Early American crime writing

In 1851, Herman Melville confessed to possessing a criminal democratic philosophy. He worried, however, that his chosen interlocutor, Nathaniel Hawthorne, might not appreciate this subversive formulation and instead cleave to an "aristocracy of the brain." "So," he wrote Hawthorne, "when you see or hear of my ruthless democracy on all sides, you may possibly feel a touch of a shrink, or something of that sort." Melville presumed that Hawthorne's "shrink" would stem not merely from intellectual or class prejudice but from a *moral* repugnance, admitting, "It is but nature to be shy of a mortal who boldly declares that a thief in jail is as honorable a personage as Gen. George Washington."[1]

Melville should have been nervous. His equation between the thief and the founder promoted a version of America and its literature that many writers in Hawthorne's circle found deeply objectionable. While Melville suggested that a truly "ruthless" America would embrace egalitarianism through sympathy with the criminal, authors, such as Hawthorne's favorite literary critic, Edwin Whipple, attacked popular crime writing precisely because it promoted this leveling identification. He lambasted what he called the "Romance of Rascality" for teaching "the fact that a man excites moral reprobation is his claim upon our sympathy" and that "the old gentlemen of '76 ... fought for an equality in evil as well as good."[2]

The following essay sketches a brief history of this "equality in evil." It tracks popular American crime writing from seventeenth-century execution sermons through eighteenth-century novels and then concludes with the courtroom journalism that electrified the antebellum era. In short, it examines how debates over sympathy for the criminal structured these texts and, ultimately, shaped Melville's "ruthless" American literature.

City of saints

In seventeenth-century England, rogues, fiends and "penitent thieves" or "murderers" appeared in criminal biographies with titles such as *The Witty*

Rogue Arraigned, Condemned, & Executed: Or, the History of That Incomparable Thief Richard Hannam, and *Natures Cruell Step-Dames: Or, Matchless Monsters of the Female Sex* and *A Full and True Account of the Penitence of John Marketman, during His Imprisonment in Chelmsford Gaol for Murthering His Wife*.[3] Instead of such "accounts" and "histories," however, seventeenth-century New England popularized the "execution sermon." These sermons accompanied judicial executions and were usually delivered during the week or hours preceding the solemn event – often with the condemned in the audience. Formally, they did not differ from other Puritan sermons. Using the basic three-part sermon structure, they began with a scriptural extract or "text," then continued with a "doctrine" section explicating that text, and concluded with a lengthy "application" transforming the doctrine into practical behavioral prescriptions. Yet, execution sermons drew notably larger audiences than most other lectures, with many auditors traveling long distances to hear them. In one illustrative instance, the thousands who gathered to hear a sermon delivered by Increase Mather had to flee the meetinghouse when their weight threatened to collapse the gallery. (Mather and his audience immediately reconvened in a sturdier church.)

Encouraged by this popular response, New England's most respected ministers strove to reach even larger audiences by rushing their orations into print. Increase Mather, for example, published his 1675 *The Wicked Man's Portion* so "that it might thus be exposed to the view of the world."[4] Between 1674 and 1825, when the first and last execution sermons appeared, New England printers produced a substantial corpus of such pamphlets – at least 75 distinct sermons distributed in varying combinations with other texts. Furthermore, these sermons often spawned multiple editions and became perennial bestsellers, consumed for years after the unfortunate malefactors that occasioned them had dissolved in the grave.[5]

This consistent and widespread popularity made the printed execution sermon a powerful jeremiad for ministers hoping to enforce the dictum of Massachusetts' first governor, John Winthrop, who had designated New England "a city upon a hill," a community of saints set apart by God to act as a beacon of true religion to a faltering and fallen world.[6] (This principle ultimately translated into an ideology of US exceptionalism, typified by Ralph Waldo Emerson's call in "The Young American" (1844) for a moral nation to rejuvenate and reform the world.) During the 1670s, when the first execution sermons appeared, however, many colony leaders feared that the younger generation's commitment to this "city" was flagging. Therefore, execution sermons typically focused on youthful sins – disobeying parents, hanging out with the wrong crowd and committing sexual "uncleanness" – as the precipitating factors in a sinner's fall into criminality. For instance, the very first execution sermon, Samuel Danforth's *The Cry of Sodom Enquired Into* (1674), was provoked by a teenage boy caught *in flagrante* with a mare. Subsequent discourses written for less explicitly sexual crimes, such as murder and infanticide, also insistently linked youthful disobedience and illicit sexuality with capital crime. In a sermon on the infanticides – such as Elizabeth Emerson and an unnamed African-American woman, for example – Cotton Mather acknowledges that there "may be *Old* Hypocrites" that practice "uncleanness … [b]ut it is the Young people that are this way most Extravagant." He continues emphatically, "If all the *Young People*, that have many ways, *Polluted themselves, from their Youth up*, were turned out of our Assemblies we should have Thin Assemblies Left!"[7]

While this harangue certainly spits fire and brimstone, it also demonstrates one of the more unusual and influential conventions of the execution sermon: sympathy for the condemned. At a time when most popular English genres labeled malefactors as "cruel monsters" or heroic "rogues" beyond ordinary human experience, execution sermons typically humanized their objects. Calvinist theology taught that because of Adam's fall all human beings shared an innate depravity, which only the grace of God kept in check. Ministers thus warned their listeners not to "exult" over the criminal; for he or she had only taken one more short step down the "slippery slope" than they had – an exemplum of their own possible future if God removed His restraining grace. Mather thus reminds his listeners and readers that, while they have not literally committed murder yet, many of them have moved toward it and "*Polluted themselves*" just as the condemned infanticides had.

Despite the execution sermon's reliance upon shared sinfulness, this identification with criminals was nevertheless not exactly the egalitarian connection that Melville felt with thieves, but rather was intended to reaffirm theocratic hierarchy. For instance, Benjamin Colman's sermon for another infanticide, entitled *The Divine Compassions Declar'd and Magnified* (1715), claims that he must open her "Wounds"; for "[t]he greatest Compassion and *Tenderness* to thee at present is, to *awaken in thee … a sense of the Terrors of God, and of His Wrath impending over thee*, unless you find Grace from Him."[8] In other words, "Compassion" should help inspire fear of the authority "impending" over her. Ministers such as Colman often spent months wielding this particular brand of compassion in long pastoral visits with particularly infamous criminals, whom they encouraged to admit their own depravity and their judges' righteousness. Only after the criminals' submission did ministers exert their tender rhetorical efforts on behalf of these repenting "monuments of grace." On the other hand, those who did not submit themselves to ministerial guidance and affirm sacred and temporal authority – rebellious pirates, Irish crypto-Catholic infanticides, etc. – could still be tagged with alienating labels such as "Cockatrice" or at least "Tragical Spectacle."[9]

Much of the execution sermon's energy was thus devoted to walking a line between (1) a sympathy that reinforced the proper moral authorities and reintegrated the community and (2) a sympathy that threatened to encourage rebellion and induce centrifugal disorder. For instance, a century and a half before Melville deconstructed the moral distinction between criminal and saint, Cotton Mather's 1693 *Warnings from the Dead* attacked that mistaken, leveling form of sympathy as the source of crime. He blamed the condemned malefactors' transgressions on "their Observing, *That there is one Event unto all*. Many a man is too *Pore-blind* to see any Difference between *Good* and *Bad* men in the World." In other words, instead of obeying God and his "*Good*" surrogates – parents and ministers – criminals embarked upon their slide into crime by equating sinners and saints. This lack of discrimination between people translated into an inability to make proper moral choices. Foreshadowing nineteenth-century arguments over poisonous popular literature, Mather added: "He Drinks all that he sees before him, and he never ponders, *Is there no poison in it?*" Mather thus positioned his execution sermon as an instrument to correct this mistake and restore the social and moral discrimination necessary to maintain theocracy and a city of the elect.[10]

Unfortunately for New England's ministers, their audiences increasingly displayed the same lack of discrimination that set the criminal at odds with authority, as New Englanders began to join their English brethren in a preference for more secular forms of crime writing. In the seventeenth century, New England's isolation had allowed its theocracy to exert an iron-clad hold on local printers, who could not print the "trash" that characterized the secular crime literature of England. New Englanders could thus only feed their desire for crime writing by turning to ministerial pamphlets. By the end of the seventeenth century, however, the crown reasserted direct political control over the colony, and the burgeoning population grew more secular and socially diverse. This process of "Anglicization" eventually released printers from religious censorship, enabling them to compose cheap gallows literature: one-page "broadsides" that claimed to be authentic autobiographies, final words and confessions, melancholy ballads, and eventually lengthier criminal histories – genres which characterized England's popular street literature.

Puritan ministers, however, did not relinquish their hold on popular crime writing without a fight. As the Enlightenment sped onward, public attention turned to historical and environmental explanations for social phenomena. Ministers responded by adding documentary supplements to their published sermons that, with the exception of the conversion narrative, were often indistinguishable from secular accounts. But the ministers' authority was wedded to the universalizing narrative of sin and punishment or redemption, and this attempt to play to public taste only channeled attention toward individual historical details, further undermining sacred explanations.

This historicizing impulse played into the hands of a group that would dominate the eighteenth century's discourse of crime: novelists. Execution sermons had connected ordinary Americans and criminals by a vibrating chord of sympathy, but when ministerial influence declined, theological narratives largely ceded control of this connection to imaginative writing. The "wrong" kind of sympathy increasingly prevailed, and novels egged it on – or at least reopened the question of how bad it really was to sympathize with the "bad."

Sympathy for the devil

After the decline of the ministerial hegemony, American crime writing experienced a renaissance of the rogue. Eighteenth-century audiences devoured autobiographies of rakes, thieves and confidence men, such as Stephen Burroughs and Levi Ames, or of righteous rebels wronged by unrighteous legal authority, such as Whiting Sweeting. Americans who enjoyed these narratives returned to an old English tradition of class resistance mediated by vicarious pleasure in the adventures of outlaws, which allowed the lower orders to mock their betters and let off steam but did not radically alter forms of power. In other words, the rogue played with social order. This play seemed more attractive to English than American novelists, however, and, while rather benign picaros featured in important early texts like Royall Tyler's *Algerine Captive* (1797) or Hugh Henry Brackenridge's *Modern Chivalry* (1792–1805), the early republic's most significant novelists were mesmerized by another criminal type: the fiend.

Although critics generally sort America's first novels into sentimental or gothic categories, authors such as William Hill Brown, Susanna Rowson, Hannah Webster Foster and Charles Brockden Brown crossed these standard literary boundaries to construct "true crime" narratives focused on actual rapes, seductions and bloody mass murders.[11] These novelists found crime writing irresistible because they aspired to be "moral painters" inculcating virtue in the new nation.[12] They found the fiend even more irresistible because the virtue these novelists aspired to teach depended upon sympathy as its first principle, and the fiend threatened that foundation. Unlike the rogue, the fiend did not play with social order but destroyed it – ripping apart affective bonds by slaughtering friends, lovers and family. The fiend's radical evil defied explanation, and by inhabiting a sphere beyond human understanding it also passed beyond the reach of human sympathy.

Influenced by the work of the French philosopher Michel Foucault, scholars have generally explained this American obsession with fiends as part of a larger cultural transition from a sympathetic seventeenth-century model of the criminal to an alienating eighteenth- and nineteenth-century paradigm, which cast the criminal as radically other and mysterious.[13] But this movement did not go unopposed, and the early republic's "true crime" novels sought to protect a liberal moral system by worrying the fiend into palatable forms that could fit within a framework of sympathy, such as the misunderstood victim or the mentally ill "lunatic." Their efforts at revision centered on two fiends in particular: the infanticide and the familicide.

Close to fifty years before these novelists started writing, colonial society had begun redefining the woman who killed her infant as a victim rather than a fiendish "unnaturall mother." In the 1730s, New England juries suddenly began refusing to convict women suspected of infanticide. This abrupt move departed from the seventeenth century's draconian legislation, which had used the infanticide to enforce patriarchal authority over women and the sexually undisciplined lower orders. English statute law had defined infanticide as a crime that only "lewd women," that is, unmarried and "unclean" women, could commit, and further linked it to witchcraft by making it the only other capital offense that assumed the defendant's guilt. Not surprisingly, the percentage of alleged infanticides convicted and executed in England and its colonies far exceeded the percentages condemned for other forms of homicide. The New England public's actions better than reversed this disproportion.[14]

New England's ministers reacted to this shift with trepidation. The infanticide's connection to youthful and lower-class crimes of disobedience had made this criminal a favored and effective subject for the execution sermon's jeremiad. Although modern scholars have connected the dramatic turnaround in the conviction rates of accused infanticides to various social movements, ministers thought they knew the source of the trouble: sympathy – and not the right kind of sympathy for the "Good" but the wrong kind of sympathy for the "Bad." In the seventeenth century, divines such as Cotton Mather had to work against their congregation's initial antipathy for the "unclean" woman in order to enforce a chastising identification. By 1738, however, the Reverend Eliphalet Adams harangued his audience about their overly enthusiastic empathy with the convicted infanticide, Katherine Garret, and begged them not to forcibly "stay" her execution. He fretted that criminals' "moving Expressions," "affecting Language" and embodied emotion ("They faint, They swoon away …") had tempted legal officials and the general public to "neglect justice." That justice, he argued, now required that the public view infanticides as aliens "who have forfeited all Claim to be suffered any longer among men." Yet the genie of sympathy was out of the bottle, and, instead of ousting these fiends, "The Spectators are struck with concern; The Judges are melted into tears."[15]

Sympathy for rogues was a long English tradition, but tears for a fiend that earlier English crime pamphlets would have labeled a "Matchless Monster" signaled a significant cultural shift. Adams's description of his auditors' weepy response to Garret's tears, faints and "affecting Language" identifies this shift with the advent of a sentimental literary paradigm. What became known as "sensibility" linked virtue to a capacity for sympathetic identification with suffering underdogs. Novels perpetuated this new structure of feeling, and, in the mid to late eighteenth century, one subgenre, in particular, helped it along: the phenomenally popular "novel of seduction." While seventeenth-century authorities had singled out the "lewd" or "unclean" woman as almost inevitably a monstrous infanticide, seduction novels generally followed a plot line that radically revised this conclusion and generated sympathy for the fallen: A virtuous maiden is lured away from home by a rake, he rapes or seduces her, she dies in a state of saintly contrition, often after giving birth to "a monument of [her] guilt," the rake repents and spends the remainder of his life "weep[ing] over the grave" he has filled, and the community joins together in shedding tears of sympathy for the departed angel.[16]

The "lewd" or "unclean" woman had thus metamorphosed into a saint, and a narrative that clerical authorities claimed led down a slippery slope into infanticide had now been reconfigured as a tale of victimized virtue. In fact, seduction novels taught that sympathy with the "lewd" woman, now only "fallen" like all humanity, proved and even produced virtuous sensibility. As the epigraph to chapter twenty of Rowson's bestselling *Charlotte Temple* (1794) asserts, "Virtue never appears so amiable as when reaching forth her hand to raise a fallen sister." Later in that chapter the husband of such a virtuous woman supports the "sensibility" that urges her to reach forth that hand, saying, "Let prudes and fools censure if they dare, and blame a sensibility they never felt; I will exultingly tell them that the heart that is truly virtuous is ever inclined to pity and forgive the errors of its fellow-creatures."[17] In the aptly named *The Power of Sympathy* (1789), William Hill Brown goes even further, arguing that sympathy for the fallen woman does not merely urge on the virtuous but actually reforms the vicious. In the moment of his return to morality, the novel's young seducer declares: "Hail sensibility! Ye eloquent *tears of beauty*! ... it was these that corrected my faults."[18] By thus metamorphosing the infanticide into a victim subject to sympathy, seduction narratives transform a challenge to republican virtue into its guarantee.

Charles Brockden Brown performed a similar alchemy with the familicide. After the American Revolution, reactionary elements held up the man who exterminated his family as proof that the free-thinking principles unleashed by republicanism would also release radical evil that could not be controlled by a moral system based on sympathy. Brown refuted this argument by creating an alternative explanation for this seemingly inexplicable fiend: he becomes the victim of errors or mental illness. This theory encouraged Brown's audience to rethink its notions about these "monsters" so that they too could be included in the circle of sympathy. Brown's most famous novel, *Wieland* (1798), thus fictionalizes and revises the infamous case of William Beadle, who, in 1782, dispatched his sleeping wife and four children with an ax and carving knife and then shoved a pistol into each of his ears and fired. Apparently, Beadle had invested a little too heavily in the Revolution – both its deflating currency and its deistical free-thinking – until, according to the pamphlet account penned by Stephen Mix Mitchell, the bankrupt speculator began to receive "sundry intimations, he really thought from God himself."[19]

By contrast to *Wieland*, Mitchell's pamphlet maintains a distant tone and spares almost no sympathy for Beadle. On the contrary, it lingers over the murders' gory details and limits its perspective to witnesses discovering or later touring the scene, who express empathy for the victims alone. According to Mitchell, "sorrow and tender pity for the lady and her innocent babes ... melted every heart ... [T]he very inmost souls of the beholders were wounded at the sight." This response demonstrates the community's virtuous sensibility, but such virtue has a distinct limit, however, because those sympathetic "inmost souls" are also "torn by contending passions." Sympathy for the victims was "succeeded by furious indignation against the author of the affecting spectacle" and in a "frantic rage" the neighbors toss Beadle into a shallow grave like "the carcase of a beast." Mitchell joins them in demonizing the "unnatural murderer" and substantiates his unsympathetic assessment by using Beadle's own journals against him. He includes extracts from a sermon that selectively quotes the journals – affirming passages where Beadle describes himself as "small and mean" and then analyzing his attempts at free thought as evidence of his cold calculation and unreasonably "high opinion of his intellectual abilities." Ultimately, the pamphlet agrees with the minister and attributes Beadle's actions to the "[s]hocking effects of pride and false notions about religion."[20] In other words, the pamphlet places blame solely on Beadle and his sinful arrogance bred by liberty.

Brown, on the other hand, refutes Mitchell's illiberal conclusion by revising the pamphlet narrative in a way that builds sympathy for Wieland/Beadle and throws into question the morality of community "rage." The novel acknowledges that Wieland's bloody deed was "inhuman ... [and] worthy of savages trained to murder, and exulting in agonies," but it does not let us forget his humanity in the inhumanity of his action. Succeeding lines describe him as an enlightened man of sensibility, a perfect citizen: "[t]hat man of gentle virtues and invincible benignity! placable and mild – an idolator of peace!" While the pamphlet only uses Beadle's journals to sustain its ugly portrait of him, the novel reproduces Wieland's own detailed and wrenching narrative of the murders in order to shed light on his thought processes and enable understanding. Furthermore, while the viewpoint of an outraged crowd governs the pamphlet, the novel presents Wieland through the eyes of his devoted sister, Clara. Through her more empathetic judgment, the audience can view her brother as a "victim" and "sufferer" led to his crimes by "errors," which could have been avoided "[i]f Wieland had framed juster notions of moral duty, and of divine attributes; or if I had been gifted with ordinary equanimity or foresight."[21] With that last conditional phrase, Clara is not reductively blaming the victim. Rather, she is extending responsibility out into the community. She thus refuses to exorcise criminality by attaching it solely to a fiend who can be simply abused and tossed aside like "the carcase of a beast." In the early republican crime novel, apparently even the devil deserved sympathy.

Later American writers, such as Edgar Allan Poe and Herman Melville, would continue to puzzle over the limits of sympathy for the fiend. But, unlike Brown and his fellow early republican novelists, antebellum writers wove their narratives under the influence of powerful new legal and journalistic approaches to crime.

Republic of sinners . . . and jurors

Charles Brockden Brown initially trained for the law but abandoned it because he believed that writing fiction gave him greater scope to delve honestly into moral questions. During the next century, however, lawyers would challenge this novelistic freedom as the legal profession orchestrated a closer fusion of law and literature. This synthesis created "legal romanticism," a discourse which inserted sentimental literary tropes into legal argumentation and drew legal discourse into popular crime literature.[22] The 1830s thus witnessed American printers conducting a brisk business in trial transcripts and sensational "true crime" pamphlets (some of which were fake), while newspapers invented court reporters and filled their front pages with long stretches of courtroom wranglings.

This juridical transition in public taste was driven not only by the increasing power of the legal profession but also by the advent of a modern mass media, particularly the rise of modern crime reporting. Before the 1830s, most newspapers catered to a small elite readership interested in shipping, business and some political news, but in 1833 Benjamin Day started the first major "penny paper," the *Sun*, followed in 1835 by his rival James Gordon Bennett, who published the *Herald*. These cheap dailies billed themselves as the papers for the "common man," and the common man apparently wanted sex and death – and lots of it. Bennett especially pioneered tactics of modern crime reporting: he was credited with conducting and printing the first interview (with an infamous Madame) and with inventing the media sensation by keeping a single crime on the front page and thus in public consciousness for weeks, months and even years at a time.[23]

This obsession with lurid crimes may sound very familiar and modern, but the sensational pamphlets, trial transcripts and newspaper stories of the early antebellum era differed in one important respect from crime publications in our own day: they were produced in a world that had not quite professionalized crime. The detective, the police officer, the forensic pathologist existed mainly as amateurs, and their often bumbling enthusiasm rightfully raised "reasonable doubt" in the public mind. Furthermore, because the rise of crime reporting accompanied the "democratization" of newspapers, it created an atmosphere in which citizens exercised their power through an active engagement with crime. In effect, the prominence of the adversarial legal system along with crime journalism aimed at the masses made the decades before the Civil War the great era of the juror, in which the public positioned itself as a kind of mass jury inquiring into and judging the facts of alleged crimes for themselves.[24]

At the same time, the "romanticism" in legal romanticism guaranteed that sympathy would play a significant role in these judgments, and, as a result, literary representations of "true crime" continued to stretch sympathy's limits. Whereas eighteenth-century novels had evoked empathy for criminals victimized by patriarchal power, the popular "city mystery" novels and pamphlets of the 1840s and 1850s tempted their readers to fall just a little in love with the sadistic monsters, who tortured and murdered the elite agents of that power. Antebellum crime novelists, such as George Lippard, George Thompson and Ned Buntline, reconfigured the fiend as both the unfathomable "alien" recognized by Foucauldian critics and as a hero fighting for "the Democracy." They pushed the criminal to the farthest margins of humanity but invited the American public to come along. As the fiend's radical evil enabled its audiences to imagine radical liberty, crime writing traced the ragged edge of the saintly republic's "ruthless democracy."

NOTES

1. Melville to Hawthorne, 1? June 1851, in *Moby Dick*, ed. Harrison Hayford and Hershel Parker (New York: Norton, 1967), pp. 556–7.

2. E. P. Whipple, "Romance of Rascality," *Essays and Reviews*, vol. II (Boston: Houghton Mifflin, 1850), pp. 76–7; this introduction also draws on David Reynolds, *Beneath the American Renaissance: The Subversive Imagination in the Age of Emerson and Melville* (Cambridge, MA: Harvard University Press, 1988).

3. Lincoln Faller, *Turned to Account: The Forms and Functions of Criminal Biography in Late Seventeenth- and Early Eighteenth-Century England* (Cambridge University Press, 1987), pp. 290, 294, 301.

4. Increase Mather, *The Wicked Man's Portion, or a Sermon* (Boston: John Foster, 1675), front matter.

5. Daniel Cohen, *Pillars of Salt, Monuments of Grace: New England Crime Literature and the Origins of American Popular Culture, 1674–1860* (New York: Oxford University Press, 1993), p. 10. Cohen's valuable work has greatly informed this discussion of execution sermons.

6. John Winthrop, *A Model of Christian Charity* (1630).

7. Cotton Mather, *Warnings from the Dead, or Solemn Admonitions unto All People but especially unto Young Persons to Beware of Such Evils as Would Bring Them unto the Dead* (Boston: Bartholomew Green, 1693), pp. 58–9.

8. Benjamin Colman, *The Divine Compassions Declar'd and Magnified: To Engage and Encourage the Greatest Sinners unto a Speedy and Earnest Repentance* (Boston: T. Fleet, 1715), pp. 45–6.

9. Cotton Mather, *The Vial Poured out upon the Sea. A Remarkable Relation of Certain Pirates Brought unto a Tragical and Untimely End* (Boston: T. Fleet, 1726), p. 1; and *A Sorrowful Spectacle. In Two Sermons, Occasioned by a Just Sentence of Death, on a Miserable Woman, for the Murder of a Spurious Offspring* (Boston: T. Fleet, 1715), p. iv.

10. Mather, *Warnings from the Dead*, pp. 2, 9.

11. See Cathy Davidson, *Revolution and the Word: The Rise of the Novel in America* (New York: Oxford University Press, 1986).

12. Charles Brockden Brown, *Wieland or The Transformation, An American Tale* (New York: Penguin, 1991), p. 4; see also the prefaces to William Hill Brown, *The Power of Sympathy* (New York: Penguin, 1996), p. 7, and Susanna Rowson, *Charlotte Temple* (New York: Oxford University Press, 1986), pp. 5–6.

13. See especially Karen Halttunen, *Murder Most Foul: The Killer and the American Gothic Imagination* (Cambridge, MA: Harvard University Press, 1998), and the extensive introduction by Daniel Williams to his *Pillars of Salt: An Anthology of Early American Criminal Narratives* (Madison, WI: Madison House, 1993).

14. Peter Hoffer and N. E. H. Hull, *Murdering Mothers: Infanticide in England and New England, 1558–1803* (New York University Press, 1981), pp. 20, 44, 77.

15. Eliphalet Adams, *A Sermon Preached on the Occasion of the Execution of Katherine Garret, an Indian-Servant* (New London: T. Green, 1738), p. 14.

16. Hannah Webster Foster, *The Coquette* (New York: Oxford University Press, 1986), p. 146, and Rowson, *Charlotte Temple*, p. 118.

17. Rowson, *Charlotte Temple*, pp. 71, 75.

18. Hill Brown, *Sympathy*, p. 70.

19. Stephen Mix Mitchell, *A Narrative of the Life of William Beadle* (Windsor, VT: Alden Spooner, 1795), p. 13. This text is the latest English reprint of the Mitchell

pamphlet, which first appeared in 1783. A German-language edition was printed in 1796.

20. *Ibid.*, pp. 7–9, 23.
21. Brockden Brown, *Wieland*, pp. 198, 278.
22. Cohen, *Pillars*, pp. 191–2.
23. John D. Stevens, *Sensationalism and the New York Press* (New York: Columbia University Press, 1991), pp. 48–9, 41.
24. For how "new legal narratives effectively treated readers as jurors," see Halttunen, *Murder*, pp. 116–17.

3

STEPHEN RACHMAN

Poe and the origins of detective fiction

"These tales of ratiocination," Edgar Allan Poe explained to a correspondent in 1846, "owe most of their popularity to being something in a new key."[1] Poe was referring to his three stories written in the early to mid 1840s featuring C. Auguste Dupin ("The Murders in the Rue Morgue," "The Mystery of Marie Rogêt" and "The Purloined Letter"). The "new key" was, of course, what we have come to call "detective fiction," and Poe, as the form's first truly modern exponent, was aware that his stories were enjoying an unprecedented popularity with the reading public. In "The Murders in the Rue Morgue," Poe introduced readers to the Parisian polymath, Dupin. He was a man for whom ordinary men "wore windows in their bosoms."[2] Such are Dupin's powers that not only can he seemingly read the narrator's thoughts at the very instant he is thinking them, but he can explain the whole chain of reasoning that had led to his thoughts merely by observing the sequence of expressions on his face. Coming across a case in the newspaper – the grisly killings of Madame L'Espanaye and her daughter in their apparently locked lodgings in the Rue Morgue – Dupin displays his analytical prowess, unraveling the seemingly insoluble mystery.

Even in outline, readers will recognize many of the features of the detective genre in its classic or analytic form: the metropolitan setting, the violent crime scene in an apparently locked room, the vain, befuddled law enforcement official, the wronged suspect, the confession, the cleverly convoluted solution (in which murder turns out not to be murder) with an exotic perpetrator (razor-wielding "Orang-Outang"), the class antagonisms implicit in the genteel detective's apprehension of the violent working-class criminal, and the masculine camaraderie of a supercilious gentleman mastermind and his credulous companion/narrator (by the third tale, pipe-smoking would make its appearance). In these three stories, Poe offered, in Terence Whalen's estimation, "a genre in miniature."[3] Poe had given the form its initial shape, created its first great detective, knew that the tales were popular and yet, after 1845, in the four years left in his brief life, wrote no more of Dupin.

In fact, Poe deprecated the attention paid to the Dupin stories at the expense of other aspects of his work. "I do not mean to say that they are not ingenious," he explained,

> but people think them more ingenious than they are – on account of their method and *air* of method. In the "Murders in the Rue Morgue," for instance, where is the ingenuity of unravelling a web which you yourself (the author) have woven for the express purpose of unravelling? The reader is made to confound the ingenuity of the supposititious Dupin with that of the writer of the story.[4]

Poe privately asserted that the cleverness of these stories was deceptive and overrated.[5] From the author's point of view, Poe suggests that detective fiction plots entail a schematic operation in which a mystery is not properly explored, but revealed after being systematically concealed. Poe suggests that writing detective fiction is not an act of imaginative expression, explanation, clarification, or, perhaps, even genuine analysis, but a program of deception that is eventually explained. Small wonder Poe admitted to a degree of disillusionment with the form. Like a revealed magic trick, the act of writing detective fiction perforce involves a necessary stripping of illusions. From the mythical ball of yarn (a clew) that Ariadne gave Theseus to help him find his way out of the Minotaur's labyrinth, the clues of detective fiction have come down to us as things that point the way to a solution. Poe describes the act of composing a mystery as one of coiling and uncoiling a narrative thread, a concept of classical antiquity presented in a modern urban guise. A structural irony that Poe bequeathed to the genre consists of his avowed commitment to analysis and analytic processes, while creating narratives that at best, from the writer's point of view, seldom offer opportunity for genuine analytical discovery, and at worst present spurious reasoning, especially if Dupin was nothing more than a mere cipher designed to mystify the reader. One can see why an author might dismiss these tales as little more than an old tune played in a new key.

But whatever reservations Poe may have had about the literary merits of detective fiction from the author's point of view, he recognized that he had created something that struck many readers of the 1840s as not only fresh and new but central to modern experience. Philip Pendleton Cooke, the correspondent to whom Poe dismissed the supposititious Dupin, indicated that he found "those stories of criminal detection" to be "certainly as interesting as any ever written, and that he shared them with a local "prosecuting attorney" who declared them "miraculous."[6]

While Poe was aware of the commercial viability of these tales of ratiocination, he did not see himself as he would come to be seen in the twentieth century as the founder of a popular literary genre. Rather, the Dupin tales were novelties, keyed to the texture and tone of the modern world. In "The Murders in the Rue Morgue," Poe signals this by setting his detective fiction in Paris, the epitome of the nineteenth-century modern metropolis. With London, Paris was one of the first to establish a police force, and Poe connects his tales to the rise of urban life, which began to require institutions of policing and surveillance. By making the prefect of police a foil for the great detective, Poe connects the detective's plight with the growing sense that these police forces, generally manned by working-class men, were perceived as inadequate to the mysteries of the great city; and by focusing on the urban crime story as reported in the metropolitan daily newspaper, Poe connects his tale to the mass media by which vast readerships would come to follow crime stories with unprecedented avidity.

The central action of the first detective story consists primarily, as John Irwin has remarked, of reading "newspaper accounts of the crime and talking with the Prefect of police and the narrator in the privacy of his apartment."[7] "Not long after this," begins a relevant passage,

> we were looking over an evening edition of the *Gazette des Tribunaux*, when the following paragraphs arrested our attention.
>
> "EXTRAORDINARY MURDERS. – This morning, about three o'clock, the inhabitants of the Quartier St. Roch were roused from sleep by a succession of terrific shrieks, issuing, apparently, from the fourth story of a house in the Rue Morgue, known to be in the sole occupancy of one Madame L'Espanaye, and her daughter, Mademoiselle Camille L'Espanaye."[8]

Detective fiction propels itself forward as a critique of the representation of actuality as presented in the city dailies. The reader encounters the L'Espanayes with the same depersonalized avidity familiar to all tabloid junkies. We learn of them solely as victims and bodies, objectified as any chalk outline.

If detective fiction is often accused of gleefully producing corpses for the callous delectation of its readership then it acquired this from the newspaper by way of Poe. The *Gazette*'s extraordinary headline implies that ordinary murder is commonplace in the metropolis and not worthy of full caps. When the investigation of the Rue Morgue crime scene yields more interesting details it provokes in Dupin a greater empathy for the problem and the killer, not the victims. The paper's representation of the crime is found wanting. "The *Gazette*," Dupin explains to his interlocutor,

> has not entered, I fear, into the unusual horror of the thing ... It appears to me that this mystery is considered insoluble, for the very reason which should cause it to be regarded as easy of solution – I mean for the *outré* character of its features.[9]

It is as if the newspaper's investment in normalcy and the quotidian prevents it from being able to fully or properly represent the outré and unusual aspects of the case, and as the detective finds himself competing with the prefect for the proper solution, detective fiction finds itself in competition with the newspapers in its depiction of reality and its ability to isolate the case's salient features. Indeed, Dupin will further his solution of the case by luring the sailor through an advertisement in "a paper devoted to the shipping interest, and much sought by sailors";[10] as master-reader the detective can harness the power of the press for his own ends. If the urban newspaper helped to constitute "imagined communities" of the nineteenth century, as Benedict Anderson described national consciousness, then the detective tale was a second-order operation within that community, a viral form in which readers recognized a new fictive expression of a modern social order.

Anderson argues that a citizen's ability to apprehend the world required, in part, daily newspapers as a technical means for "re-presenting" the broader imagined community "that is the nation" or, in terms of detective fiction, the metropolis.[11] For Anderson, the newspaper created a "mass ceremony: the almost precisely simultaneous consumption ('imagining') of the newspaper-as-fiction."[12] Reading the newspaper became a way to participate with fellow readers: "the newspaper reader, observing exact replicas of his own paper being consumed ... is continually reassured the imagined world is visibly rooted in everyday life."[13] In Poe's usage, the newspaper confirms this hold on imagined reality, or reality-fictions, as it were, by allowing the detective, while seated in his armchair, to trace and solve actual crime by way of its representation in the daily papers. The detective's task becomes one of exposing, as Dupin does in the instance of the *Gazette*, the relative accuracy or inaccuracy of any given newspaper account even as it binds him more deeply to the newspaper as a means of imagining the city and solving its problems.

The central problem that detective fictions take up over and over again as their special province, that of interpreting crime, comes to the fictional Dupin in the same way that they typically reached actual ordinary readers in the nineteenth century – through the city newspaper. In this way, Poe's detective becomes the master paper-reader who, through the use of dispassionate logic and calculation, fathoms what is inscrutable or unconnected. Through the use of the newspaper as the medium of criminal representation, detective fiction situated itself from the outset in a complex negotiation between worlds of facts and worlds of fictions. "Ripped from the headlines," runs the slogan of *Law & Order*, one of television's long-running crime shows. Since Poe, detective stories have sought to explore the interpenetration of reality and fiction surrounding the discourse of crime. To solve crime, detective fiction teaches us, one must imagine crime in all its psychological and forensic complexity, activating by necessity our deepest fantasies and fears. In its use of the newspaper, detective fiction yields more than evidence of imagined communities; it indicates that our sense of community is bound up in a web of potentially real or potentially imaginary scenarios.

One of the apparent paradoxes of literary history is how Poe, an author whose fiction is, as J. Gerald Kennedy has observed, "preponderantly devoted to terror, madness, disease, death and revivification,"[14] came to invent a form committed to reason and solution. Part of the answer lies in Poe's abiding themes of terror, haunting and the irrational, and his skepticism about all forms of certainty. Prior to "The Murders in the Rue Morgue" Poe had written what Walter Benjamin labeled "an x-ray picture of a detective story"[15] entitled "The Man of the Crowd." It recounts an incident in which a *flâneur* who fancies himself an expert in Dupin's specialty, the reading of faces and social types, pursues an old man through the labyrinthine streets of London for twenty-four hours, convinced that he is "the type and genius of deep crime," only to learn nothing specific.[16] Richard Wilbur has argued that Dupin's commitment to rationality is counter-balanced by his ability to mirror or empathize with the doubled, often irrational, mentalities of his criminal antagonists.[17] Indeed, the Dupin stories thematically reproduce this opposition using cool analysis as they deal with brutal murders in the case of the first two, and, in "The Purloined Letter," a dangerous and exacting kind of revenge.

When the detective story first emerged, its generic lineaments were unclear. Poe originally conceived of the stories as "tales of ratiocination," emphasizing the delineation of a chain of logical reasoning and analysis. According to the *Oxford English Dictionary*, "detective" first appeared as an adjective in 1843 in reference to "detective police," two years after the original publication of "Rue Morgue," the noun form appearing in 1856. Dupin is Poe's vehicle for tracing a train of thought and the tale a way to analyze, as he put in the prefatory comments that open "The Murders in the Rue Morgue," "that moral activity which *disentangles*."[18] It was an interest in the ratiocinative process, not the character of the detective *per se*, that led Poe to his innovation and led him away from it as well. He left it to others, notably Sir Arthur Conan Doyle, to explore the possibilities of the character of the detective, of which his deductive methods would be but one facet. When Watson, upon learning of Holmes's deductive method, remarks that he reminds him of Dupin, Doyle has Sherlock Holmes comment in *A Study in Scarlet*, "'Now, in my opinion, Dupin was a very inferior fellow ... He had some analytical genius, no doubt; but he was by no means such a phenomenon as Poe appeared to imagine.'"[19] Doyle cagily puts his finger on the point with which Poe would have agreed. When

Poe referred to Dupin as "supposititious" he was in a sense recognizing the binary oppositions of rational/irrational, truth/fiction and solution/mystery at the heart of the genre. The central fiction underlying the reasoning that detective fiction invokes consists of a presumption that the detective's inferences which are proffered with the utmost certainty may not be necessarily true. Detective fiction of necessity entails supposing, fiction-making and scenario-constructing – in short, the imaginary. If detective fiction presents the hard certainties of solution at one pole of its imaginative spectrum, then at the other pole stands the possibility of unlimited suspicion. This is a nearly paranoid condition in which the would-be investigator whirls, as it were, in a darkened stairwell, casting the panicky flashlight of accusation on all suspects. Poe understood from the outset that ratiocination moves between these possibilities and that, in a sense, all detectives are potentially mere hypothesizers and that for every accurate solution that might be provided, there may be countless false accusations.

The intersection of fact and fiction has, therefore, been central to detective stories from its inception, and as much as this might be relevant to the development, for example, in the 1960s of the true-crime novel, it also derives from the cultural preoccupations of the 1830s and 1840s. Poe's pseudo-factual sea adventures, such as *The Narrative of Arthur Gordon Pym* (his only novel) and "The Balloon-Hoax," attempted to address and tap into the growing power and potential of mass culture. As Neil Harris has shown, Poe's hoaxes and ratiocinative fictions were, like the humbugs of P. T. Barnum's American museum, part of a modern public interest in the line between truth and fiction. There was, Harris writes, "a profusion at this time of large amounts of information, sometimes in statistical tables, sometimes in long lists of data. In large enough quantities, information gave the illusion of problem-solving by presenting previously unknown facts."[20]

The social, economic, and technological transformations of the United States during the 1830s and 1840s were quite pronounced. Eastern cities were beginning to develop metropolitan qualities (e.g. infrastructures, police forces). Rail transportation, telegraph communications and photography all promised to usher in a new era of technological advancement. The period was marked by Jacksonian democracy, questions of slavery, abolition and expansion, Indian removal, financial booms and panics, and a veritable explosion of print media, and Poe's development as an author in the turbulent magazine culture of the 1830s and 1840s was tied to the rise of other popular forms such as the penny press. Magazines and newspapers, addressing themselves to large urban and even national audiences, attempted to keep pace with these developments.

As Terence Whalen has argued, the emergence of detective fiction as a form was the result of "the most profound engagement between Poe's material imagination and the developing capitalist economy."[21] By the late 1830s, Poe found himself pursuing another of his ratiocinative interests – the science of cryptography and decoding. He ran contests in Philadelphia magazines challenging readers to send encrypted messages for him to solve. As he would in the Dupin stories, Poe exploited puzzle-solving analysis to reach a mass audience. Eventually, he was inundated with encoded messages and had to end his contest, but this work deepened his sensitivity to ratiocinative processes. "The ratiocination actually passing through the mind in the solution of even a simple cryptograph," he observed, "if detailed step by step, would fill a large volume."[22]

Poe would insert a cryptographic motif into "The Gold-Bug" but it was through Dupin that Poe found a narrative structure in which one might detail the steps of a ratiocinative process through to a solution. Poe's ratiocinative writings, with their treatise-like openings and air of method, allowed readers to enter into a fictional world of urban mystery and crime and through analysis impose order and reason on it. "The Murders in the Rue Morgue" exploited this notion by making the core of Dupin's analysis reliant upon careful readings of accounts of crime in the Parisian newspapers. In "The Mystery of Marie Rogêt," Poe used the parallel universe of Dupin's fictional Paris to solve the real murder of Mary Cecilia Rogers whose corpse was discovered in the Hudson River in the summer of 1841.

In this case, Poe followed the details of the investigation in the Philadelphia newspapers and, in an attempt to have his tale keep pace with developments, went to the New York area to investigate. Scholarship has shown that Poe suppressed his knowledge that Mary Rogers likely died of a botched abortion; we can see Poe's engagement with the newspaper as the medium through which urban reality is perceived and regulated as a key to the tale of ratiocination.[23] In an 1842 letter, Poe explained that

> under pretence of showing how Dupin (the hero of the Rue Morgue) unravelled the mystery of Marie's assassination, I, in fact, enter into a very rigorous analysis of the *real* tragedy in New-York. *No point* is omitted. I examine, each by each, the opinions and arguments of our press on the subject, and show (I think satisfactorily) that this subject has never yet been *approached*. The press has been entirely on a wrong scent. In fact, I really believe, not only that I have demonstrated the falsity of the idea that the girl was not the victim of a gang – as supposed – but have *indicated the assassin*.[24]

"Marie Rogêt" becomes a critique of journalistic practice and its popular reception. Dupin arrives at the "analytic sublime,"[25] as Shawn Rosenheim has described the promise of detective fiction, not through the transparent power of reasoning in a vacuum as it were, but through an attempt to correct for the necessary distortions of the print media whose biases are implicitly sensational. "'Several of the morning papers of the day,'" Dupin quotes from an article on the murder, "'speak of the *conclusive* article in Monday's "Etoile."'" To me, this article appears conclusive of little beyond the zeal of its inditer."[26] Dupin finds nothing conclusive about the paper's investigation except for its own self-satisfied air of certainty, that is to say, of supposititiousness. Geoffery Hartman has charged detective fiction with being manipulative. Its trouble is, among other elements, "not that it lacks realism but that it picks up the latest realism and exploits it."[27]

If this is a common enough criticism of detective fiction, "Marie Rogêt" indicates the ways in which Poe was wrestling with the same phenomenon, the exploitation of reality. For Poe, however, it is a journalistic problem. As Dupin explains,

> We should bear in mind that, in general, it is the object of our newspapers rather to create a sensation – to make a point – than to further the cause of truth. The latter end is only pursued when it seems coincident with the former. The print which merely falls in with ordinary opinion (however well founded this opinion may be) earns for itself no credit with the mob. The mass of the people regard as profound only him who suggests *pungent contradictions* of the general idea. In ratiocination, not less than in literature, it is the *epigram* which is the most immediately and the most universally appreciated. In both, it is of the lowest order of merit.[28]

If the first detective story placed the newspaper at the center of the action, the second one demonstrated a deeper level of engagement with Anderson's imagined communities to the extent that it describes a media feedback loop through which erroneous or potentially erroneous conclusions become consensus. The market-driven desire to create sensational realities promotes a culture of striking assertions that operate on contrast rather than accuracy, or what Dupin calls "pungent contradictions." In striving to be epigrammatic, newspaper headlines distort, and Dupin suggests that literary epigrams have an analogous effect – they are more quotable than true.

Any reader of "Marie Rogêt," however, will notice that its vexed attempts to arrive at a convincing conclusion suggest that detective fiction may take up more difficulties than any solitary correction for journalistic sensationalism may allow. But Poe's intervention in the representation of journalistic reality was generically fundamental, and while he was the first he was not the only one to take up detective fiction as a means to solve real crimes. In 1860, a murder in an English country house and its subsequent investigation by

Scotland Yard detectives set off a national obsession with crime and detection that would preoccupy the British press and many prominent Victorian novelists (chiefly Charles Dickens and Wilkie Collins) for decades. As theories and suspects proliferated and circulated in the English press, and numerous individuals attempted "to play detective," using the techniques of detective fiction to solve a real murder, the boundary between fact and fiction blurred. In the national obsession with the murder at Road Hill House, the first subgenre of detective fiction was born, the English country-house mystery, and with it emerged another generation of readers and writers who styled themselves, as did one English pamphleteer promising a definitive solution to that murder mystery, "A Disciple of Edgar Allan Poe."[29]

Through the example of Poe, mass culture began to participate more widely in the modern fantasy of rendering the mysteries of the great city suddenly legible by analyzing the details of cases in newspapers. The Oxford editions of Sherlock Holmes reveal the extent to which Conan Doyle raided *Tit-Bits*, a London magazine of miscellaneous information, for the germs of stories, and indeed it is no accident that Sherlock Holmes flourished in another urban magazine, London's *The Strand*. While Conan Doyle had Holmes disparage the showy Dupin in *A Study in Scarlet*, the author made plain in a more candid assessment the influence that Poe had on his work and the genre of detective fiction:

> Poe is the master of all. To him must be ascribed the monstrous progeny of writers on the detection of crime ... Each may find some little development of his own, but his main art must trace back to those admirable stories of Monsieur Dupin.[30]

With the last of the Dupin tales, "The Purloined Letter," Poe, in a sense, effaced the messy proliferation of newspaper-oriented detail that clutters "Marie Rogêt," only to expose detective fiction's inherent analytical mechanisms, recasting the problem of imagined reality as one about analyzing the minds of others. In place of the newspaper texts and the problems of fiction and reality that these entail, "The Purloined Letter" offers a brilliant set of literary abstractions in its place, a king and queen, a ministerial jack, and a stolen letter, the secret contents of which can never be divulged or circulated. As Dupin outwits the Minister D — by, in John Irwin's words, "doubling an opponent's thought processes in order to turn his own methods against him,"[31] Poe's tale establishes the modern paradigm (which Dashiell Hammett and John Huston followed in *The Maltese Falcon*) of the hermetically sealed fiction of cross and double-cross in which spirited antagonists pursue a prized artifact of dubious or uncertain value, only to find themselves either being outplayed by their own techniques or caught up in an increasingly vertiginous cycle of self-consciousness. By stripping away the acts of newspaper reading that marked the earlier stories, Poe reveals the acts of analysis central to detective fiction.

"The Purloined Letter" transmutes the analytical game of the newspaper crime fiction into a game of analysis in which the central object of inquiry – the text of the stolen letter – has been withheld from the reader. While the first two stories of the detective genre were structured around the presentation of published newspaper accounts, Poe's last innovation was effectively to privatize the genre, to demonstrate that it could traffic in private (as opposed to public) representations and mysteries. This is achieved by shifting from murder to theft and making a private text the object of crime and not just the medium of its representation. While the personages involved in the first two stories had a journalistic specificity – the L'Espanayes, Adolphe Le Bon, and Marie Rogêt – in "The Purloined Letter" the characters are as personalized as a pack of cards. By withholding the central text from the reader Poe effectively exposes ever more clearly the game-like structure of the speculation involved in detection and analysis. Implicit in Dupin's critique of urban journalism (and the prefect of police) was an ability to determine the motives for the press's habits of thought (chiefly sensationalism and promotion of its own circulation) and then to calibrate his responses to their theories accordingly. In "The Purloined Letter," Dupin applies this kind of calibration to the Minister D —. In Shawn Rosenheim's words, "the central problem of Poe's fiction is that of the existence of other minds," and in detective fiction exemplified by "The Purloined Letter" this problem expresses itself as an attempt by the rational and rationalizing mind "to steer a course between the rocks of identification and the whirlpool of solipsism."[32] This formulation amounts to an abstract revision of the problem of supposititiousness exhibited in the earlier tales in which the detective navigates a course between the unique solution and the proliferation of random suspicion.

With "The Purloined Letter," Poe laid out the full range of a generic template that would be taken up by a succession of writers from Conan Doyle to Jorge Luis Borges to Paul Auster. With the success of Sherlock Holmes, the figure of Poe's analytic detective was entrenched in popular culture and wedded to adventure narratives. Dozens of detective stories invoke Dupin or Poe, either directly as in Jeanette Dobson's *Nevermore* and Thomas Harris's Hannibal Lecter novels, or indirectly as in Dashiell Hammett's *The Maltese Falcon*, in which the protagonists chase after a mysterious black bird. At times, in the twentieth century, the analytical aspect has been foregrounded, as in the psychoanalytic work of Jacques Lacan and the subsequent criticisms of it by Jacques Derrida and Barbara Johnson. In the 1840s, the generic arc of detective fiction was laid out by Poe in all its supposititious glory, from questions of the inherently fictional texture of reality as represented in the urban newspaper to the dizzying self-reference potential in all analytical entanglement. As John Irwin has suggested, Poe's genius was to recognize the impossibility of the detective fully comprehending his own act of analysis, and that the solution of any mystery leaves us with another mystery.

NOTES

1. Poe to Philip Pendleton Cooke, August 9, 1846, in *The Letters of Edgar Allan Poe*, vol. II, ed. John Ward Ostrom (New York: Gordian Press, 1966), p. 328.
2. Edgar Allan Poe, "The Murders in the Rue Morgue," in *Edgar Allan Poe: Poetry, Tales, & Selected Essays*, ed. Patrick F. Quinn and G. R. Thompson (New York: Library of America, 1996), p. 401.
3. Terence Whalen, *Edgar Allan Poe and the Masses: The Political Economy of Literature in Antebellum America* (Princeton University Press, 1999), p. 226.
4. Cooke to Poe, p. 328 (see note 1).
5. Poe's sentiment has been echoed throughout the commentary on detective fiction. In 1850, Rufus Griswold, Poe's libelous literary executor, published a withering assessment of Poe's career in which he proffered Poe's remarks verbatim as if they were his own critical dismissal of the Dupin tales ("Edgan Allan Poe," *International Monthly Magazine*, vol. 1 (October 1850): 331). In 1898, the "Contributor's Club" column in the *Atlantic Monthly* complained that the mass of detective fiction contained exhibited "none of this analytic, this unfolding art" that Poe described; the typical author of detective fiction conceives of a crime and then "proceeds carefully to cover up his own tracks, and, having got them into the requisite state of concealment, elaborately to withdraw the veils" ("Contributor's Club: Detective Stories," *Atlantic Monthly*, vol. 81 (April 1898): 573).
6. Cooke to Poe, p. 328 (see note 1).
7. John T. Irwin, "Mysteries We Reread, Mysteries of Rereading: Poe, Borges, and the Analytic Detective Story," in *Detecting Texts: The Metaphysical Detective Story from Poe to Postmodernism*, ed. Patricia Merivale and Susan Elizabeth Sweeney (Philadelphia, PA: University of Pennsylvania Press, 1999), pp. 27–8.
8. Poe, "The Murders in the Rue Morgue," p. 405.
9. *Ibid.*, pp. 413–14.
10. *Ibid.*, p. 425.
11. Benedict Anderson, *Imagined Communities: Reflections on the Origin and Spread of Nationalism*, rev. edn. (London: Verso, 1991), pp. 22, 25.
12. *Ibid.*, p. 35.
13. *Ibid.*, pp. 35–6.
14. J. Gerald Kennedy, "The Limits of Reason: Poe's Deluded Detectives," *American Literature*, 47 (1975): 184.
15. Walter Benjamin, *Charles Baudelaire: A Lyrical Poet in the Era of High Capitalism* (London: Verso, 1983), p. 48.
16. Poe, "The Man of the Crowd," in *Edgar Allan Poe: Poetry, Tales, & Selected Essays*, p. 396.

17. Richard Wilbur, *Responses: Prose Pieces, 1953–1976* (New York: Harcourt, 1976), pp. 135–6.
18. Poe, "The Murders in the Rue Morgue," p. 397.
19. Arthur Conan Doyle, *A Study in Scarlet* (1887; repr. London: Penguin, 1981), p. 25.
20. Neil Harris, *Humbug: The Art of P. T. Barnum* (Boston: Little, Brown, 1973), p. 88.
21. Whalen, *Edgar Allan Poe and the Masses*, p. 226.
22. Poe, "Secret Writing [Addendum III]," *Graham's Magazine*, 19 (December 1841): 306.
23. John Walsh, *Poe the Detective: The Curious Circumstances Behind the Mystery of Marie Roget* (New Brunswick, NJ: Rutgers University Press, 1968), pp. 69, 92.
24. Poe to J. E. Snodgrass, June 4, 1842, in *The Letters of Edgar Allan Poe*, vol. I, p. 246.
25. Shawn James Rosenheim, *The Cryptographic Imagination: Secret Writing from Edgar Poe to the Internet* (Baltimore, MD: Johns Hopkins University Press, 1997), pp. 65–86.
26. Poe, "The Mystery of Marie Rogêt," in *Edgar Allan Poe: Poetry, Tales, & Selected Essays*, p. 521.
27. Geoffrey Hartman, *The Fate of Reading and Other Essays* (Chicago University Press, 1975), p. 225.
28. Poe, "The Mystery of Marie Rogêt," p. 521.
29. Kate Summerscale, *The Suspicions of Mr. Whicher* (London: Bloomsbury, 2008), pp. 173–4.
30. Arthur Conan Doyle, *Through the Magic Door* (New York: McClure, 1908), pp. 117–18.
31. Irwin, "Mysteries We Reread," in *Detecting Texts*, p. 33.
32. Rosenheim, *The Cryptographic Imagination*, pp. 27–8.

4

CATHERINE ROSS NICKERSON

Women writers before 1960

For most, if not all, of the twentieth century, a consensus has existed among fans, collectors and critics of detective fiction about its development in the United States. The origin is in Edgar Allan Poe's "tales of ratiocination" of the early 1840s. There follows a long dry spell, a "fallow" period of about fifty years until Sherlock Holmes takes America by storm, and inspires some famous but ultimately minor writers (such as Jacques Futrelle). Between the 1890s and the 1920s, the real action is in Great Britain, where a "golden age" of tightly woven puzzles and country houses full of amusing guests is presided over by Agatha Christie and imitated by Americans like S. S. Van Dine. American detective fiction only comes into its own with the emergence of the hard-boiled style out of the "pulps" in the 1920s. In rebellion against a British style that seemed contrived and dull, Dashiell Hammett and Raymond Chandler produced something quintessentially American, like jazz. The iconic American detective novel is an improvisation on the themes the early hard-boiled writers laid out: urban settings, conspiracies among thugs and powerful men, deceptive women, and an underlying pessimism about human nature and American society.

This is a pretty good story, but it is not the whole story by any means, as Maureen Reddy and Sean McCann argue elsewhere in this volume. American writers were experimenting with Poe's detective story structure at least as early as the 1860s,[1] and the most innovative and successful ones were women. They created a style I have come to refer to as "domestic detective fiction," a tradition of women's writing that lasted for at least three generations. Poe's "tales of ratiocination" bring together two of his interests: the workings of the human mind and the nature of terror. Women writers saw the possibilities of intensifying that exploration of fear and knowledge as twin subjects by drawing on several longstanding traditions of female writing about danger and women's experience, including female gothic novels, sensation fiction, seduction narratives and the more recently developed domestic novel. Into that mixture, they implanted the figure of the detective and the narrative structure of detective fiction. For what Poe established was not just a subject – crime and its investigation by intellectually superior people – but also a distinctive way of structuring and organizing that subject.

Tzvetan Todorov explains that structure as a double narrative.[2] One story is the narrative that we follow from page one on through to the end. It is a narrative of the process of investigation: discovering a crime, determining the identity of the victim, gathering the physical evidence, interviewing witnesses and suspects, checking alibis, and ultimately making sense out of all those disconnected bits of information. The other story is a narrative of secrecy: the motives and methods of the miscreants, their attempts to cover their tracks and destroy things (and sometimes people) that connect them to the crime, grudges against and unexpected alliances with other characters, and their efforts to guide the detective away from themselves. While the criminals want desperately to keep their story fragmented and illegible, the detective is working just as hard to put the pieces back together into a coherent narrative. The resolution of the narrative disarray that makes up the bulk of a detective novel comes at the point at which the detective can retell the tale of the crime; detective fiction is ultimately about how and why to tell a story. It is for this reason that the narrator of "The Murders in the Rue Morgue" speaks of his "fancy of a double Dupin – the creative and the resolvent."[3]

The women writers who followed Poe picked up on another kind of tension in the doubled narrative structure of detective fiction, a tension that shows its roots in the gothic mode. While one narrative line is driving forward to revelation and enlightenment, another is working in the opposite direction, toward concealment and erasure. There is as much admiration for the clever hiding of evidence as there is for the brilliant discovery of it. When an investigation into a crime within a family circle gathers momentum, all sorts of secrets – embarrassing, hurtful, criminal – threaten to come to light. For various reasons, innocent characters and even detectives wish to keep these secrets under wraps. Sometimes these secrets seem to be minor subplots that have nothing to do with the crime, but they almost always turn out to be connected to it in the end. And of course, offstage, the author of the story is dropping hints to us and creating clues for the investigator to find, even as she makes sure they don't make complete sense immediately. This oscillation between concealment and revelation, obfuscation and explication, is a feature of all kinds of detective fiction, but is amplified in this women's tradition.

These writers used the transatlantic gothic mode to critique hypocrisy among the moneyed classes, in the tradition of E. D. E. N. Southworth, Harriet Beecher Stowe, Mary Elizabeth Braddon and the Brontë sisters. The female gothic is about terrible things happening to women in domestic spaces. Haunted houses and various kinds of imprisonment within the home (the worst being live burial) are strong metaphors for a broader notion of danger and unhappiness within the vaunted "women's sphere." But the female gothic is not interested solely in the victimization of women. Rather, a gothic heroine receives training in problem solving, learns to challenge platitudes and discovers that she is braver and smarter than she thought she was. The state of fear, in other words, has an epistemological component. If the first rule of the hard-boiled is "follow the money," the first rule of early women's detective fiction might be "turn toward the things that make you afraid."

The first appearance of a detective in fiction after Poe comes in a short story by Louisa May Alcott called "V. V., or Plots and Counterplots." This 1865 thriller was one of many that she published under pseudonyms. While best known for the series of children's novels that began with *Little Women* (1869), she was a prolific and savvy writer for the magazines and story-papers that arose in the 1850s. "V. V." centers on the attempt of a young Scottish aristocrat to determine the true identity of an adventuress and to prove that she has killed his fiancée and his cousin. At a certain point he calls in a famous private investigator from Paris to assist him; Antoine Dupres (who sometimes uses the alias of Dupont) is an open parody of Poe's Auguste Dupin. The narrator of Poe's "The Murders in the Rue Morgue" famously characterized Dupin's mind as analytical, as the mind that *"disentangles."*[4] Alcott's detective, though, is more like that narrator's "fancy of a double Dupin." Staging a dramatic unmasking of the killer is his primary concern; he asks his client to

> promise me that you will not call in the help of your blundering constabulary, police, or whatever you name them. They will destroy the éclat of the *dénouement* and annoy me by their stupidity ... [T]his brain of mine is fertile in inventions and by morning will have been inspired with a design which will enchant you by its daring, its acuteness, its romance.[5]

Alcott sets a pattern that we will see elsewhere in early women's detective fiction; she is more interested in the side of Poe's doubled prototype that is creative, generative, an author of counterplots to the ones that he uncovers; his mind may work to "disentangle," but he himself becomes entangled in the drama of the story.

We see the same entanglements in the two detective novels written by Metta Fuller Victor, *The Dead Letter* (1867) and *The Figure Eight* (1869), under the pseudonym of Seeley Regester.[6] Here she takes the skeleton of the detective short story as conceived by Poe and – for the first time in America – fleshes it out into a full-length novel. In what would come to be a foundational plot for domestic detective fiction, a brutal crime occurs in an apparently placid, prosperous household. Someone emotionally involved with that household becomes an amateur investigator, either to aid the police detectives or to show them that they are on the wrong track. In Victor's earliest version of this formula, our narrator is a lawyer-in-training under a wealthy attorney. A tragedy has occurred: the fiancé of the elder daughter in the household is found murdered on the road near the family home. As in the domestic novel, the erotic energies of the household are this novel's main concern; understanding an interlocking set of love triangles and professional rivalries is the way to identify the murderer. Our narrator is part of one of the most volatile of these triangles: both he and the nephew of his employer are secretly in love with that employer's daughter, and both also have high expectations of taking over the family law firm.

Likewise, in *The Figure Eight*, our narrator, Joe Meredith, is a medical student and adopted nephew of a wealthy doctor; he is also secretly in love with his cousin. When the doctor is found poisoned at his desk, Meredith goes about trying to solve the crime, at first to protect the financial interests of his cousin, and later to prove his innocence when he is accused of the crime. Partly because he is a suspect in the case, Meredith uses a number of disguises to track the people he thinks are behind the crime; his ruses include blackface and a fake medical practice. Both of these early novels are preoccupied with issues of class position, class climbing, the emergent professional class and people on the verge of a downward slide. Meredith is in a precarious class position; having been rescued by his kindly uncle from a rude upbringing, he is vulnerable to accusations of ingrained criminality. Many other characters have anxieties about their current or future class positions, including the doctor's second wife, an adventuress from Cuba; a governess infatuated with her employer; and the governess's brother who falsely represents himself as a wealthy man of leisure to court women in the highest social circles. Victor's novels of fatal rivalries and unreliable self-presentations show the homes of the upper middle class as places in need of surveillance and correction. Greed and betrayal lie just below the surface of households that appear to be models of genteel values and behaviors, and young people of the professional class seem especially well equipped to bring their secret scandals into plain view.

Victor, who was married to the editor of the powerful dime-novel publishing house, Beadle and Adams, wrote scores of dime novels in multiple genres under various pseudonyms. She also wrote, under her own name, novels that argued directly against slavery – *Maum Guinea and Her Plantation Children* (1861) – and polygamy – *Lives of Female Mormons* (1860) – and she edited a women's magazine, *Beadle's Home Monthly*. Alcott's and Victor's bibliographies may sound incomprehensibly eclectic, but we can see in them documentation of what Richard Brodhead calls "a major re-articulation of the literary field" beginning in the 1850s and 1860s. He argues that magazines like

The Atlantic established the category of "the nonpopular 'high' culture that came to exist 'above' the domestic or middlebrow world of letters in the later nineteenth century just as the new story-papers of the 1850s helped to organize the 'low' one that came to exist 'below' it."[7] While the American women's detective story first appeared in a story-paper, it took only a little over a decade for detective fiction by women to move "upward" to the level of the middlebrow novel. Victor's two hardbound novels were an important first step in that process. They are a complicated, and not entirely harmonious, blend of genres, some lowbrow, like the adventure stories that Victor was so adept at producing as a dime novelist, and some more middlebrow, like the sensation novel.

Anna Katharine Green's work firmly established the detective novel as respectable reading for educated adults. Her first novel, *The Leavenworth Case*, was the bestseller of 1878. Its ability to gain entry into the middle-class home is due in large part to the way it uses the framework and tone of the domestic novel of mid-century; much about the book would be familiar to readers of that declining popular form. The focus of *The Leavenworth Case* is on the emotional aftermath of a tragic event. It is energetic in evoking sympathy for its characters, it explores the circumstances and prospects for young women in detail, and there is a moralistic sensibility, especially about the abrogation of duty – qualities the book shares with domestic novels. The basic premise of the domestic detective novel is that the bourgeois home harbors depravity and pretends it does not; we can understand it as a more radical version of the domestic novel's moral agenda. Within sentimental culture, there was an impulse toward the correction of misguided desires and errant behavior; Green reworks it as criminal investigation. She uses the extremity of a situation of unsolved murder to explore, in literal and metaphorical ways, how women are damaged by the values of the market-place and limited by the force of propriety.

Green's novels argue that the discovery of the hostilities and selfishness in an upper-class household can only be undertaken by someone who may be an outsider to the household, but who is insider to its ways of operating by virtue of membership of the same social class. In *The Leavenworth Case*, the police detective, Ebenezer Gryce, enlists the help of a young lawyer in his investigation of the murder of the patriarch of a New York City family. Gryce explains that, like any detective, "I cannot pass myself off for a gentleman," and that "when we are in want of a gentleman to work for us, we have to go outside of our profession."[8] Of course, for members of the upper middle and professional classes turning detective, the idea of listening at doors, snooping through bureau drawers, scrutinizing the envelopes of other people's mail – in other words, spying – forces them to set aside their genteel reverence for privacy and forthrightness. The ethics of spying comes up over and over in the novels of Victor and Green, and their detectives justify it as a means to the greater end of protecting someone they love from harm or false accusation. Sneaking around seems to be the only way to get past the elaborate façades that wealthy, seemingly respectable families put up around their less savory private affairs.

While Green's early works were almost always narrated by men and featured male detectives, she did create more female detectives and narrators beginning in the 1890s. Amelia Butterworth, the first of these, is the prototype of all the meddling spinster-sleuths who have followed.[9] Her motives for detecting are mixed: she believes in justice, she believes in protecting the innocent, she believes in avenging the mistreatment of young women by their husbands and suitors, and she also believes that she is a better detective than Ebenezer Gryce, who infuriates her with his patronizing attitude. When he refuses to treat her as an equal, she conducts her own investigation, withholding the solution she has found until she can help a deserted wife spoil her husband's bigamous wedding to another woman. At the same time, Butterworth is not a proto-feminist. She is proudly blue-blooded and old-fashioned, and feels that most of the young women of her class are shallow, materialistic and unrefined. She muses about the fate of upper-class womanhood: "we have lost our manners in gaining our independence." To her, the proper ambition of a Victorian lady is to strengthen her character and find a way to "make her mark" in the world, through good works and the defense of good taste.[10]

Green's other female detective is Violet Strange, a debutante from a wealthy and well-connected family, who appeared in the 1910s.[11] She is hired by the police because she can go places in high society and ask questions that they cannot. Both Butterworth and Strange may be shaken by the secrets they uncover, dismayed by the deception they must practice from time to time, and frightened by the situations in which they find themselves – such as being locked in bedrooms or pursued down dark corridors – but they never doubt their right to be detectives. Gryce originally invites Butterworth to advise him, in a very limited way, based on her "women's eyes for women's matters."[12] However, in the social worlds that Green constructs, all things are "women's matters" in one way or another. Women are vulnerable to the greed and ambition of men seeking to constantly increase their wealth and social standing in the Gilded Age. In her tales of murder, women are deserted after marriage or jilted after betrothal, they are trapped, literally and metaphorically, in their homes by the mores of the time, they are unable to control their money or their property. Depending on their father's or husband's class position, they may work themselves to the bone in menial labor or be forbidden to earn an independent income. Green's detectives, male and female alike, recognize the effect of male arrogance and ambition on women, and draw the reader's attention to this general inequity as they pursue the perpetrators of specific crimes.

Green produced almost fifty volumes of detective novels and short stories, and her very successful career continued into the 1920s. She inspired a number of writers, including Agatha Christie. Among her American followers, the most talented and successful was Mary Roberts Rinehart, who began publishing detective stories in *Munsey's* magazine in 1904, and published her last almost fifty years later. She is, by several methods of accounting, one of the bestselling writers of the twentieth century and was one of the earliest women to step into the newly created category of "literary celebrity." Though she is remembered today mainly for her mysteries (sixteen novels and dozens of short stories), she also wrote a long-running series of humorous stories about a set of exuberant spinsters for the *Saturday Evening Post*; realistic, and sometimes bleak, novels about romance and marriage; a handful of plays; and a monthly column for the *Ladies Home Journal* in the early 1930s.[13]

Almost all of Rinehart's mystery novels are narrated by women, and the exploration of women's experience is her real subject. She is especially interested in how to tell a story from a woman's perspective, and how to focus our attention on the importance of women telling the stories of their lives. One of her techniques for reminding us that we are listening to a woman representing an extraordinary experience is retrospection. One heroine pauses at the point where she is telling us about a decision to leave her gun behind to say: "I suppose that is funny, really, when I look back over it. But it is not really funny at all. Later on I planned to go back one day and get it; but it would not have done me any good, as I know now."[14] Another opens her narrative this way: "We have just had another flood ... [It] brought back to me the strange events of the other flood five years ago, when the water reached more than half-way to the second story, and brought with it, to some, mystery and death."[15] Yet another narrator-heroine ends the first chapter of her tale with the disclosure that "I've got a joint in my right foot that throbs when it is going to rain or I am going to have bad luck, and it gave a jump then. I might have known there was trouble ahead."[16]

This backward glancing, which is also very effective for building suspense, earned her work – and the work the many women whom she inspired – the derisive label of the "Had-I-But-Known School." The critique that "the heroine rarely behaves in a way that bears much relation to common sense" and "invariably and inevitably finds herself in a situation she has been warned to avoid" is typical of influential male connoisseurs.[17] The assessment is clearly gendered: Howard Haycraft opines that this was "a school of mystery writing about which the less said the more chivalrous," and Julian Symons complains that these stories have "the air of being written specifically for maiden aunts."[18] Feminist critic Kathleen Maio counters by summarizing the significance of the narration in this style succinctly: "This woman is trying to tell us something. Something worth listening to."[19]

Rinehart's women with stories to tell are usually spinsters, sometimes older women, and sometimes younger women who fall in love with a man in the course of the novel. She created one series detective, a nurse so adept at solving crimes that the local police nickname her "Miss Pinkerton" (after the famous Allan Pinkerton and his detective agency). Her narrator-heroines are witty and intelligent, and can summon great courage when the investigation requires it. "Miss Pinkerton" is drawn into investigating a series of crimes because people she loves are apparently involved; at times she is afraid that these people are in fact guilty of crime, deception and betrayal. These investigators, like Green's Amelia Butterworth, are goaded into action by the patronizing attitude of the police, or into writing their narratives by journalists who mangle the story.

The settings of Rinehart's mystery novels are frequently large country estates, but the tone is very different from the British Golden Age novels and their weekend parties. These elaborate houses become the source of fear and dread, and they provide a symbolic language for discussing women's lives and the development of courage. In *The Yellow Room* (1945), a young spinster discovers a corpse when she comes to open her family's summer home: a woman has been beaten to death, stuffed into a linen closet, and set on fire with cooking oil. The circumstances of this death reveal how easily familiar domestic items and spaces can be made uncanny. Internment of a woman's body within this house echoes what we hear about the heroine in the opening passages of the book. Her recently widowed mother has become a

> peevish semi-invalid, and Carol at twenty-four, her hopes killed by the war, found herself in the position of the unmarried daughter, left more or less to wither on the maternal stem ... What she wanted was to join the Wacs or the Waves ... She was young and strong. She could be useful somewhere. But the mere mention of such activity was enough to bring on what her mother called a heart attack.[20]

Rinehart frequently uses the gothic trope of seclusion or imprisonment within a house to comment on the waste of women's talents among those classes to whom the appearance of propriety is everything. The mansions in which she usually sets her story should be sanctuaries of luxury, order and peace; instead they become places that are subject to surveillance and intrusion, dystopias where one murder leads to another and everyone seems to have a plausible motive. Everyone also seems to have a secret, or at the very least knows something about the proliferating crimes that she or he is not telling.

The work of the Rinehart heroine is to find out the dangerous secret that is always behind the initial, obvious crime (it is often a covert marriage, financial fraud or blackmail). She also needs to find out everyone's relationship to that secret – the part they played, the evidence they have accidentally discovered, the facts they know but do not understand. Over the course of the narrative, she tells us not only what happens, but how she feels about it all. And mostly those feelings run to anxiety and fear. We might well ask why this kind of book was so very popular; what reader willingly puts herself into a world of dread, confusion and physical violence? One reason might be that we watch the heroine become stronger and more knowledgeable over the course of events. While she may express a lack of confidence in her investigative skills, we are so assured of her intelligence and determination that we know she will prevail.

But perhaps the more powerful reason is that Rinehart's blend of gothic atmosphere and detective story structure allows her readers to see the situation of women in the twentieth century dramatized in a satisfying way. The female gothic tradition is a discourse of anger, and Rinehart's heroines express the resentments felt by most American women at some point in their lives. Because we are in the world of gothic mystery, it is in fact true that our heroine is – purely by virtue of her sex – patronized, demeaned and confronted with physical peril. She confirms what many of us suspect or know about the power structures of the real world. And she fights back with humor, with the conviction that her own instincts are correct, and ultimately by claiming the authority to tell the story better than anyone.

Rinehart is a major figure in women's popular literature, and inspired many followers. One group of women took up the basic formula she created and worked often powerful variations, including Carolyn Wells, Dorothy Disney, Mabel Seeley, Leslie Ford and Mignon Eberhart. Another group took that formula in another direction, producing what came to be called gothic romance or romantic thrillers. Joanna Russ best described these highly popular books in the title of her classic article on the subject: "Somebody's Trying to Kill Me and I Think it's My Husband." While they contain many of the elements of a Rinehart novel, including the huge mansion, an atmosphere of suspense, a big secret and murders, they are far more focused on the romantic dramas of young women. But the most significant difference is the utter helplessness and passivity of the heroine. Russ speculates that these novels arose out of the anxieties and internal conflicts of women negotiating the "feminine mystique" that Betty Friedan identified in the 1960s.[21]

Rinehart's most famous follower was Mignon Eberhart. She wrote nearly sixty novels and numerous short stories from 1929 through 1989. Despite her popularity, Eberhart's work has received scant scholarly attention. LeRoy Panek, one of the few to take a close look at her vast opus, concludes that, while she began by writing something clearly identifiable as detective fiction up until 1934, she soon drifted closer to the sort of romantic thrillers described above. The heroines of those novels are passive and easily led: Panek argues that "to them she applies techniques both ancient and modern, which make them helpless."[22] Eberhart's women are alone and friendless – orphaned, conspired against, forced into marriages that are loveless at best and predatory more often. They are falsely accused of crimes, and cannot defend themselves because they have some secret (unconnected to the crime) that will shame themselves or those they love.

However, Eberhart did begin differently, with a well-regarded set of five novels featuring Nurse Keate, who works alongside Lance O'Leary, private eye, and a series of short stories featuring a woman mystery writer, Susan Dare. While Keate's narration includes a general tone of apprehension and dread, the books also show the influence of the Golden Age school and its love of complex but self-contained puzzles. *The Mystery at Hunting's End* (1930) includes a favorite device of that style, the locked-room murder. This hybridization of what are sometimes described as divergent styles – the gothic and the puzzle – is an example of how vigorously the many subgenres of detective fiction have hybridized and recombined over the course of the twentieth century. Eberhart's legacy may have suffered from a problem of classification – is the work detective fiction, or even mystery? Or is it, after 1934, really romance? Her closest heir is Mary Higgins Clark, who began writing mysteries in the 1970s and is still a publishing phenomenon.

Zenith Brown began publishing mysteries under the pseudonym Leslie Ford in 1929.[23] She chronicles the culture of the upper-middle class in the era after the Crash, through World War II, and into the 1950s, with many of her novels set in or near Washington DC, and including intrigue among the political elite. Her best-remembered novels are a series featuring a middle-aged widow named Grace Latham and her friend Colonel Primrose, which debuted in 1934. While Latham resembles a Rinehart spinster-sleuth in some ways, particularly in the way that she "restores order so that the young might have their chance at life," she is far less involved in the actual work of investigation (which is left to the professionals). The atmosphere of the books is thus more consistently light-hearted than Rinehart's detective fiction, though Latham finds herself in danger with remarkable regularity. Betty Richardson argues that novels of the late 1930s and early 1940s are especially valuable because Ford was "writing at a time when the war's outcome was still unknown" and thus "reveals the fears, prejudices, and anxieties of US citizens coping for the first time with threats of air raids, rationing, and espionage."[24]

With her close attention to the lives of the moneyed classes, Ford might seem to be Rinehart's rightful heir. But Ford's novels emit a thick haze of nostalgia for life before the Depression, whereas Rinehart's heroines, at least in her last batch of detective novels published in the 1950s, wish to rid themselves of the burdens and preoccupations of a bygone era. In *The Swimming Pool* (1952), our heroine is living with her brother in a decrepit mansion that is the sole legacy to her generation, her father having committed suicide after being ruined in the Crash. She tells us "there should be a law against families who, in the luxurious years before two world wars, built vast country places and then left them to their descendants," who cannot afford to maintain the lavish estates.[25]

Mabel Seeley, who published six detective novels between 1938 and 1954, explored the potential for this style of detective fiction to express American women's experience. Most notably, her books are narrated by quite ordinary middle-class women who have actual jobs as nurses, librarians and stenographers. While these characters are sometimes related to very wealthy people, Seeley does not make the world of the upper crust normative, as Rinehart, Ford and Eberhart do. Her work, while most strongly influenced by Rinehart, has a tinge of noir in the plots and attitudes of the characters. In *The Whistling Shadow* (1954), our middle-aged narrator learns that her recently deceased son was secretly married; when she finds the bride, heavily pregnant, she takes on her care, all the while suspecting that she is being conned, though willing it not to be so. Seeley takes up the style's preoccupation with the heroine's emotional state and produces far more nuanced and realistic studies of a mind in turmoil than the rest of the Rinehart school.

Like Rinehart's heroines, Seeley's narrators look back at what they learned through their entanglement in a crime. In the opening sentences of *The Chuckling Fingers* (1941), our narrator gives us a classic "had-I-but-known" moment: "heaven defend me from ever again having to stand hopelessly by while it becomes more and more apparent to everyone but me that the person I love most in the world is murderously insane."[26] But Seeley is playing with that convention; it turns out the "person I love most in the world" is the narrator's sister, not a boyfriend or a husband. What Seeley recognized was that the lives and experiences of women are at the heart of this tradition of female writing. Crime and danger serve to throw the vulnerabilities and strengths of women into high relief. In the course of these stories, women learn that they can take on all sorts of fearful things: male authority figures, disapproving mothers, physical pain, disillusionment, betrayal – and survive. The structure of detective fiction allows them to articulate the crucial insight that finding the solution to a complex problem is both difficult and possible. Answers do not come easily to fictional detectives, but they do come.

Sara Paretsky argues that the goal of women writers of detective fiction is nothing more and nothing less than that of all women writers, which is "to broaden the range of their voices, to represent their age for women, to describe women's social position, their suffering – and their triumphs."[27] The earliest women writers of detective fiction, like Victor and Green, were famous in their own day but sank into obscurity in the early decades of the twentieth century. Rinehart and her successors were phenomenally popular, but took heat from the largely male corps of promoters and critics for creating situations and characters that were both predictable and illogical. However, these writers and their many fans knew what this tradition of writing was really about. At the end of *The Beckoning Door*, Seeley's heroine reflects on what she has learned from her involvement in the investigation of murder: "maybe the trouble with me is that I've rested back, waiting, wanting other people to open doors for me, when I should have done my own opening … What's been happening to me is a story; maybe I can write it so people will want to read it."[28] And she did, and they did.

NOTES

1. See LeRoy Lad Panek, *The Origins of the American Detective Story* (Jefferson, NC: McFarland, 2006), pp. 5–28. There are so very many women writing detective fiction in the vein that I trace that I have not been able to include them all; some significant names include Meredith Nicholson, Emma Murdoch Van Deventer and Isabel Ostrander.
2. Tzvetan Todorov, *The Poetics of Prose*, trans. Richard Howard (Ithaca: Cornell University Press, 1977), pp. 58–9.
3. Edgar Allan Poe, *The Murders in the Rue Morgue: The Dupin Tales* (New York: Modern Library, 2006), p. 7.
4. *Ibid.*, p. 3.
5. Louisa May Alcott, "V. V., or Plots and Counterplots," in *The Hidden Louisa May Alcott: A Collection of Her Unknown Thrillers*, ed. Madeleine Stern (New York: Avenel, 1984), pp. 382–3.
6. *The Dead Letter* first appeared in serial form in *Beadle's Home Monthly* in 1866. Both novels were originally published by Beadle & Company, and have been reprinted in a single volume, *The Dead Letter and The Figure Eight* (Durham, NC: Duke University Press, 2003).
7. Richard Brodhead, *Cultures of Letters: Scenes of Reading and Writing in Nineteenth-Century America* (University of Chicago Press, 1993), pp. 80, 79.
8. Anna Katharine Green, *The Leavenworth Case* (1878; repr. New York: Dover, 1981), pp. 106, 107.
9. Butterworth appeared in three novels: *That Affair Next Door* (1897; repr. Durham, NC: Duke University Pres, 2003), *Lost Man's Lane* (1898; repr. Durham, NC: Duke University Press, 2003) and *The Circular Study* (New York: McClure's, 1900).
10. Green, *That Affair*, pp. 194, 27.

11. Green, *The Golden Slipper and Other Problems for Violet Strange* (1915; repr. Whitefish, MT: Kessinger, 2008).
12. Green, *That Affair*, p. 47.
13. For a meticulous bibliography, see Jan Cohn, *Improbable Fiction: The Life of Mary Roberts Rinehart* (University of Pittsburgh Press, 1980).
14. Mary Roberts Rinehart, *Miss Pinkerton* (New York: Farrar & Rinehart, 1932), p. 5.
15. Rinehart, *The Case of Jennie Brice* (Indianapolis, IN: Bobbs-Merrill, 1913), p. 1.
16. Rinehart, *Where There's a Will* (Indianapolis, IN: Bobbs-Merrill, 1912), p. 11.
17. Chris Steinbrunner and Otto Penzler (eds.), *Encyclopedia of Mystery and Detection* (New York: McGraw Hill, 1976), p. 180.
18. Howard Haycraft (ed.), *The Art of the Mystery Story* (New York: Simon & Schuster, 1946), p. 319; Julian Symons, *Mortal Consequences* (New York: Schocken, 1972), p. 97.
19. Kathleen L. Maio, "Had-I-But-Known: The Marriage of Gothic Terror and Detection," in *The Female Gothic*, ed. Juliann Fleenor (Montreal: Eden, 1983), p. 90.
20. Rinehart, *The Yellow Room* (1945; repr. New York: Kensington, 1988), p. 6.
21. Joanna Russ, "Somebody's Trying to Kill Me and I Think it's My Husband: The Modern Gothic," *Journal of Popular Culture*, 6.4 (1973): 671.
22. LeRoy Lad Panek, "Mignon Good Eberhart," in *Mystery and Suspense Writers*, vol. I, ed. Robin Winks and Maureen Corrigan (New York: Charles Scribner's, 1998), p. 351.
23. Brown's bibliography is very long and very complicated, as she published two series in the US and two in the UK under different pseudonyms. For a logically arranged bibliography, see Betty Richardson, "Leslie Ford," in *Great Women Mystery Writers*, ed. Kathleen Gregory Klein (Westport, CT: Greenwood Press, 1994), pp. 108–12.
24. *Ibid.*, 108, 109.
25. Rinehart, *The Swimming Pool* (1952; repr. New York: Kensington, 1985), p. 18.
26. Mabel Seeley, *The Chuckling Fingers* (New York: Doubleday, 1941), p. 1. This and several other of her novels have been reprinted by Afton Historical Press, 1998–2000.
27. Sara Paretsky, *Women on the Case* (New York: Delacorte, 1996), p. xi.
28. Seeley, *The Beckoning Door* (Garden City, NJ: Doubleday, 1950), p. 218.

5

SEAN McCANN

The hard-boiled novel

"Hard-boiled" is the style most people think of when they refer to the American crime story: tough-talking, streetwise men; beautiful, treacherous women; a mysterious city, dark, in Raymond Chandler's famous phrase, "with something more than night";[1] a disenchanted hero who strives, usually without resounding success, to bring a small measure of justice to his (or, more recently, her) world. The main elements of the style are so widely known that they have achieved something close to mythic stature. Merely invoking a few of its hallmarks is enough to plunge us into a deeply familiar world whose features seem to well up out of the dark recesses of the collective imagination.

That resonance at once illuminates and conceals the writing it surrounds. On the one hand, the sheer familiarity of its conventions points to the genuinely central place of the hard-boiled crime story in the popular culture of the United States. Along with a handful of comparable popular narratives, it is one in the repertoire of mass cultural codes whose rules are instantly recognizable and endlessly available for variation. On the other hand, the very familiarity of the hard-boiled style tends to over-inflate its prominence and to tie it too closely to a narrow idea of national character, while also obscuring the richness of the fiction itself. The once commonplace assumption that the American crime story simply *is* the hard-boiled story downplays the variety in the history of American crime narrative. It also threatens to reduce hard-boiled fiction to a kind of unauthored mythos, making it too easy to forget that the style emerged out of a distinct time and place and that it has been put to use by a number of talented artists who found in its elements the means to pursue quite varied ambitions.

The hard-boiled crime story first appeared as a distinct style of adventure narrative in the pulp magazines of the 1920s, at the height of the crime wave that followed World War I, and made audiences eager for fiction that acknowledged the realities of the industrial metropolis. At the time, pulp magazines (named for the low-cost paper on which they were printed) were a thriving industry, providing cheap entertainment for millions of readers and employment for hundreds of writers who churned out piece-work at the rate of a penny or two per word. Intense competition and constant demand for innovation made the pulps highly responsive to shifting popular tastes. When the wave of crime that accompanied Prohibition leapt to attention and drew public awareness to the new phenomenon of racketeering, pulp writers and editors responded by producing what they called "a newer type of detective story" – one that set aside the genteel features of "golden-age" detective fiction for an emphasis on the corruption and violence that seemed to characterize the rapidly growing metropolis.[2]

In the minds of its creators and fans, the new hard-boiled style was distinguished above all by its grimly realistic depictions of crime and urban life. "The characters you read about are real human people," the influential pulp editor Joseph Shaw told his readers. "When they are wounded they bleed; when they are hurt, they feel it . . . That is vastly different from reading stories of dummies stuffed into the clothes of the parts they are supposed to act."[3] His comment was meant to rebuke the "classic" detective story, which was in the midst of a great vogue during the twenties. Following the example of Sherlock Holmes, "classic" detective fiction put a premium on the specialized knowledge and brilliant ratiocination of an eccentric detective. In the most extreme versions of the form – typified by the era's most popular writer, S. S. Van Dine – the detective was arch and refined, the story took place in the isolated world of the sybaritic leisure class, and the plot was built around the detective's effort to solve the puzzle of the murderer's elaborate schemes. The hard-boiled writers who, championed by Shaw, began to take over the pulp magazines during the twenties set out to challenge that classic style by displacing its pleasing artificiality with a stark emphasis on "the seamy side of things." As Raymond Chandler remarked in praise of his predecessor Dashiell Hammett, hard-boiled fiction "took murder out of the Venetian vase and dropped it in the alley."[4]

Along with Chandler and Shaw, most of the hard-boiled writers liked to think of their fiction as representing merely a "realistic style" of crime writing. Hard-boiled fiction "gave murder back to the kind of people who commit it for reasons," Chandler proclaimed, "put those people down on paper as they were, and . . . made them talk and think in the language they customarily used for these purposes."[5] But, despite its often vivid depictions of the contemporary city, the hard-boiled story at its core was no less a popular fantasy than "the old cut-and-dried type of detective story" it sought to displace.[6] Before beginning his career as a writer, Hammett had been a Pinkerton detective, and he colored his fiction with details of crime and investigation that he had learned on the job. But most of the hard-boiled writers actually had little experience of the worlds they described; one of the most influential among them tried never to leave his home in suburban Yonkers. Like the secluded mansions of the golden-age detective story, their urban landscape was a dreamworld, an exaggerated image of the metropolis as a battlefield of crime lords and corrupt officials that drew as much from the traditions of pop imagery and urban folklore as it did from direct observation.

Indeed, the hard-boiled style bore the hallmarks of two traditions of popular narrative that had been prominent in the late-nineteenth-century dime novels from which the twentieth-century pulp magazine descended. Against the artificiality of the classic detective story, the hard-boiled writers reached back to the example of once widely popular dime-novel detectives like Cap Collier and Nick Carter – adventure heroes who were distinguished not by their learning or ratiocination but for their ability to call on cunning and disguise to navigate the farthest reaches of the city. Less directly, hard-boiled fiction invoked the closely related tradition of the western, importing the conventions of frontier adventure to the territory of the industrial metropolis. Combining those two narrative strands, hard-boiled crime fiction imagined the city as a labyrinthine world of dark and mysterious powers and, at the same time, as an urban frontier, where the rule of law came into confrontation with disorder. The detective's often overwhelming task was to lay the hidden places open to light and, ultimately, through mortal combat, to bring a savage world under control. The central conflict, as one early story put it, lay between "gangdom" and "society."[7] The detective hero stood agonistically on their boundary.

Rather than viewing the hard-boiled detective story as simply more realistic than other forms of crime fiction, then, it would be more accurate to say that the hard-boiled writers displaced one popular fantasy (emphasizing status competition and what was then called "brain work") with another, combining two themes that had assumed increasing resonance in the US in the years following World War I: the tension between bureaucratic organization and personal autonomy, and the violent struggle, as Shaw put it, between "civilization" and "barbarity."[8] Alongside the sudden prominence of organized crime, which transfixed popular attention in the twenties, the recent growth of corporate enterprise and of the federal government each appeared to portend fundamental transformations in American society during the twenties. So, too, did the expansion of the nation's cities, the personal liberties and cultural and ethnic diversity of which had become the central grievance in a wave of xenophobic suspicion that coursed through every corner of public life in the years after the war.

The hard-boiled crime story took those concerns about bureaucracy and about cultural disorder and made them into the materials of a resonant popular myth. Like the western hero before him, the hard-boiled detective struggles between counterpoised (yet often mutually complicit) antagonists. He resists the official, but not quite legitimate, authority of a decadent society, now elevated into the towering bureaucratic impersonality of the law. And he battles the brute enemies of civilization – with the role once played by savage Indians in frontier myth now being filled by swarthy denizens of the urban underworld. Where the western hero snubbed ranch owners and vanquished desperadoes or Native Americans, the hard-boiled detective resists the police and battles the foreign menace of the criminal mob. Much as in the western, justice and fairness always appear to be swamped by illegitimate power and sheer brutality. But, in his struggle with the enemies of civilization, the hard-boiled detective, like the frontier hero before him, has at least the chance to seize his heroic mission and remake his world.

The single writer who did the most to create this new version of popular myth is now almost completely forgotten. Carroll John Daly was the epitome of the pulp industry hack, churning out hundreds of stories that earned him an enthusiastic popular audience but little critical recognition. (Like most pulp writers, he scorned artistic ambition in favor of craftsmanship and sheer labor. "If I ever had an inspiration, I have not had the wit to recognize it," he bragged. "With me it's mostly work.")[9] But Daly had a gift for action and for understanding the demands of his readers. It was Daly who, in the stories he wrote for the now legendary pulp *Black Mask*, did most to resuscitate the forgotten example of the dime-novel detective, making his private eye a hero who thrived less on mental acrobatics than on fisticuffs and gunplay. In addition, Daly hit on two elements that would be crucial to the success of the hard-boiled style. Following the example of the western, he made his hero a liminal figure who was stranded between legal authority and the criminal underworld – "just a halfway house between the dicks and the crooks."[10] And he emphasized his hero's insubordinate character by making him a first-person narrator who addresses the reader in sardonic vernacular. A canny pathfinder of the metropolis, Daly's private eye vanquishes his enemies with a wit revealed equally in physical struggle and slangy repartee. "My life is my own and the opinions of others don't interest me," a typical Daly story begins, "so don't form any, or if you do, keep them to yourself. If you want to sneer at my tactics, why go ahead; but do it behind the pages – you'll find that healthier."[11]

That brashly confrontational persona was an immediate sensation when Daly published his first hard-boiled story in 1923. ("Pay no attention to the spelling or grammatical errors in this tale," *Black Mask* warned its readers, explaining that the story was narrated in the detective's "own language."[12] The readers responded by boosting the sales of the magazine by 15 percent whenever Daly appeared.) And it soon attracted imitators, who took up

Daly's tales of urban combat and aped his colloquial diction. Within a year, the example shown by Daly and then by Hammett, who quickly followed Daly and became along with him a fan favorite, transformed *Black Mask*, turning it from an undistinguished miscellany of narrative styles into a celebrated vanguard of the new fiction. Within but a few years more, the hard-boiled detective story had migrated beyond *Black Mask* to inspire off-shoots in numerous other pulp magazines. By the later twenties, the hard-boiled style ruled the pulp universe.

In a small way, that transition pointed to developments that would assume much wider significance in the coming years. For, although he was a limited writer who relied on melodramatic plotting and crudely one-dimensional characters, Daly was also a shrewd reader of popular tastes who discovered a possibility latent in the unusual market position of the pulp magazines. At the time, the pulps were both a large entertainment industry and yet never-theless marginal to the era's booming consumer economy. By contrast to the dominant media of the day – the "big slick" magazines and the nascent radio industry – the pulps drew minor revenue from the rapidly expanding adver-tising business, and they could do little to develop the glossy features that appealed to aspiring middle-class readers. Despite being confined to a largely urban, working-class audience, however, the pulp magazines at first did little to differentiate themselves from their up-market competitors. A typical story in the early *Black Mask* introduced "Dr. Darius Y. Porter, wealthy and famous specialist in diseases of the eye, ear and throat, as he strolled leisurely homeward after dinner and bridge with a neighbor."[13] In the language of marketing, the pulps had not yet defined their niche.

Daly's example changed all that, tapping into the pulp readership's latent hunger for fiction that would thumb its nose at pretense and sophistication. In the hard-boiled universe, learning and refinement would henceforth look like vices. Bravado, physical prowess and street smarts would become the key virtues. Rather than manners and brain work, the hard-boiled story would foreground the detective's craft knowledge, his physical strength and skill. (It was not incidental that Joseph Shaw appealed to his readers by contrasting the authenticity of bodily pain – "when they are hurt, they feel it" – to the artificiality of dummies stuffed in clothes.) Above all, the hard-boiled detec-tive was not, like Darius Porter or Philo Vance, a gentleman amateur, but a skilled worker whose life was dominated by the necessities of the job and hinged round by the abrasive demands of clients, bosses and officials. In a venue that spoke mainly to working-class readers, the hard-boiled detective emerged as a popular hero who knew how to handle himself and whose abilities gave him the capacity to assert his independence and rudely put his ostensible betters in their place.

Indeed, Daly's heroes, who were proudly tough guys, were, only slightly less evidently, sentimental defenders of the underdogs of the city. Time and again, they squared off against two kinds of criminal enemy, each of whom the official agencies of the law were powerless or unwilling to control: the parasitic representatives of a wealthy elite, and the savage forces of the criminal underclass. In his first novel, *The Snarl of the Beast*, for example, Daly placed his hero Race Williams between two antagonists: the foppish son of a declining English aristocracy, and the brutish leader of a criminal gang – "a great organization" headquartered in the "teeming tenements of the Lower East Side." Those two antagonists turn out to be linked by genealogy and by their mutual greed, but they are joined by a more substantial logic as well. Each represents a clannish group implicitly foreign to America and to the decent people of the city. Only when Race has defeated both, vanquishing the criminal Beast of the title in a final bloody showdown, can he free Milly, the novel's good-hearted working girl, from the life of prostitution to which she seemed fated.[14]

At the ethical core of Daly's stories, in short – and of much of the hard-boiled fiction to follow – lay the outlines of an emergent white, working-class populism that would play a defining role in American culture and politics in the decades to come. The detective, who speaks the vernacular of the working-class city, is also its champion. Navigating the furthest corners of the metropolis, he ranges across its social and geographic terrain, tying the disparate features of the urban landscape into a legible map. But, less obviously, he also does battle on behalf of the hard-working people of the metropolis, and he struggles to defend their interests against the illegitimate wealth, criminal violence and official indifference that otherwise seems to dominate their world.

Over the course of the twenties, that populist vision expanded throughout the pulp universe as a generation of talented writers built on Daly's example. It was the subsequent two decades, however, that gave hard-boiled fiction its true golden age. During the Depression and the New Deal, as the white working class moved to the center of the political order, and as the industrial city came to seem not an insidious threat to American civilization but its very heart, the hard-boiled style leapt beyond the confines of the pulps. It was during these years that the movies and radio, experiencing their own golden age, discovered the character types and storylines the pulps had been cultivating and enshrined the tough-talking private eye as a durable face of the mid-century metropolis. During the same years, the big slick magazines also began mining the hard-boiled style. The former pulp writer Rex Stout began the most popular detective series in American history by cleverly merging the characteristics of the classic and the hard-boiled styles (a synthesis neatly achieved by partnering the reclusive genius Nero Wolfe with his city boy sidekick Archie Goodwin). He published his first novel in the *American* magazine, one of the most popular big slicks of the day.

While Stout was bringing elements of the hard-boiled story to that mainstream mass success, more prestigious critics and readers were likewise coming to appreciate the appeal of the hard-boiled style. During the Depression years, elite literary publishers like Alfred A. Knopf discovered first Hammett and subsequently Chandler, and prominent critics began to regard them as the creators not of mere "escape literature," but, as W. H. Auden wrote of Chandler, genuine "works of art."[15]

The surprising leap that Hammett and Chandler each made from pulp obscurity to elite critical recognition points to an important curiosity in the history of the hard-boiled style. A strong populist strain ran through the core of the fiction, but the most important advances in the style were made by ambitious writers who often scorned the middlebrow success achieved by writers like Stout. Writing to Knopf as he set out on his journey from the pulps to literary respectability, Hammett addressed his publisher in terms that could also apply to Chandler and others among the most important hard-boiled writers. His goal was "to make literature" of the detective story, Hammett explained.[16] In that often frustrating effort, he and his peers would bring to their work tensions and desires that revealed unexpected expressive depths in their form.

Hammett himself had discovered in the hard-boiled style pioneered by Daly a vehicle perfectly suited to his gifts. Before writing his first detective story, he had published a handful of supercilious, yet unremarkable, stories and essays. Daly's example showed Hammett his *métier*. Beginning in 1924, Hammett poured out a series of stories for *Black Mask* featuring an unnamed San Francisco private eye, the Continental Op, who negotiates the confusing metropolis by wit and experiment – or, as he often repeats in his first-person narratives, by "stirring things up."[17] Like Daly's Race Williams, Hammett's detectives are not puzzle-solvers, but aggressive huntsmen who pursue knowledge through direct and disruptive personal experience. His stories were written, Hammett explained to *Black Mask*'s readers, for "customers who don't like their sleuths to do too much brain work."[18]

But if in his broad outlines Hammett's detectives resemble Daly's private eye, in all other ways the two writers differed greatly. Where Daly's city was fantastic, his plotting melodramatic and his characterization simplistic, Hammett's writing is remarkably subtle and veristic. His stories take place in a recognizable world with plausible features; his characters are vivid and three-dimensional; his plots are full of neat turns and surprising moral ambiguities; and his style resembles the cool sleekness of modernist art. "I knocked him on the noodle with my borrowed crutch," the Op reports of one episode where he disarms an unprepared criminal. Describing a fleeing felon, he pauses to provide a rendition of her appearance that sounds like imagist poetry: "She walked without haste to the door, her short skirt of gray flannel shaping itself to the calf of each gray wool-stockinged leg."[19] In his scenes of action, he provides not the breathless rendition of tumult and bravery that Race Williams trumpeted, but a defamiliarizing, camera-eye view that makes the actors resemble manikins in a perversely comic silent film:

> The gray-mustached detective who had sat beside me in the car carried a red ax.
> We stepped up on the porch.
> Noise and fire came out under a window sill.
> The gray-mustached detective fell down, hiding the ax under his corpse.
> The rest of us ran away.[20]

Most importantly, Hammett's detective departs from the heroic model presented by Race Williams. Short, fat and middle-aged, he is not the triumphant image of the common man that Daly presented, but more nearly the reverse – a truly ordinary-seeming person who turns out to conceal extraordinary cleverness beneath his commonplace exterior. In his struggles with his clients and his employer, moreover, and in his battles with the criminals he encounters, Hammett's detective is not always completely victorious, and his victories when they come can seem strangely anti-climactic. Daly's Race Williams liked to brag that he was indifferent to the ethical codes of polite society and ruled only by his own needs, while all along making it clear that he was in fact governed by the noblest of desires: to crush evildoers and protect nice kids like Milly. Hammett's detective, by contrast, truly does present an often disturbing image of moral neutrality. His motivation, the Op explains, stems not from conviction or interest or desire, but solely from the fact that he likes his work. "And liking work makes you want to do it as well as you can ... I don't know anything else, don't enjoy anything else, don't want to know or enjoy anything else." That professional commitment could also, as Hammett's stories increasingly emphasized, make his hero eerily unresponsive not only to greed or lust, but to pity, compassion and love – as the Op shows, for example, in one throwaway moment where, without remarking on the action, he pistol-whips a client who has failed to follow instructions out of anxiety for the woman he loves. "There's nothing human" about such behavior, the Op admits.[21]

As he expanded beyond the pulps, however, Hammett's fiction took on still greater depths. In the novels he wrote for Knopf, Hammett drew on the scenarios favored in the pulp universe, while at the same time subtly undermining them. In *Red Harvest*, for example, Hammett sends the Continental

Op to Personville, a small Montana city dominated by corrupt officials and a ruthless gang of mobsters and gamblers. As in any Race Williams tale, in other words, the detective is a solitary warrior faced with the need to bring a disordered frontier under control, while simultaneously eluding the demands of decadent social authority.

In pointed contrast to the stark clarity of his prose, however, everything about Hammett's story is messy and morally ambiguous. The Op's client Elihu Willsson is an autocratic mineowner who has introduced gangsters into the city in order to crush organized labor. (The story was inspired in part by Hammett's experience working as a Pinkerton in Butte, where he narrowly avoided being enlisted in the notorious lynching of International Workers of the World organizer Frank Little.) His method is to set the various factions of the town's criminal organizations against each other, and the consequence is a wave of bloodshed that rattles the confidence of his colleagues and raises doubts even for the Op himself. After the eighteenth murder provoked by his intrigue, the Op begins to wonder if he is not "going blood-simple like the natives." Despite the fact that his efforts involve not merely manipulation and cruelty, but the betrayal of nearly everyone who trusts him, moreover, the campaign ultimately serves little purpose. Though he can impose order on the city, Hammett's detective can do little to produce justice or peace. The criminals he subdues will soon be replaced by new gangsters. And, while he momentarily frustrates and embarrasses his client, the victory is trivial; he can do nothing to scratch Willson's wealth or power. "You'll have your city back, all nice and clean," the Op acknowledges, "and ready to go to the dogs again."[22]

Where Race Williams triumphed over decadent aristocracy and savage criminality, Hammett's Op can achieve against those enemies little more than symbolic victories. The result is typical of Hammett's mature fiction. Though they make deft use of pulp conventions, his novels handle those conventions in ways that make the satisfactions of the hard-boiled story appear dubious. His second novel, *The Dain Curse*, for instance, is a captivity narrative like *The Snarl of the Beast*, in which the Op must work to save the young heiress Gabrielle Dain from her predatory aristocratic family and from vicious criminals who are painted with hues of ethnic corruption and moral subversion (in this case a crew of con men posing as one of the spiritualist cults that flourished in California at the time). But, as the Op eventually discovers, Gabrielle is kept captive less by brute coercion than by false, yet addictive, beliefs about her own degeneracy that she cannot keep herself from cherishing, and which can only be countered when the Op offers her a new, and perhaps no less confining, narrative about herself.

To make matters worse, as irrational as they are, Gabrielle's misguided beliefs are not at all unusual, but merely typical of the way human beings process information. "Nobody thinks clearly," the Op explains. "Thinking's a dizzy business, a matter of catching as many ... foggy glimpses as you can and fitting them together as best you can."[23] The detective who works to piece together a coherent story of a case, and who operates mainly by *disproving* the false stories that are manufactured by other people, is a model of a pragmatic way of dealing with that condition. Gabrielle Dain, who clings to misguided beliefs even as they harm her, is an example of the person who cannot accept the sheer contingency of life and thus becomes a victim of imprisoning fictions.

But even this subtle variation on the traditions of the detective story is more complex than it first seems. At first glance, Hammett's fiction looks like a celebration of the Op's skeptical pragmatism and a running critique of the danger of superstition and irrationality. But, on closer inspection, this attitude, too, is open to question. In Hammett's subtly self-undermining novels, the detective's professional amorality, and the detective story itself, begin to look like Gabrielle Dain's misguided self-understanding. They are indispensably comforting narratives that make sense of the world while nevertheless leaving their believers captive to potentially confining beliefs.

Hammett deepened that theme in his most brilliant and powerful work, *The Maltese Falcon*, which tells of the intrigues of a group of international criminals competing to gain possession of the mythical, jewel-encrusted statue named in the book's title. That novel's colorful gang of criminals – the jovial and ruthless fat man Caspar Gutman, his gunslinger and lover Elmer, the effeminate cosmopolitan Joel Cairo, and the devious femme fatale Brigid O'Shaughnessy – are bound together in a web of mutual lies and emotional entanglements, so that, like the Dains, they resemble a gothic vision of the bad family. In their efforts to deceive and ensnare each other and to mislead the detective, Sam Spade, the members of that criminal family are like Owen Fitzstephen; they manufacture one misleading story after another – none more exquisitely than the inventive and murderous Brigid, who casts herself like Gabrielle Dain as a captive of malevolent criminals and then follows up that disproven lie with a series of additional, enticing fables. But Hammett's criminals are not just the authors of false stories; they are believers as well, as they reveal through their unwillingness to give up their "quest" for the legendary statue at the novel's center.

In its use of the bird, Hammett's novel mocks and subverts the quest romance, much as *Red Harvest* undermines the western. The Maltese Falcon itself is first cast as a "*rara avis*" that speaks of a mythic spiritual inheritance stretching back to the Crusades and then treated as a "dingus" pursued for its material value.[24] But the most important purpose of the central symbol in Hammett's novel is to show that even people who conceive of themselves as ruthlessly calculating pursuers of self-interest will gladly submit themselves to the most outlandish fantasies so long as they provide a sense of meaning. Although the falcon they have pursued for years is revealed to be a fake, Hammett's criminals simply cannot give up their hope that the true object will materialize at the conclusion of their next escapade. The belief in the falcon in this light is like the belief in love, with which the novel strongly associates it, or in honor or beauty – an implausible but endlessly alluring fable.

Fittingly, then, in the novel's dramatic climax, Spade explains to Brigid why, although he loves her, he must turn her into the police for murder. As she appeals to his passions, his face sweats, his eyes go bloodshot, his voice shakes and the muscles of his cheeks stand out like welts. Even a ruthlessly unsentimental detective like Sam Spade can avoid falling prey to enticing stories of love and romance, in other words only through a supreme effort of will that makes him repellent to other people. In the novel's conclusion, the detective's secretary Effie, seemingly one of his few friends, rebukes him for his action. "I know you're right," she remarks. "But don't touch me." As far as Effie is concerned, the price of the detective's freedom is his humanity. And even that freedom does not look very free. In the novel's final scene, Spade shivers as Effie vengefully sends his nagging former lover Iva, the widow of his murdered partner, into his office. Though Spade has managed to dispatch Brigid, the emotional entanglements that women represent in Hammett's world still have him surrounded.

For Hammett, in short, making literature of the detective story meant turning it into a slyly self-reflexive meditation on the dangerous yet inescapable power of fiction. (Four of his five novels include concealed self-portraits, so that Hammett in effect casts himself as both the author and captive of his own writing.) Not surprisingly, the approach inspired few imitators. Though many pulpsters admired Hammett's skill, few wrote stories that much resembled his. Raymond Chandler, for instance, admired the style ("hard and clean and cold and ventilated"), but not the attitude that accompanied it. "Hammett," he noted, "never really cared for any of his characters."[25]

Caring, by contrast, was the key ingredient that Chandler brought to the detective story. Where Hammett's detectives were cool professionals, Chandler's heroes are men who feel things intensely – who act on personal impulse, find their way by intuition, and pursue their cases not for money (which they typically end up losing) or professional determination, but out of profound emotional commitment.

That different approach was partly the result of the writers' differing backgrounds. Chandler had come to the detective story by a route unlike Hammett's – beginning his work in the pulps in the depths of the Depression not as a cocky young man looking for a break, but as a middle-aged failure who had lost his career as an oil executive to alcoholism. Lacking Hammett's experience in the Pinkertons, Chandler could call up few of the details of crime and investigation that Hammett used to give his fiction the ring of truth. What he could bring to the hard-boiled story was a version of the sensibility he had cultivated in his youth, when he had been an aspiring poet in Edwardian London writing of idealized love and enchanted worlds. When he set out to restart his literary career in the thirties, Chandler joined that wistful attitude to the discipline of the detective story form, giving it a bite absent in the writing of his earlier years. In the process, he also turned the hard-boiled story from a vision of urban warfare into a covert vehicle of longing and sensibility – a kind of concealed romantic poetry. The aim, he later wrote, nearly inverting Hammett's approach, was "the creation of magic by words."[26]

That romantic attitude is evident in nearly every feature of Chandler's work. It can be seen, for example, in the way Chandler magnified possibilities latent in the hard-boiled tradition to make his fiction a powerful vision of the conflict between romantic idealism and an existing world of squalor. In the hard-boiled story as it flourished in the pulps, the city is a place of violence and illegitimate power; in Chandler's fiction Los Angeles blossoms into a baroque landscape of corruption and perversity. Likewise, in the conventional hard-boiled story, the villains are often deceitful women like Brigid O'Shaughnessy who use their sexual allure to mislead the detective. Chandler's femmes fatales are not merely greedy and selfish, but often bizarre pathological creatures – like *The Big Sleep*'s Carmen Sternwood who has "little sharp predatory teeth" and a face that assumes a "bony scraped look" when she falls into the seizures that lead her to murder. Finally, the hard-boiled detective as he descended from Carroll John Daly is a hero concealing himself as a mercenary, but in Chandler's Philip Marlowe he is almost explicitly a reinvention of the courtly knight of medieval romance (an early incarnation was named Malory), struggling desperately to hold the grail of justice and love above the seas of corruption that surround him. Where for Hammett crime (and the crime story itself) was a symptom of popular irrationality, in Chandler's fiction it is an index of the way the world fails to live up to our dreams, a theme to which Chandler's novels return time and again. "Knights had no meaning in this game," Marlowe remarks in *The Big Sleep*, referring directly to a chessboard on which he plays a practice game, but indirectly to his profession. "It wasn't a game for knights."[27]

That regretful vision accounts for the potent emotional tone of Chandler's fiction – which is rife with expressions of distaste, regret, disappointment, and above all loneliness. The detective who is brash in Daly, and icy in Hammett, is a sorrowful man in Chandler. It also informs the feature for which Chandler is usually celebrated – his extraordinary style. Building on a possibility latent in hard-boiled fiction's conventional first-person narrative, Chandler splits his protagonist's voice into two distinct levels. In the dialogue he engages in with other characters, Marlowe preserves the combative manner pioneered by Carroll John Daly. Indeed, the action of Chandler's novels is largely constructed of character contests in which Marlowe jousts verbally with various antagonists and displays his sangfroid while forcing cracks in the composure of his opponents. But to this combative dialogue, Chandler adds the interior monologue through which Marlowe narrates his experiences to the reader. Here, the voice is laden with emotion and rich with imagery – especially Chandler's trademark outlandish similes. Consider, for example, the famous description of the gigantic ex-con Moose Malloy which begins *Farewell, My Lovely*. Moose has shown up on Los Angeles's Central Avenue looking for his former lover Velma, not realizing that while he was in jail the white working-class neighborhood has become part of the African-American ghetto. Standing outside the nightclub where Velma once sang, Moose stares at the windows with "ecstatic fixity, ... like a hunky immigrant catching his first sight of the Statue of Liberty." In the context of the crowd surrounding him, however, he looks "about as inconspicuous as a tarantula on a slice of angel food."[28]

Such unlikely similes emphasize the detective's intense responsiveness to the world he records. Their effect is like that set up by the two levels of Chandler's narrative method in general, and, by the same token, like that created by the two, disparate similes for Moose Malloy in particular. They emphasize the tension between a public world of conflict and struggle (where Moose Malloy looks like an unwelcome and lethal creature), on the one hand, and the reverie of private consciousness (where he is a grand dreamer at the gate of the promised land), on the other. Only the detective, and the readers who understand him, Chandler implies, have the capacity to appreciate the genuine truth of the dream.

What gave Chandler's fiction its power (and distinguished it from the poetry of his youth) was the way he used that romantic vision to illuminate the world in which he lived. The city through which Marlowe moves is a dreamscape of the corrupt and perverse. But it is also a world constructed from distinct details of the Los Angeles Chandler had come to know and informed by the writer's minutely attentive eye for the social geography of class and status. Under the pressure of his imagination, LA's byways and obscure corners – low-rent office buildings, second-rate hotels, stately mansions, secluded subdivisions, anonymous apartment buildings – shine forth as dim clues in an only partly decipherable map. The flotsam and jetsam of its commercial nexus – faith healers, drug dealers, gamblers, torch singers, hustlers, grifters, pornographers – stand out as minor figures in an obscured pageant whose passages provide a resonant means of reading the social life of the city. In the story of Moose Malloy, who had been in jail throughout the thirties and returns to LA to find the Runyonesque city he knew gone – displaced both by the African-American migrants who have streamed into the city throughout the Depression and, less directly, by the greed of a wealthy elite who have prospered even as the working-class city declined – Chandler provides a whole history of interwar LA.

That romantic vision of the city and its observer would make Chandler by far the most influential writer of the hard-boiled detective story. In the decade following World War II, just as the hard-boiled style was becoming familiar enough to look clichéd, striking new variations in the form began to appear. Prompted by the postwar "paperback revolution," which sparked a new demand for popular fiction and opened paths to aspiring authors, a generation of young writers redefined the conventions that had developed in the interwar pulp magazines. Mickey Spillane looked back to his favorite author, Carroll John Daly, and re-invented Daly's swaggering protagonist, making his own variation on the detective hero, Mike Hammer, into a relentless enemy of Communist subversion and sexual freedom. His tales of jubilant vigilantism made Spillane a massive bestseller and the most popular author of the 1950s by far. In the least prestigious fractions of the paperback industry, meanwhile, a cohort of little-known writers, led by the pulp avant-gardist Jim Thompson, fashioned a distinctively dark literature of criminal failure. Building on James M. Cain's novels of the thirties – *The Postman Always Rings Twice* and *Double Indemnity* – which had featured first-person narratives by criminals whose desperate stratagems only ensured their demise – Thompson and a group of like-minded writers (David Goodis, Charles Willeford, Peter Rabe) wrote fatalistic stories of loners on the outskirts of society who schemed for brief criminal pleasures and almost always doomed themselves in the effort. During the same years, writing in Paris, Chester Himes recalled his own youthful experience reading *Black Mask* in prison, and began to adapt the conventions of the genre to craft an account of the segregated life of Harlem. Building his novels around two African-American detectives, Coffin Ed and Gravedigger Jones, Himes created an extraordinary vision of Harlem as a carnivalesque maelstrom boiling out under injustice and repression. In his stories of his detectives' brutal, yet ultimately ineffective, efforts to impose order and achieve justice, Himes resembled no one so much as Hammett.

But it was Chandler's version of the hard-boiled detective story that would prove to exercise the farthest-reaching influence. One version of that influence can be seen in the critically acclaimed novels Ross Macdonald began writing during the fifties. In Macdonald's fiction, which, building quite directly on

Chandler's model, follows the development of California into the new postwar suburbs, the detective becomes a man of sorrows who is distinguished by his emotional insight and the pity he feels for the sufferings of psychically mal-formed people. But Chandler's legacy can be seen in less direct ways as well. His view of the detective as a lonely figure, pained by injustice and intensely sensitive to the social landscape he inhabits, would prove deeply attractive to numerous crime-fiction writers, many of whom would otherwise share little with their predecessor. The countercultural detective stories (James Crumley, Kinky Friedman) that began to appear in the seventies would make use of those qualities. So, too, would the feminist revision of the hard-boiled form crafted by Sara Paretsky and Sue Grafton in the 1980s, as would Michael Nava's novels of gay Chicano lawyer and investigator Henry Rios. Perhaps most impressively, in the series of novels he began in the 1990s, Walter Mosley would reimagine the whole map of Chandler's Los Angeles by adapting Philip Marlowe's attributes for his African-American detective Easy Rawlins – using Chandler's form to take up the struggles and suffering of the people in Watts who had been a largely invisible boundary to Chandler's imagined city.

All of these revisions of the Chandlerian detective tale are also transfigura-tions of the industrial metropolis that was the original setting of the hard-boiled story. Following the path marked by Macdonald, they chart the transformation of the postwar city as its contours and its social geography have been reshaped by the decline of American industrialism and the rise of a postindustrial economy. But all of them, too, use the features of the hard-boiled story to remap their social landscape and render its history into a knowable story. All of them, furthermore, preserve in some form the populist vision that lay at the core of the hard-boiled crime story – of the failures of the legal and social order to protect decent people from elite predation and criminal abuse and of the detective hero's pained awareness of his or her limited ability to redress that injustice.

NOTES

1. Raymond Chandler, "Introduction," *Trouble Is My Business* (1950; repr. New York: Vintage, 1988), p. viii.
2. Joseph Shaw, Editorial Note, *Black Mask* 16, No. 10 (December 1933): 7.
3. *Ibid.*
4. Chandler, "The Simple Art of Murder: An Essay," *The Simple Art of Murder* (1950; repr. New York: Vintage, 1988), p. 14.
5. *Ibid.*, pp. 14–15.
6. Shaw, Editorial Note, 7.
7. Erle Stanley Gardner, "Hell's Kettle," in *The Black Mask Boys: Masters in the Hard-Boiled School of Detective Fiction*, ed. William F. Nolan (New York: Mysterious Press, 1985), p. 126.

8. Shaw, Editorial Note, *Black Mask* 17, No. 11 (January 1935): 7.
9. Carroll John Daly, Letter to the Editor, *Black Mask* 6, No. 5 (June 1, 1923): 127.
10. Daly, "Knights of the Open Palm," *Black Mask* 6, No. 5: 33.
11. Daly, "Three Gun Terry," *Black Mask* 6, No. 4 (May 15, 1923): 5.
12. Editor's Introduction, *ibid.*: 5.
13. Walter Deffenbaugh, "Hear Not, See Not, Speak Not Evil," *Black Mask* 4, No. 3 (December 1921): 55.
14. Daly, *The Snarl of the Beast* (1927; repr. New York: Harper Perennial, 1992), pp. 213, 14.
15. W. H. Auden, "The Guilty Vicarage," in *The Complete Works of W. H. Auden: Prose: Vol. II, 1939–1948*, ed. Edward Mendelson (Princeton University Press, 2002), p. 265.
16. Dashiell Hammett, quoted in Diane Johnson, *Dashiell Hammett: A Life* (New York: Fawcett Columbine, 1985), p. 72.
17. Hammett, *Red Harvest* (1929; repr. New York: Vintage, 1992), p. 85.
18. Hammett, Letter to Editor, *Black Mask* 6, No. 23 (March 1, 1924): 127.
19. Hammett, *The Big Knockover* (1966; repr. New York: Vintage, 1989), pp. 35, 36.
20. Hammett, *Red Harvest*, p. 121.
21. *Ibid.*, p. 33.
22. *Ibid.*, pp. 154, 203.
23. Hammett, *The Dain Curse* (1929; repr. New York: Vintage, 1989), p. 181.
24. Hammett, *The Maltese Falcon* (1930; repr. New York: Vintage, 1992), p. 203.
25. *Selected Letters of Raymond Chandler*, ed. Frank MacShane (New York: Columbia University Press, 1981), pp. 173, 23, 54.
26. *Ibid.*, p. 273.
27. Chandler, *The Big Sleep* (1939; repr. New York: Vintage, 1988), p. 154.
28. Chandler, *Farewell, My Lovely* (1940; repr. New York: Vintage, 1988), p. 3.

6

ANDREW PEPPER

The American roman noir

There is an infamous moment in Dashiell Hammett's 1929 novel *Red Harvest* where his detective, the Continental Op, wakes up bleary-eyed from a laudanum-induced slumber to find his right hand wrapped around "the blue and white handle" of an ice pick whose "needle-sharp blade" has been "buried in Dinah Brand's left breast."[1] Its significance lies not in the fact that Brand has been murdered but rather for the way in which it seems to implicate Hammett's detective in the act itself. Just as revealing is the Op's inability to discount himself as a suspect, at least until the end of the novel when his innocence is finally confirmed. *Red Harvest* is often cited as the first hard-boiled American crime novel, but the fact that it might also constitute the first American roman noir draws attention to the close relationship between what we might tentatively call these different subgenres of crime writing. In the end, the Op's investigative prowess brings order, and the law, to the western US city of Personville and, as such, it might be premature to argue for its classification as a noir novel (as opposed to a hard-boiled *detective* novel), but in other ways the similarities between *Red Harvest* and works by writers such as Horace McCoy, James M. Cain, David Goodis and Jim Thompson are beyond refutation. Before Cain's *The Postman Always Rings Twice* (1934) and even Paul Cain's *Fast One* (1932), Hammett deployed many of the traits or features that would later be cited as characteristic of a "noir" sensibility: an unknowable, morally compromised protagonist who is implicated in the sordid world he inhabits, an overwhelming sense of fatalism and bleakness, and a socio-political critique that yields nothing and goes nowhere.

If nothing else, this example highlights the difficulties associated with categorization. To illustrate this point, Lee Horsley asks quite rightly whether "noir" is best understood as "a visual style, tone, a genre, a generic field, a movement, a cycle, a series – or just a helpful category?"[2] To complicate matters further the term roman noir – literally translated as black novel – was only deployed in relation to a particular kind of American crime fiction as late as the 1980s and, as a term denoting a field of critical study, it has only been operative for about the past twenty years. In a similar fashion, the related label "film noir" did not describe a dedicated cinematic genre, with its own codes and conventions that film-makers self-consciously borrowed from and adapted, but was coined retrospectively by French critics, notably Nino Frank and later Raymond Borde and Étienne Chaumeton. They noticed shared stylistic and thematic preoccupations across films as diverse as *The Maltese Falcon*, *Laura*, *Double Indemnity* and *The Woman in the Window*.[3] In most early accounts of film noir, there is an attempt to differentiate film noir from the hard-boiled school of writing, even while acknowledging the influence of writers like Hammett and Chandler. Borde and Chaumeton, for example, locate this difference in the shift of perspective from investigator to criminal and from the "social" to the "psychological." They also argue that while the hard-boiled school should be seen as part of the emerging police genre, since its primary focus is on the *detection* of crime, film noir is better or more appropriately characterized as the "criminal adventure," or better still the "criminal psychology," a type of movie centrally preoccupied with the "dynamism of violent death."[4]

Richard Gray offers the term "detectiveless crime novels" and Stephen Knight the term "psycho-thriller";[5] if this distinction between committing and investigating crime, and an emphasis on the psychic traumas of its protagonists, constitutes the jumping-off point for my chapter, then all kinds of further caveats and qualifications are necessary. The business of appropriating definitions of film noir in order to characterize what I am calling the American roman noir perhaps poses more methodological problems than it solves, not least because there is very little consensus on how to define or characterize film noir. While most critics are happy to cite hard-boiled fiction, French poetic realism, German expressionism and perhaps even American naturalism as significant cultural antecedents, the question of whether film noir is best understood in terms of its visual style, iconography, narrative patterns, conditions of production, preoccupation with sexuality, philosophical stance or a response to particular historical moments like World War II has been the subject of much debate.[6] More to the point, such an approach threatens to overlook the very significant differences between writing and film-making as artistic and cultural practices. Nonetheless, the debates surrounding film noir have inevitably spilled over and influenced the critical reception of a particular kind of "black" crime fiction, and consequently the question of whether a body of writing characterized by writers like Cain, Goodis and Thompson is best understood as a product of the Depression years (Mike Davis), the emergence of mass consumerism and the rise of the mass market paperback (William Marling, Geoffrey O'Brien), Cold War paranoia (Woody Haut) or the failure of New Deal liberalism (Sean McCann) has *also* been fiercely debated.[7]

For the purposes of this chapter, I do not intend to outline or negotiate a path through this burgeoning field of criticism; rather, I want to build up a picture of what has retrospectively been characterized as the American roman noir through an analysis of particular novels and particular thematic concerns. Literary noir defies straightforward categorization. Still, while any such account that tries to shoehorn writers as diverse as McCoy, Cain, Goodis, Charles Willeford, Thompson and Patricia Highsmith into the same descriptive straitjacket is surely bound to fail, there *are* similar thematic and political concerns that unite these writers, notably relating to the corrosive effects of money, the meaninglessness and absurdity of existence, anxieties about masculinity and the bureaucratization of public life, a fascination with the grotesque and a flirtation with, and rejection of, Freudian psychoanalysis. Indeed, rather than trying to offer an overarching account of the historical development of the American roman noir from the 1930s to the 1950s, I will focus on three of these thematic tropes and demonstrate how particular writers, notably McCoy, Cain, Goodis, Willeford, Thompson and Highsmith, created parables of Americana united by an at times unfocused but politically angry anti-authoritarianism. This is why David Schmid describes noir as a "heretical" category: that is to say, one premised on its opposition to all cultural and political orthodoxies.[8] In this sense, it is tempting to situate noir as a form of popular or pulp modernism: what Horsley calls "the popular expression of the kind of modernist pessimism epitomized in *The Waste Land*"[9] or what Paula Rabinowitz describes as "the peculiar way in which America expressed its uniquely hokey modernism."[10] David Cochran, too, argues for the roman noir as an underground culture that "kept alive the critical impetus of modernism."[11] Still, in looking to expand our definition of modernism beyond its traditionally quite narrow foundational core, and in looking to justify noir in intellectual terms, we must not allow ourselves to get too carried away with this kind of project. For all their heretical energies, noir writers occupy an uneasy space between the academy and the street corner. Thus while "noir" is, indeed, deeply critical of all forms of authority and institutional arrangements and "official" or traditional narratives about social progress, this does not make it an elitist or avant-garde form of culture imposed from above on an unthinking mass audience; as O'Brien says of noir's populist roots, "the public wanted gunfights and Lana Turner, not existentialism and *l'acte gratuit*."[12] To forget this framework, as I will try and show, is to forget who wrote these novels and for whom.

Marxist noir: "All mass culture under monopoly is [not] identical"[13]

The fact that Hammett's *Red Harvest* depicts an orgy of bloodletting and a smattering of sex does not preclude it from offering a coruscating critique of

US society as it is organized under capitalism. The same could be said of Horace McCoy's *They Shoot Horses, Don't They?* (1934). The bestial ugliness of the town in *Red Harvest*, a place physically scarred by the effects of mining and further despoiled by the rapacious business practices of mine owner Elihu Willsson and the proto-capitalist gangs trying to usurp his preeminent position, is testament to Hammett's nascent political anger. Similarly, the dance marathon in *Horses* analogizes the dehumanizing conditions of the workplace whereby contestants endlessly circulate around the arena and in doing so mimic the deadening routine of the factory production line. This is Horkheimer and Adorno's "culture industry" laid bare: the creation of safe, uniform cultural products that bear the indelible imprint of the system that has spawned them and that reflect or indeed produce a new pliant, passive and, above all, imitative subject.[14] In their rush to denunciate the standardized products of mass culture, however, Horkheimer and Adorno overlooked pulp novels like McCoy's *Horses* which, to all intents and purposes, anticipated their criticism; the mechanized, circular motions of the dance marathon contestants speak about exactly the same loss of individuality that would later preoccupy Horkheimer and Adorno. As one of the characters puts it, "There is no new experience in life."[15] The contestants are differentiated from one another only by the products they have been assigned to endorse (surely a perfect embodiment of the concept of the commodity self?). Even McCoy's protagonists, Robert Styverten and Gloria Beatty (who O'Brien describes as representing a "borderline of the human personality, beyond which it cannot be said that there is a person there")[16] are little more than anonymous ciphers; a man and a woman without a past or a future, replaceable and, as with knackered horses, disposable. Indeed, rather than struggling against their circumstances, the contestants, perhaps understandably given the Depression-era context, internalize the values of a dog-eat-dog capitalism and are rewarded for their efforts with just enough sustenance and medical care to keep them alive and in the competition.

But in McCoy's skillful hands, a novel about exploitation and dehumanization is subtly transformed into a commentary on the subversive potential of the kind of violent, brutalizing "entertainment" epitomized by the dance marathon and, by implication, the American roman noir. For one thing, the dance's organizers, Rocky and Socks, are not the unreconstructed capitalist exploiters that a simple reading of the novel would have us believe; at the end when the marathon ends in tragedy and farce they agree to share the prize money equally between the contestants. For another thing, the dance marathon itself is actually by no means banal and predictable, at least in comparison with most of the sugar-coated Hollywood films made by the actors and directors who pay to watch the contestants shuffle around the arena. Indeed what marks the dance marathon as different is both its unpredictability – the fact that any of the contestants might fall or collapse at any moment – and its inherent nastiness. It is an uncomfortable truth that some people might take pleasure in watching or indeed reading about the suffering of others, but McCoy is making an important point: life is constant struggle and art needs to reflect some of this unpleasantness. Like Horkheimer and Adorno, he offers us what amounts to a Marxist critique of capitalist society but with no unrealistic revolutionary hopes. As with *Red Harvest*, McCoy's is a critique which, in the end, yields nothing and goes nowhere: capitalism is not about to implode under the weight of its contradictions. What *Horses* demonstrates, and what Horkheimer and Adorno fail to see, is the subversive possibilities inherent in a popular form that is somehow able to reflect upon, or compel its readers to reflect upon, its own grimly exploitative vision.

Alienation and absurdity: "Does the absurd dictate death?"[17]

The dance marathon in McCoy's *Horses* can be read in one of two ways; either as a particular response to the stultifying effects of the Great Depression and the barbarity of life organized under capitalism, or as a general response to a world that, as Richard Pells puts it, has grown "pointless and absurd."[18] By the same logic, the alienation experienced by the contestants is either a direct product of their commodification within a highly diversified capitalist economy or a general condition of existence in an absurd universe. James M. Cain's *The Postman Always Rings Twice* is structured by this same tension, but while *Horses* ultimately favors a Marxist rather than an existentialist reading, Cain's novel is more finely balanced. Certainly the particular registers of the Depression are visible in *Postman*; as Richard Bradbury argues, Cain's is "a world in which the quintessentially American posture of individual effort being rewarded with security has been shattered by the economic collapse."[19] This is Cora's dilemma: having killed her husband, Nick, with the assistance of drifter-come-lover, Frank Chambers, she wants nothing more than to turn Nick's roadside diner into a thriving commercial concern. "We've got it good. Why wouldn't we stay here?" she says to Frank, when it becomes apparent that he favors a life on the road. "You've been trying to make a bum of me ever since you've known me, but you're not going to do it. I told you, I'm not a bum. I want to *be* something."[20] As in many noir tales, sexual desire, for Cora at least, is yoked to a yearning for material betterment and, in the context of the Depression, this yearning can only be realized through violence; perhaps that is why Mike Davis describes the "Los Angeles Novel of the 1930s" as exemplified by Cain's oeuvre as "the moral phenomenology of the depraved or ruined middle classes."[21]

Frank, however, is a potentially more intriguing character, not least because his motivation – beyond instant sexual gratification – is hard, if not impossible, to fathom. He neither seems to want to usurp Nick's position as petit-bourgeois businessman nor marry and settle down with Cora, but he still agrees to help her kill her husband. In a world where there are no fixed moral absolutes (or where all fixed moral absolutes have been shattered by the economic collapse), Frank's actions may, at times, appear to be irrational but this, I think, is Cain's point. Unable to define himself through his actions and the choices he makes, and possessing little or no self-insight, his life is ruled by contingency and fate; whether he succeeds or fails in the tasks he undertakes is arbitrarily determined by forces beyond both his control and his comprehension, though he half-suspects this when he tells Cora: "We thought we were on top of the mountain. That wasn't it. It's on top of us, and that's where it's been ever since that night."[22] The mountain here – one of the few metaphors employed by Cain in what is otherwise a remarkably spare narrative – adds to the fatalistic tone. When, at the end of the novel, just as Frank and Cora have reconciled themselves to each other, a car crash results in Cora's death and Frank's arrest for her murder, Cain's point seems to be *not* that Frank is going to be justly punished either because the law is omnipotent or because he has behaved in a morally unacceptable manner but rather, and quite simply, that blind chance has intervened.

While McCoy achieved little domestic recognition in his lifetime, he was widely admired in France, particularly by Parisian noirist Marcel Duhamel, who thought him a worthy contemporary of Hemingway and Faulkner. Cain's influence on a new generation of French writers was arguably even greater; famously Camus has cited *Postman* as an influence for his masterpiece *L'Étranger* (1942).[23] What, then, is the relationship between American noir and French existentialism? Certainly one needs to be wary about deploying a term as contested as "existential" too glibly. However, whereas Sartre in *Existentialism and Humanism* (1946) is at pains to identify the positive aspects of his philosophical stance – namely, that in a world devoid of God and fixed moral absolutes "man is nothing else but that which he makes himself"[24] – the American roman noir, as Robert Porfirio notes, tends to dwell on its negative aspects, emphasizing "life's meaninglessness and man's alienation" and "its catch-words include 'nothingness,' 'sickness,' 'loneliness,' 'dread,' 'nausea.'"[25] In Cain's novel, for example, Frank tries to "make himself" but finds only dead-ends and death. The work of David Goodis is also littered by characters who have fallen a long way from grace but who, as James Sallis notes, have often collaborated in their demise and even accepted it, "blurring the hard edge of loss with alcohol, masochistic relationships and, finally, a passivity reflecting utter disengagement with life."[26] Eddie in *Down*

There (1956) – later remade by Truffaut as *Shoot the Piano Player* (1962) – is typical; a man for whom "the sum of everything was a circle, and the circle was labelled Zero."[27] Once a concert pianist who debuted at Carnegie Hall, Eddie's exploitation at the hands of his promoter has resulted in tragedy, and his subsequent descent into the abyss has led him finally to Harriet's Hut in the Philadelphia ghetto where he plays the piano for drunken mill-workers. Numb and detached even from himself, Eddie's cocoon-like existence is threatened first by the arrival in the bar of his wayward brother and then by his attachment to Lena. "It was happening suddenly and much too fast and he tried to stop it,"[28] Goodis writes, describing Eddie's terror at the prospect of feeling a connection with another human being. Ultimately Lena is murdered and Eddie returns to the bar to play the piano, the trauma of death once again enacting a mind/body split. "That's a fine piano, he thought. Who's playing that? He opened his eyes and saw his fingers caressing the keyboard."[29] Still, it is Eddie's capacity to feel and his ability to *act* – his willingness to help others – that distinguishes Goodis's novel and reminds us of Sartre's assertion that we are "condemned" to be free.[30] This particular notion is also picked up and developed by Charles Willeford's 1955 novel *Pick-Up*. Failed artist Harry Jordan and alcoholic heiress Helen Meredith form a suicide pact but, while Harry kills (or believes he kills) Helen, he fails in his efforts to end his own life and, having been exonerated of Helen's murder by a stroke of blind luck, he is set free "to wash dishes . . . smash baggage, carry a waiter's tray, dish up chile beans as a counterman."[31] For me, *Pick-Up* poses the same question raised by Camus in *The Myth of Sisyphus* (1942), namely "Does the Absurd dictate death?" For if "dying voluntarily implies that you have recognized . . . the absence of any profound reason for living,"[32] this seems to describe the nihilistic worldview of Harry and Helen. However, just as Camus ultimately rejects the logic of his own question, Harry's perseverance *in spite* of life's meaninglessness suggests that the real effort, as Camus puts it, is indeed "to stay there."[33] More to the point, whereas Goodis – and Camus for that matter – are less interested in casting the plight of their characters in purely economic terms, Willeford (perhaps with one eye on McCoy rather than Cain) remains stubbornly anti-consumerist and thereby re-orientates noir back to its materialist roots. The world is not Harry's or Helen's because it is absurd, but rather because life, art and all human relations have been hopelessly and grotesquely distorted under capitalism.

The sexual abyss: "We might just be cold-blooded and smart as hell"

If noir is, as Schmid argues, a heretical category – that is to say, a type of writing committed to overturning or debunking cultural and political orthodoxies – one cannot assume that its transgressive impulses are necessarily politically progressive. The treatment of sexual desire is a case in point. From the moment where Frank Chambers "sunk his teeth into [Cora's] lips so deep [he] could feel the blood spurt into [his] mouth"[34] sexual desire in the American roman noir, as it is exercised by men against women, has adopted both misogynistic and violent overtones. For Frank, as for many noir protagonists, sexuality remains something of an abyss, a primeval force that he neither understands nor can control, and which compels him to act in ways that defy conventional explanation. It is no coincidence that noir came of age at a time marked by what Frank Krutnik describes as an extensive popularization of "Freudian psychoanalysis" in American culture, and in this sense Krutnik is right to point out that film noir led the way.[35] Emblematic of this convergence was the film adaptation of Cain's 1935 novel *Double Indemnity*, directed by Billy Wilder and only released in 1944, partly because of the limitations imposed on Wilder by the Hollywood censors. If sex could not be treated as explicitly and gratuitously on the screen as on the page, this did not mean that it disappeared altogether. Rather, as Marling notes, "salacious events had to be figured in icons, symbols, gestures, stage business, costumes, lighting, expression and intonation."[36] In *Double Indemnity*, for instance, Phyllis Dietrichson's (Barbara Stanwyk) rank sexuality is coded via her ankle bracelet (and its longstanding associations with prostitution), a fetish object that cuts into her bare skin and in doing so entrances insurance salesman Walter Neff (Fred McMurray). Many critics have discussed how the coding of sexuality into symbols evokes "Freud's notion of the dream work,"[37] and this particular association is strengthened by self-conscious attempts on the part of film-makers to deploy a popularized version of psychoanalysis in their movies. *Double Indemnity* has proved to be a particularly rich ground for contemporary critics wanting to read the film through various psychoanalytic lenses, not least because it seems to actively encourage such readings. For example, Walter's motivation for doing what he does is explained not by his sexual attraction for Phyllis but via his desire to transgress the Law of the Father as represented by his mentor and boss Barton Keyes (Edward G. Robinson).[38]

Still, while film noir, for the reasons outlined above, has, by and large, opened itself up to psychoanalytic ideas and criticism, American noir *novelists* have not shared this preoccupation and have tended to eschew psychological or familial explanations for the deviant actions of their protagonists in favor of ones that foreground their characters' social and political circumstances. Willeford's *Pick-Up* contains a withering assault on the inadequacies of psychoanalysis as a tool to explain motivation, but Jim Thompson's *The Killer Inside Me* (1952) is perhaps the best example of this maneuver. Lou Ford, the sheriff of a small west Texan town, might describe himself as "a typical Western-country peace officer,"[39] but he suffers from a self-diagnosed malady or "sickness" – a condition which apparently causes him to launch a sickeningly brutal assault on prostitute Joyce Lakeland. Thompson offers us a neat familial explanation for this condition. Ford's youth has apparently been scarred by a sado-masochistic relationship with his father's housekeeper Helene and by his father's decision to have him sterilized as a punishment; something he cites to explain his rape and murder of a three-year-old girl and his violent antipathy towards all women. As with Cain's *Postman*, sexual desire is suggestive of a more general social and cultural transgression, but rather than yielding something progressive or liberating, it manifests itself only in acts of sickening violence and, ultimately, death. Ford's father was a doctor and in his library of medical tomes (which Ford has inherited along with the familial house) are works by "Krafft-Ebing, Jung, Freud, Bleuler, Adolf Meyer, Kretschmer, Kraepelin."[40] Indeed Ford is so well read in psychoanalytic theories that he is seemingly able to diagnose himself. "This was written about a disease or a condition, rather, called dementia praecox," he remarks, having given a description by Kraepelin that perfectly describes himself – "Schizophrenia, paranoid type. Acute, recurrent, advanced."[41] However, Thompson refuses to endorse this diagnosis and a little later Ford seems to backtrack: "We might have the disease, the condition; or we might just be cold-blooded and smart as hell."[42] Rather than explaining Ford's condition in familial or psychoanalytic terms, Thompson offers us an alternative – and more unsettling – interpretation: it is a manifestation of a much broader sickness affecting mid-century America. Cochran and McCann have both examined how noir or underground writers like Thompson map a growing disillusionment with public life and culture in the 1950s and, in this sense, Ford's banal venality simply reflects the conditions of existence in Central City (or everywhere USA), where all human relations have been debased by a rapacious form of capitalism as practiced by construction tycoon Chester Conway.[43]

It is hard not to dwell on Lou Ford's horrific sexualized violence – Ford kills men, but only because he has to, and women because, one suspects, he enjoys it – and wonder whether the roman noir itself is inherently misogynistic. Certainly most of its practitioners, women included – Dorothy B. Hughes and Patricia Highsmith come to mind – tend to dwell on male, rather than female, degeneracy and, as is the case with film noir, the depiction of female characters, especially the femme fatale, tends first and foremost to mask "a crisis in *male* identity projected onto women."[44] Film noir's potentially reactionary gender politics have been the subject of much critical debate (Janey Place, for example, argues that film noir is first and foremost a male fantasy in which women are problematically categorized as sexual)[45]. However, in so far as movies like *Double Indemnity* and novels like *Postman* feature what Sylvia Harvey calls an "absence of family" (thereby opposing a patriarchal logic in which family functions as the "locus of women's particular oppression"), noir allows "for the production of the seeds of counter-ideologies."[46] Highsmith's *The Talented Mr. Ripley* (1955) offers a similarly unusual, and potentially counter-hegemonic, perspective on the subject of male sexual deviance in so far as her protagonist Tom Ripley may or may not be a repressed homosexual, and the return of what has been repressed may or may not be responsible for the way he violently batters his friend Dickie Greenleaf to death with an oar.[47] Intriguingly, however, sexual desire, for Tom at least, is intricately bound up with class envy and bourgeois aspiration and therefore the act of killing Dickie is not necessarily the product of self-disgust (i.e. the fact that "disgust always bears the imprint of desire")[48] but rather a more complex manifestation of material and aesthetic yearnings that culminate in Tom's plan to assume Dickie's identity. What Tom ultimately seems to desire is not Dickie himself but his rings, silver lighter, cuff-links, white silk shirts and his "black fountain pen with gold initials."[49] In so far as Tom "had an ecstatic moment when he thought of all the pleasures that lay before him now with Dickie's money,"[50] sexual desire itself is figured in terms of a particular kind of bourgeois aestheticism. On the one hand, then, Tom's sexual non-conformity is potentially disruptive and threatens what Jonathan Dollimore calls the "social cohesion" and "boundaries of the larger culture"[51] but, on the other hand, his desire, like his personality, is both imitative (he wants to be Dickie) and characterized in entirely non-threatening, aspirational terms. In this sense, he is the ultimate conformist, a man with a "thoroughly forgettable face"[52] whose desire is simply a more acute and more discriminating manifestation of the same materialist impulses that grease the wheels of a generalized capitalist culture. In other words, if desire is understood in material rather than sexual terms, the incitement of desire, like the incitement of disgust, constitutes a normalizing rather than a disruptive force. As with Lou Ford, the real terror lies in the fact that Tom Ripley is not different from the rest of us, perhaps one reason we, as readers, quietly cheer for an apparently cold-blooded killer. As with Thompson, too, Highsmith's cool juggling of political critique and acquiescence would once and for all drive a nail into the coffin of any lingering desire to appropriate noir for solely politically progressive ends.

Conclusion: The rise and fall of the paperback original

From its origins in the work of writers like Hammett, McCoy and Cain, and developing through what became known as film noir in the 1940s, the

American roman noir flourished – albeit temporarily – in the paranoid, febrile atmosphere of the 1950s. Goodis, Willeford, Thompson and Highsmith all produced their best, most memorable works in this decade, perhaps as a reaction against perceived social conformism. The fact that these works set out to debunk received wisdoms, critique particular administrative arrangements, depict the futility and absurdity of existence or assault readers' expectations with their often lurid portraits of the rank unpleasantness of American life and the murderous capacities of their protagonists did not mean that writers like Goodis or Thompson were self-consciously trying to write complex or overtly political novels. Thompson and Goodis wrote quickly and primarily for money; this was pulp writing, with an emphasis on the pulp, and as such, was perfectly suited to the emerging format of the paperback original. The rise of the paperback and the high point of the American roman noir coincided not necessarily because editors and publishers in the 1950s were willing to take risks by putting out difficult, debased works like Thompson's *The Killer Inside Me*. Rather, as O'Brien notes, "publishers worked under circumstances anarchic enough to permit a few unexpected and remarkable freedoms."[53] In one sense, O'Brien is suggesting that works such as *The Killer Inside Me* might not have been published at all, if not for the sheer quantity of books rolling off the production lines – after all, in such an environment, how could an editor be expected to maintain a strict control over all content? In another sense, he is arguing for the absolute indivisibility of product and content: for, as he puts it, "the paperback's lightness enables us to bear the heaviness of what occurs inside it."[54]

It may be too simple or too schematic to argue that the earliest paperbacks "gave rise to paeans of praise to the democratic spirit," while later incarnations provoked "cries of horror at the degradation of mass taste,"[55] but such a formulation hints at two further, important insights. First, that this heyday could not last for ever, and sooner rather than later the paperback industry would be subject to the same scrutiny and regulation as other popular media; and, second, that in the hands of writers like Thompson the American roman noir deliberately sought to sully the "democratic spirit" associated with an earlier New Deal epoch and explore the extent to which the postwar world, to quote McCann, "looked not like the realization of mass democracy but a system of bureaucratic institutions and individual alienation."[56] In both cases, there were, and are, only figurative and quite literal dead-ends. The end of Thompson's 1959 novel *The Getaway*, tinged with a macabre, end-of-an-era surrealism, is indicative. Bank robbers do not die and go to heaven; like "Doc" McCoy and his wife Carol they end up in the kingdom of El Rey where "disease is unknown" and "all accommodations – everything one must buy – are strictly first class."[57] Since there is no capacity to earn a living in El

Rey's kingdom, one must bring sufficient cash to live out one's days, but the high standard of living ensures greater longevity and an eventual depletion of resources, particularly as El Rey's fees are so exorbitant; a situation that, in turn, turns couples, married or otherwise, against one another and where "the outcome depends on which of the two is the shrewder, the more cold-blooded or requires the least sleep."[58] If one has not quite understood this analogy, Thompson makes it even clearer: those who cannot pay are cast out of El Rey's kingdom and survive only by eating one another. As a police officer points out to Doc: "One need only live literally as he has always done figuratively."[59] Two further points are worth reiterating by way of a conclusion. First, the bureaucratic institutions of the state – analogized here at El Rey's kingdom – do not create the conditions necessary for collective life but rather serve the vested interests of the wealthy and powerful, to the utter detriment of an individual's ethical capacity to live and act. And second, death in such an environment is imminent and inescapable. So it is for Doc and Carol at the end of *The Getaway* and so it would be for the American roman noir, at least in its richest, most vibrant incarnation. Thompson, Goodis and Highsmith would continue to write throughout the 1960s and 1970s but all would become marginal figures in a much changed cultural and literary landscape. *The Getaway* offers us a fitting epitaph: "when people die they are dead – as who should know better than you?"[60]

NOTES

1. Dashiell Hammett, *Red Harvest*, in *The Four Great Novels: The Dain Curse, The Glass Key, The Maltese Falcon, Red Harvest* (London: Picador, 1982), p. 147.
2. Lee Horsley, *The Noir Thriller* (Basingstoke: Palgrave Macmillan, 2001), p. 6.
3. See Raymond Borde and Étienne Chaumeton, "Towards a Definition of Film Noir," in *Film Noir Reader*, ed. Alain Silver and James Ursini (New York: Limelight Editions, 1996), p. 17.
4. Borde and Chaumeton, "Towards a Definition," pp. 17, 19.
5. Richard Gray, *A History of American Literature* (Oxford: Blackwell, 2004), p. 751; Stephen Knight, *Crime Fiction 1800–2000: Detection, Death, Diversity* (Basingstoke: Palgrave Macmillan, 2004), pp. vii, 125.
6. For a good description and overview of this debate see Steve Neale, *Genre and Hollywood* (London: Routledge, 2000), pp. 151–3.
7. See Mike Davis, *City of Quartz: Excavating the Future in Los Angeles* (London: Vintage, 1992); William Marling, *The American Roman Noir: Hammett, Cain and Chandler* (Athens, GA: University of Georgia Press, 1995); Geoffrey O'Brien, *Hardboiled America: Lurid Paperbacks and the Masters of Noir* (New York: Da Capo Press, 1997); Woody Haut, *Pulp Culture: Hardboiled Fiction and the Cold War* (London: Serpent's Tail, 1995); Sean McCann, *Gumshoe America: Hardboiled Crime Fiction and the Rise and Fall of New Deal Liberalism* (Durham, NC: Duke University Press, 2000).

8. David Schmid, "Noir and Its Heretics" (Keynote Address, the Noircon conference, Philadelphia, April 3, 2008).

9. Horsley, *The Noir Thriller*, p. 1.

10. Paula Rabinowitz, *Black & White & Noir: America's Pulp Modernism* (New York: Columbia University Press, 2002), p. 6.

11. David Cochran, *American Noir: Underground Writers and Filmmakers of the Postwar Era* (Washington, DC: Smithsonian Institution Press, 2000), p. 14.

12. O'Brien, *Hardboiled America*, p. 61.

13. Max Horkheimer and Theodore W. Adorno, *Dialectic of Enlightenment*, ed. Gunzelin Schmid Noerr, trans. Edmund Jephcott (Stanford University Press, 2002), p. 95; I have added the "not" to alter their point for my purposes.

14. See, for example, Horkheimer and Adorno, *Dialectic of Enlightenment*, p. 125.

15. Horace McCoy, *They Shoot Horses, Don't They?* (Harmondsworth: Penguin, 1970), p. 53.

16. O'Brien, *Hardboiled America*, p. 117.

17. Albert Camus, *The Myth of Sisyphus* (Harmondsworth: Penguin, 1975), p. 16.

18. Richard Pells, *Radical Visions and American Dreams: Culture and Social Thought in the Depression Years* (New York: Harper & Row, 1973), p. 222.

19. Richard Bradbury, "Sexuality, Guilt and Detection: Tension between History and Suspense," in *American Crime Fiction: Studies in the Genre*, ed. Brian Docherty (Basingstoke: Macmillan, 1988), p. 89.

20. James M. Cain, *The Postman Always Rings Twice* (London: Orion, 2005), p. 90.

21. Davis, *City of Quartz*, p. 40.

22. Cain, *The Postman*, p. 108.

23. Horsley, *The Noir Thriller*, p. 71.

24. Jean-Paul Sartre, *Existentialism and Humanism* (London: Methuen, 2007), p. 30.

25. Robert Porfirio, "No Way Out: Existential Motifs in Film Noir," in *Film Noir Reader*, ed. Silver and Ursini, p. 81.

26. James Sallis, *Difficult Lives: Jim Thompson, David Goodis, Chester Himes* (New York: Gryphon, 2000), p. 49.

27. David Goodis, *Down There*, in *Crime Novels: American Noir of the 1950s*, ed. Robert Polito (New York: Library of America, 1997), p. 654.

28. *Ibid.*, p. 609.

29. *Ibid.*, p. 730.

30. Sartre, *Existentialism and Humanism*, p. 38.

31. Charles Willeford, *Pick-Up*, in *Crime Novels*, ed. Polito, p. 567.

32. Camus, *Myth of Sisyphus*, p. 13.

33. *Ibid.*, p. 17.

34. Cain, *The Postman*, p. 9.

35. Frank Krutnik, *In a Lonely Street: Film Noir, Genre, Masculinity* (London: Routledge, 1991), p. 45.

36. Marling, *The American Roman Noir*, p. 254.

37. Borde and Chaumeton quoted in Krutnik, *In a Lonely Street*, p. 50.

38. For a fuller psychoanalytic reading of the film, see Claire Johnson, "Double Indemnity," in *Contemporary Film Theory*, ed. Anthony Easthope (Harlow: Longman, 1993), pp. 135–46.

39. Jim Thompson, *The Killer Inside Me*, in *Crime Novels*, ed. Polito, p. 19.

40. *Ibid.*, p. 18.

41. *Ibid.*, p. 144.
42. *Ibid.*, p. 146.
43. See Cochran, *American Noir*, p. 13, and McCann, *Gumshoe America*, pp. 200, 212.
44. Deborah Thomas, "How Hollywood Deals with the Deviant Male," in *The Movie Book of Film Noir*, ed. Ian Cameron (London: Studio Vista, 1992), p. 64.
45. Janey Place, "Women in Film Noir," in *Women in Film Noir*, ed. E. Ann Kaplan (London: BFI Publishing, 1998), pp. 47–68.
46. Sylvia Harvey, "Women's Place: The Absent Family of Film Noir," in *Women in Film Noir*, p. 46.
47. For this reading, see Cochran, *American Noir*, p. 125.
48. See Jonathan Dollimore, *Sexual Dissidence: Augustine to Wilde, Freud to Foucault* (Oxford: Clarendon Press, 1991), p. 247.
49. Patricia Highsmith, *The Talented Mr. Ripley*, in *Crime Novels*, ed. Polito, p. 266.
50. *Ibid.*, p. 254.
51. Jonathan Dollimore, *Sex, Literature and Censorship* (Cambridge: Polity, 2001), p. 47.
52. Highsmith, *The Talented Mr. Ripley*, p. 189.
53. O'Brien, *Hardboiled America*, p. 17.
54. *Ibid.*, p. 9.
55. *Ibid.*, p. 8.
56. McCann, *Gumshoe America*, p. 212.
57. Jim Thompson, *The Getaway* (London: Corgi, 1989), pp. 202, 203.
58. *Ibid.*, p. 206.
59. *Ibid.*, p. 210.
60. *Ibid.*, p. 213.

7

ILANA NASH

Teenage detectives and teenage delinquents

Today, in the early twenty-first century, mystery series are known as a wide-spread, profitable genre of children's literature. This was not always the case; while adult mystery series thrived in the late nineteenth century, mystery series for children did not appear on the American cultural landscape until the 1920s. When they arrived, they proved immensely popular. Led by the success of the Hardy Boys and Nancy Drew mysteries, which debuted in 1927 and 1930, respectively, the literature of teen detection multiplied during the period from the 1930s to the 1950s. In those same years, youth itself commanded attention in the news and entertainment media; during the course of the early to mid twentieth century, teenagers were increasingly recognized as a distinct and potent category of social identity. As this recognition developed, so did adult concerns about the separatist nature of youth culture, its tendency to develop new cultural styles and mores that opposed white middle-class standards of decency. Youth historians Joe Austin and Michael Nevin Willard, surveying the twentieth-century discourse of adolescence, have noted in it "the bifurcated social identity of youth as a vicious, threatening sign of social decay and 'our best hope for the future.'"[1] Crime writing proved a useful venue for expressing both identities. In children's mysteries, adults wrote of teens who saved the world; in the adult-oriented genres of journalism and pulp fiction, adults wrote of teens as juvenile delinquents who augured America's doom.

In both their worst and best guises, teens in crime writing are defined as people with a subversive power to cross boundaries in the search for knowledge and experience. The mystery genre itself depends ultimately on the power of knowledge, in the detective's ability to penetrate the secrets of criminals. The Hardy Boys and Nancy Drew series offered readers the pleasures of seeing adolescents triumph over adults in their superior ability to know: the teen detectives out-perform adult police and outwit adult criminals. Juvenile delinquency stories also relied on assumptions of youth's desire to know, to break taboos and trespass into the adult world of illicit activities.

Both types of literature, written by adults, assume that adolescents have a natural drive toward transgressive knowledge.

This assumption reflected developments in the early twentieth century that influenced adult conceptions of youth. Previously, the ideologies of the Victorian era had established a construction of childhood as a condition of *not* knowing – a delightful, pre-lapsarian stage of human development, before one eats from the Tree of Knowledge and is expelled from Edenic purity. In 1904, psychologist G. Stanley Hall's book *Adolescence* described the teen years as a period of "storm and stress" in which youth lose the complacent happiness of childhood and experience emotional turmoil. As Hall's influential theories spread, social authorities discussed adolescence as a time when innocence is most threatened, not only by incipient adulthood, but by teens' innately turbulent desires to experience forbidden adventures. The literatures of teens and crime used the image of the teenager to address anxieties about social control and the future of American society.

The rise of children's mystery fiction

During the late nineteenth century, before series books were a common feature of children's literature, mystery stories reached young readers through story papers and dime novels. Story papers, in a format similar to newspapers, offered children short stories and continuing serials that focused on various kinds of adventures, with some mysteries included. Dime novels, of which mysteries were a popular subgenre, were read by a working-class audience that included adults as well as teens. In the 1880s a writer named Edward Stratemeyer started his career by writing for story papers and dime novels. In 1892 he began contributing to the already famous Nick Carter detective series, eventually writing a total of twenty-two volumes.[2] Stratemeyer gradually moved away from the milieu of dime novels into the more middle-class, "respectable" market of hardcover boys' fiction. In 1905 he founded the Stratemeyer Syndicate, where he devised concepts for series books and hired ghostwriters to develop his outlines into complete manuscripts, which he published under a variety of pseudonyms.

Though some of Stratemeyer's series (like the long-lived Bobbsey Twins books) were aimed at small children, the majority targeted readers between ten and fifteen. Series like Tom Swift presented adolescent heroes as the best of modern youth: lively, quick, forward-thinking, adept with modern technologies and active in modern pursuits. During the 1910s and 1920s, the Syndicate became the leading producer of series fiction for children. In 1926, noting that mystery series were thriving in the adult market, Stratemeyer proposed to his publishers what would become the Hardy Boys Mysteries, the longest-enduring of Stratemeyer's boys' series. The idea was ground-breaking; there had not yet been a children's series devoted solely to mysteries, with teenage detectives as recurring figures. Stratemeyer designed the Hardy Boys as two brothers, Frank and Joe, who follow in the footsteps of their father, a famous professional detective. The market proved receptive; the first few volumes of the Hardy Boys, released in 1927, sold well enough to warrant further volumes and a further extension of the format to a girls' series: in 1930 Stratemeyer released the Nancy Drew Mysteries, which surpassed the Hardy Boys in sales and would eventually become the Syndicate's most famous and most successful creation.

If penetrating mysteries was attractive to youth of both sexes, it was distinctly so to girls, because girls' literature of the early twentieth century did not often encourage its readers to penetrate anything. Even Stratemeyer's girls' series of the 1910s and 1920s tended to show their heroines as adventurous, but less so than boys. Ideologies of the day still imagined females as less ambitious, skilled and ingenious than their male counterparts. Women's intellectual abilities as "knowers" was a recent concept; women had obtained federal voting rights only ten years before Nancy Drew's debut, and many American universities still denied access to female students. In mystery stories for adults, female detectives were not entirely new; a few had appeared in earlier popular fiction. But those women were often constructed as anomalies, and their quest for knowledge was described from a condescending point of view; an early female detective in a British magazine was called "Miss Van Snoop."[3] Like the Hardy Boys, but unlike her female literary forebears, Nancy Drew is smarter and more capable than anyone else in her universe.

Often cited by professional women as one of their childhood inspirations, Nancy Drew broke ground as an icon of feminine independence. She excels at everything she undertakes and is never subjugated to negative adult authority; her widowed father, a renowned attorney, gives her total freedom to solve her mysteries, while adult authorities, like the police, treat her with respect. These qualities were rare even in other girl-centered mysteries. The Judy Bolton Mysteries, by Margaret Sutton, competed with Nancy Drew during the 1930s and beyond; but they never reached the same degree of success, partly because Sutton portrayed Judy as a normal girl with flaws and a normal subjection to adult authority. A paragon of perfection and freedom, Nancy Drew attracted a large national audience. Although the Hardy Boys' exploits were less abnormal for boys than Nancy Drew's were for girls, and hence less excitingly new, both series remained more popular than the many imitators who followed them throughout the 1930s, 1940s and 1950s – years in which youth itself became an increasing topic of public conversation.

The worrisome rise of youth culture, 1920s to the 1950s

While young teens were happily reading about powerful adolescent detectives who protect society's boundaries, adults were nervously watching older teens' assaults on traditional boundaries. When the Hardy Boys debuted in the late 1920s, the United States was experiencing its first nationwide introduction to the concept of a unified youth culture. As Paula Fass has shown, the affluence of the middle class led to a swell in college enrollments; in these relatively sheltered environments, away from parental supervision, youth in the period after World War I developed daring styles and philosophies that raised elders' eyebrows.[4] The American media spoke with alarm (and titillation) about *Flaming Youth*, the title of a 1923 book. At a time when Prohibition outlawed alcohol, youth drank bootleg liquor in speakeasies, to which they drove – recklessly – in their newly ubiquitous automobiles. Girls "bobbed" their hair in defiance of traditional styles, and wore daring fashions. Youth of the period had a more open attitude toward sex than their parents' generation, and such social innovations as "petting parties" caused widespread concern that sexual propriety was drastically eroding. Conservative cultural authorities also objected to the popularity of jazz music, considered lowly and socially degenerate because of its African-American origins. In 1921 the *Ladies Home Journal* asked, "Does Jazz Put the Sin in Syncopation?"[5] Public discourse repeatedly worried that the new youth culture was damaging the traditional hierarchies of race, class and gender upon which society relied.

The peer culture of youth spread during the following decades, assisted by an increase in high-school enrollments during the Depression of the 1930s. As more American teens found themselves commonly experiencing high-school rituals such as yearbooks, team sports and proms, a clearly definable age-based culture emerged that adult society simultaneously both worried about and exploited as a commodity. The late 1930s saw a large growth in plays and films with teenage protagonists, usually comedies in which adult writers portrayed teens as silly and frivolous creatures.[6] But the impact of teens on society was also discussed more seriously, both as a focus of concern in its delinquent aspect, and as a positive development for the American economy – starting with the fashion industry in the 1920s, manufacturers of all kinds during the 1930s to the 1950s began marketing products specifically aimed at teenage consumers.[7] The word "teenager," used only sporadically and inconsistently at first, became a commonly accepted moniker for adolescents by the end of the 1930s.[8]

World War II brought new levels of independence and social influence for American teenagers. Many dropped out of school, lured by manufacturing jobs that opened when adult men left to fight. With financial autonomy came a lack of submission to parental authority that alarmed many adults. At the same time, another threat to traditional hierarchies came in the form of the growing fields of psychology and sociology, which, since the days of Hall's influential *Adolescence*, had increasingly advised parents to take an understanding approach to their teenage children, instead of the strict authoritarianism favored in earlier generations. In 1945 the *New York Times*, the nation's most respected newspaper, published a "Teen-Age Bill of Rights."[9] In the eyes of many observers, these increased freedoms and rights were a dangerous development, because they encouraged youth to feel too important, too entitled to challenge the hierarchies of an adult-run world. How could such youngsters be trusted to reproduce the status quo when they reached adulthood?

During the 1940s and 1950s J. Edgar Hoover, head of the FBI, made dire predictions that the war's erosion of morality in America would lead to sharp increases in juvenile delinquency. The media published his and other authorities' concerns in a tone that fostered a moral panic – a widespread discourse of impending doom that surpassed the actual facts. The discussion of juvenile delinquency in the national media spiked sharply between 1953 and 1958, and, as James Gilbert has demonstrated, this rhetoric was heavily exaggerated; the statistics showing large increases in teen crime stemmed in part from new definitions of "criminal" behavior and new methods of data-gathering used by federal agencies like the FBI and the Children's Bureau, which made the incidence of such crime seem to grow more than it actually did.[10] Anxieties about the atomic bomb and the Cold War were transferred, as political anxieties often are, on to the image of the nation's youth, and many unquestioningly consumed the widespread story of teen behavior as a serious threat to postwar American society.

The delinquency discourse relied heavily on conservative hierarchies of gender, race and social class. Definitions of delinquent behavior divided along gender lines; although vandalism and violence qualified as delinquency for both sexes, sexual activity was enough to label many girls delinquent, while the same was not true for boys. As Gilbert notes, the types of behavior deemed criminal were influenced not just by actual laws, but by the morality of the white middle class – a morality which emphasized the importance of girls' chastity, as well as other well-defended boundaries, like those between the races and classes. Non-white and working-class teens often appeared as the most dangerous offenders in 1940s and 1950s reports of teen crime. When kids from "good" homes (i.e., white middle-class ones) went bad, those stories were framed in a tone of shock at society's apparent devolution, for it seemed that the future generation of citizens was being corrupted by "inferior" cultures. The popularity of rock 'n' roll music seemed proof of this downward trend; criticized for its African-American origins and sexual dances, rock 'n' roll became synonymous with dangerous youthful misbehavior in the popular imagination of the 1950s, much as jazz had in the 1920s.

The 1950s delinquency panic spawned a subgenre of pulp fiction that focused on the crimes of teenagers who were "growing up too fast," in an oft-used phrase. In titles like *Rock 'N Roll Gal* (1957), *Delinquent!* (1958), and *Teen-Age Terror* (1958), this genre portrayed high-schoolers as violent gang members and sex-crazed drug addicts. While some teenagers doubtlessly enjoyed the vicarious thrills in these lurid tales, there is little evidence to suggest that teen readers constituted a substantial audience for such texts. Like most pulp fiction, the delinquency novels addressed an imagined audience of adult males; they depicted teenagers as feral beasts driven by brutal passions, hardly a complimentary portrait. Teenagers of the postwar period had other books to read that portrayed them in a far better light; the field of adolescent literature, like many teen-oriented products, developed during the 1940s and 1950s. And, as Lucy Rollin has shown, postwar teens who favored crime stories were also avidly reading adult mysteries like the Mickey Spillane series, which allowed teens to identify with the hero-detective.[11] In its on-screen guise, however, the image of the juvenile delinquent was certainly popular with teens; serious films like *The Wild One* (1953), *Rebel Without a Cause* (1955), and many of their lower-budget imitators, portrayed delinquents as romantic heroes misunderstood by a hostile adult world. This image struck a resonant chord with teen moviegoers, and the genre of delinquency films thrived from the mid-1950s through the 1960s.[12]

The best-remembered of the delinquency novels, *The Blackboard Jungle*, reached many teen consumers because of its dual status as a book and a film. Written in 1954 by Evan Hunter, who also published mystery fiction under the name Ed McBain, *The Blackboard Jungle*'s very title reveals its vision of high-school students as wild animals. The story follows a first-year teacher at a vocational high school in a rough New York neighborhood. The students are violent, impoverished hoodlums; as one reviewer put it, the protagonist's central conflict is "Dealing with Morons in Revolt."[13] The revolts include scenes in which students beat up teachers and attempt to rape one. There is little to flatter an adolescent reader here, though some teens may have enjoyed reading about youth's power to subvert adult authority. The film version, released in 1955, attracted teens partly because it was the first film to use rock 'n' roll music on its soundtrack: Bill Haley and the Comets' hit "Rock Around the Clock" plays over the film's opening credits, and there were reports of teenagers dancing in the aisles of movie theaters. Adult response was wary; the film was banned in two states on the grounds that it would give dangerous ideas to youngsters, and was "voted the picture that hurt America most in foreign countries by the American Legion."[14] It did not help America's image during the Cold War to show the country's next generation as uncontrollable criminals.

Teenage detectives and the restoration of social order

While the media focused on the delinquent natures of high-school youth, those teens' younger siblings were avidly reading mystery series about wholesome and righteous teenagers. Sales of Hardy Boys and Nancy Drew mysteries increased during the 1950s, when the unprecedentedly large baby-boomer generation, born after 1945, reached the ten-to-fifteen age group to which publishers marketed juvenile mystery series. Parents of those children approved of the books, often having read them in their own youth. At a time when fears of delinquency led countless officials to advocate monitoring children's consumption of popular culture, the Hardy Boys' and Nancy Drew's status as "clean" entertainment assisted their popularity. Believing that children emulated what they consumed, social authorities advised giving children texts that taught sound moral values. The products of the Stratemeyer Syndicate exemplified such values, even while offering young readers the joy of seeing powerful teenagers vanquish adult criminals and surpass the achievements of adult detectives.

A shift in sensibilities had occurred around the issue of adult approval since the turn of the century, when pulp-fiction genres and early series books were decried as bad influences on the young. Dime novels, including those written by the younger Edward Stratemeyer, often contained morally questionable protagonists who indulged in such vices as drinking, smoking and gambling. As Deidre Johnson has noted, dime novels were not bought for children by parents; they were purchased by youth themselves as a form of escapist pleasure. "Consequently, [Stratemeyer] provides glimpses of a lurid world, where characters indulge in actions and activities forbidden to children."[15]

But dime novels addressed a broad audience comprised of adults as well as youth. Books intended solely for children were a different matter; they were expected to assume, and preserve, a state of innocence in their readers. The early series books' audience, and their costlier format (hard-cover books aimed at a "nicer," more middle-class readership), required consistent whole-someness in content. None of the protagonists in Stratemeyer's children's books engages in immoral behavior. There is no jazz or rock music, no sex or grisly violence. The books' central crimes are usually thefts and kidnappings. Although Nancy, Frank and Joe are often tied up, knocked unconscious, or dosed with chloroform, none sustains serious damage. Their sleuthing leads them into dangerous situations, but never an immoral locale like a racetrack or speakeasy. None of the protagonists drinks alcohol or smokes. (In a notable anomaly, the earliest printings of *The Secret of the Wooden Lady* (1950) contained an illustration in which Nancy Drew's boyfriend, Ned, holds a cigarette between his fingers. All printings after 1951 were emended to remove the cigarette.)[16]

To be sure, these series did share a familial resemblance with their dime-novel ancestors: the action is fast-paced, chapters end with improbable cliff-hangers, and convenient coincidences and simplistic characterizations abound. Critics in the early twentieth century often complained about the popularity of formulaic series books, seeing them as anti-intellectual, overly sensationalist stories that damaged children's ability to appreciate finer literature. But after the 1930s those complaints faded, as the public gradually became less worried about children's intellects and more worried about their values. Stratemeyer's series books are undeniably shallow and simplistic, but no one could fault them on moral grounds. Frank and Joe Hardy and Nancy Drew exemplified modern youth who supported the sensibilities of conservative, white, adult society.

The first Hardy Boys novel, *The Tower Treasure* (1927), establishes immediately the paradox of order and subversion that made the books simultaneously attractive to adults and to youth. Chapter One opens with a conversation between the brothers about their ambitions:

> "After the help we gave dad on that forgery case I guess he'll begin to think we *could* be detectives when we grow up ... whenever we mention it to dad he just laughs at us," said Joe Hardy. "Tells us to wait until we're through school and then we can think about being detectives."
>
> "Well, at least he's more encouraging than mother," remarked Frank. "She comes out plump and plain and says she wants one of us to be a doctor and the other a lawyer."
>
> "What a fine lawyer either of us would make," sniffed Joe. "Or a doctor, either! We were both cut out to be detectives and dad knows it."[17]

Frank and Joe have no desire to subvert the law and order of adult society; they want to support it as professional detectives who catch criminals. At the same time, this scene also demonstrates a generational conflict between teenagers and parents about proper careers and the proper time to pursue them. The Hardys are thus introduced as teens who want to wriggle free from parental restrictions, to be taken seriously by adults, and have their ambitions respected – desires familiar to many young readers. Later in the novel, when Mr. Hardy and his sons find themselves working on the same mystery, a mild competition emerges over who can crack the case first. The boys win; their ingenious work leads them to discover the hidden stash of a deceased robber, whose grateful victims give the boys a $1,000 reward (a staggering sum in 1927). Having earned money for their sleuthing, the boys have achieved the wish they expressed on the first page: they are now taken seriously as detectives.

Future volumes dispense with the parental objections; throughout the rest of the series, Mr. Hardy supports and assists his sons' detecting endeavors, while their mother recedes into the background. A general freedom from parental supervision was a common trait of Stratemeyer's series, in which protagonists can do as they please and go where they like; parents exist to finance their offsprings' activities, and to encourage them, uttering only a gentle "be careful" as their children sally forth to adventure. The Nancy Drew series followed this pattern as well; having lost her mother at an early age, Nancy is the lady of the house, and her father treats her like an equal.

This highly unrealistic portrait of parent–child relations allowed Stratemeyer's series to neatly sidestep the usual conflicts between youth and age; his protagonists are always respectful and loving to their parents, who give them so much freedom that there is no need to rebel. When parents encourage their young to go forth and sleuth, rebellion actually looks a lot like obedience. This formula allows the series to conduct a clever sleight-of-hand, outwardly portraying teens as perfectly respectful of parental authority, which allowed adults to give children these books with an easy mind. But at a symbolic level, teen sleuthing is fundamentally a transgressive act; charged with the detective's duty to learn and know, Nancy, Frank and Joe must cross the barriers that exclude them from knowledge of the criminal world. In real life, this is the same knowledge which adult authorities anxiously strove to hide from children, whose innocence had to be protected lest they be seduced into delinquency.

Moreover, the adult–teen conflicts that are conspicuously absent from the characters' family lives are not wholly absent from the books: they simply transfer to a different relationship, that between detective and criminal. Significantly, the Hardy Boys and Nancy Drew mysteries contain no juvenile-delinquent villains; criminals are always adults. In this context, the conflict between youth and age is disguised as a conflict between law and crime. Since the teenagers represent the law, they are free to trespass where they do not belong; to penetrate (adult) criminals' secrets, and undermine their plans; to use their superior energy and intelligence to ruin (adult) criminals' lives. The perfect parent–child relationships disguise these series' commitment to celebrating the triumph of the young and the modern. This message proved highly attractive to children, but it also made clear that teen power was only acceptable in its law-abiding form. By separating teens from criminal behavior, the books serve to keep negative "role models" away from impressionable readers.

Significantly, in the first decade of the series' production, Nancy Drew and the Hardy Boys occasionally had conflicts with the police – not because they misbehaved, but because they were better detectives than the professionals. To heighten their portrayal of youth as paragons of intelligence and fast action, the series' ghostwriters created adult policemen as slower and dumber foil-figures. In *The Tower Treasure*, Frank and Joe Hardy encounter Chief Collig of the Bayport Police, "much given to telling long-winded tales," who can usually be found "with his feet on the desk, reading the comic papers."[18] He and his assistants, Detective Smuff and Officer Riley, repeatedly hamper the Hardys' more efficient investigation and are made to look like dunces. Ghostwriter Leslie McFarlane used the bumbling Keystone Kops, of silent-movie fame, as his inspiration for scenes of humor at the police's expense. But after using this formula in the earliest volumes, McFarlane soon received different instructions:

> Stratemeyer felt that the volumes already written suggested a grievous lack of respect for officers of the law! He regretted that I seemed to regard Mssrs. Collig, Smuff, and Riley as figures of fun. He did not think this was wise. The effect on growing boys must be considered. In future volumes it would be well to treat the Bayport constabulary with the respect to which they were entitled.[19]

McFarlane found this strange, considering that Stratemeyer's original outline had prescribed the name Smuff, which seemed to invite comic treatment: "How could any lad with a scrap of intelligence stand in awe of a cop named Smuff?" McFarlane wondered.[20] His own, plausible conclusion was that Stratemeyer had initially envisioned some comedy in these characters, but had changed tack after receiving complaints about the first few books from the moral watchdogs of children's culture.

Mildred Wirt Benson, who ghostwrote the early Nancy Drew books, did not make police the butt of silly humor, but she did portray them initially as aggravating impediments to Nancy's sleuthing. In *The Hidden Staircase* (1930), Nancy's solution of the mystery depends in the climactic moments on her persuading the sheriff to arrest a man who she knows is a thief and kidnapper. The sheriff raises a not unreasonable objection: "I dasn't proceed without evidence. You can't arrest a man unless you've got some proof he's guilty."[21] But the sheriff's use of "dasn't," a dated, regional variant of "dare not," marks him as unrespectable. Throughout both the Hardy Boys and Nancy Drew mysteries, grammatical errors and regional dialects usually signal undesirable traits: working-class, unsophisticated, and uneducated. The teen protagonists and their circle speak standardized and grammatically correct English, modern but not slangy, which marks them as culturally superior. Nancy's superiority in this encounter is magnified by readers' knowledge of her knowledge; they have watched her track the criminal. With a "rising temper," Nancy snaps at the sheriff until he agrees to act, then scolds his sloth: "'Well, it seems to me you've taken plenty of time to make up your mind,' Nancy said sarcastically." As Nancy drives off, readers see her thoughts: "'The sheriff may be stupid enough to refuse to arrest him unless he finds *evidence* on the place,' she thought in disgust."[22] Readers are encouraged to sympathize with Nancy's perspective.

But again, this portrayal of a teen detective in conflict with lawmen did not continue in later volumes. The first three Nancy Drew books were published in the same year that Edward Stratemeyer died; when his daughter Harriet Stratemeyer Adams took control of the Syndicate shortly thereafter, she brought a more consistently conservative perspective to the construction of Nancy Drew. In various interviews, both Adams and Wirt Benson subsequently noted that Adams insisted upon a more genteel characterization for Nancy; under her direction, Nancy soon stopped having a "temper," stopped speaking "sarcastically" to adults, and stopped showing disregard for police procedure.[23]

Another method by which the Syndicate promoted conservative values appeared in its adherence to traditional hierarchies of class, race and gender. As the example of the sheriff in *The Hidden Staircase* demonstrates, working-class characters are usually denigrated. The Hardys' and Drew's social circles do not include anyone of a non-white race. In both series, the detectives assist the "deserving poor," who have become impoverished through crime; when Nancy and the Hardys solve the crimes, these victims are restored to financial security. Characters born and bred in the working class, as well as racial and ethnic minorities, usually appear only as servants or criminals.

In addition to showing a preference for the white moneyed classes, both series conform to traditional ideologies of gender. Early Hardy Boys texts portray their teen characters as boys who spend Saturdays romping through fields and forests in the company of other boys, swimming and rough-housing goodnaturedly. This image of boyhood draws on a tradition stretching back to Twain's *Adventures of Tom Sawyer*, where male youth is exuberant, adventurous and happiest when in nature, away from the restrictions of females and adult society. The Nancy Drew series also draws on traditional gender codes, but presents something of a paradox; while Nancy's many skills include such "masculine" activities as changing flat tires and fixing outboard motors, her portrayal in every other respect conforms to her culture's expectation that proper teenage girls be lady-like in their behavior. The books' illustrations depict Nancy sleuthing in fashionable dresses and high heels; at all times she comports herself with propriety. In *Nancy's Mysterious Letter* (1932), for example, Nancy resists her urge to open the titular letter while her friends are visiting, because it is impolite to read mail in front of guests.[24]

Nancy adheres to the prescribed behaviors for lady-like conduct, not only in her good manners, but in her refusal to identify herself as a wage-earning professional – a role traditionally proscribed for white women of the higher classes. While the Hardy Boys strive to be recognized as professionals, and earn cash for their sleuthing, Nancy insists on her amateur status and refuses remuneration when it is offered. In *The Hidden Staircase*, two elderly women seek Nancy's aid in solving mysterious thefts at their home.

> "If only you will take the case, Miss Drew," Rosemary begged, "we'll be glad to pay you well for your work."
>
> "But I'm not a detective," Nancy protested …
>
> "I'll be glad to do anything I can," Nancy promised willingly. "But of course I'll not take money."[25]

As the daughter of a well-to-do attorney with high social standing, Nancy is too genteel a lady to take cold hard cash for her altruistic actions.

During the 1950s, Harriet Adams took further steps to ensure the consistent respectability of her characters: she began rewriting the series' earliest volumes, to remove problematic material. Her primary goal was to update the books, since many contained outdated references that children of the 1950s did not recognize. A secondary motivation came from the new sensibility about ethnicity and race in the postwar years; as the civil rights movement grew, the Syndicate received more frequent complaints about racial stereotypes in their older books. Ever concerned with meeting the demands of public morality, Harriet Adams addressed these complaints in her revisions by removing most of the racist language and characterizations. But during these revisions, she and her staff of writers also removed the taint of anti-authoritarianism in the teens' characters. McFarlane's bumbling police, and Wirt Benson's slow-witted sheriff, were completely erased in the 1950s revisions, replaced by competent police officers who enjoy a cooperative relationship with deferential teenagers. When these revisions were published, they catered perfectly to anxieties about youth's relationship to law and order, portraying a world to young readers in which adult authorities are always benevolent and correct.

The nationwide moral panic over juvenile delinquency did not extend into the 1960s; although the genres of pulp fiction and exploitation film continued to churn out delinquency stories, newspapers and magazines diminished their coverage of this topic after 1958. But anxieties about youth did not disappear in the 1960s; they transferred to older teens who, by the middle of the decade, were launching significant rebellions against adult society as activists on college campuses and as "hippies" who rejected the values and moralities of the white middle class. The cultural revolution sparked by these older youths surpassed the threat of high-school hoodlums in the national spotlight. As American media coverage of the counter-culture rose, the Hardy Boys and Nancy Drew mysteries, always popular with child readers, found a new level of popularity with adults. Newspapers and magazines of the 1960s increasingly celebrated these series as comforting proof that the old, "square" values were still available to, and popular with, children. In 1968, a *New York Times* article about the Stratemeyer Syndicate proclaimed in its headline, "100 Books – and Not a Hippie in Them."[26]

In every decade of their production, the Hardy Boys and Nancy Drew capitalized on the growing cultural fascination with adolescence as a time of disruptive power. As youth culture rose, so did the public's knowledge of youth as knowers, seekers and innovators, who have the power to change the world – for good or ill. While the American media and the pulp-fiction genre of juvenile delinquency focused on adults' fears of uncontrollable youth, children's mystery series offered a consistently positive image of youth's power to triumph while upholding traditional values, thereby appealing both to young readers' and to adults' desires.

NOTES

1. Joe Austin and Michael Nevin Willard (eds.), *Generations of Youth: Youth Cultures and History in Twentieth-Century America* (New York University Press, 1998), p. 2.
2. Deidre Johnson, *Edward Stratemeyer and the Stratemeyer Syndicate* (New York: Twayne, 1993), p. 21.
3. Patricia Craig and Mary Cadogan, *The Lady Investigates: Women Detectives and Spies in Fiction* (New York: St. Martin's Press, 1981), p. 23.
4. Paula S. Fass, *The Damned and the Beautiful: American Youth in the 1920s* (New York: Oxford University Press, 1977).
5. A. S. Faulkner, "Does Jazz Put the Sin in Syncopation?" *Ladies Home Journal*, 38 (August 1921): 16.
6. Ilana Nash, *American Sweethearts: Teenage Girls in Twentieth-Century Popular Culture* (Bloomington, IN: Indiana University Press, 2006).
7. Kelly Schrum, *Some Wore Bobby Sox: The Emergence of Teenage Girls' Culture, 1920–1945* (New York: Palgrave Macmillan, 2004).
8. Erroneously, the *Oxford English Dictionary* lists 1941 as the first known appearance of the word in print, in an issue of *Popular Science Monthly*. However, the *Readers Guide Restrospective* database and the *Proquest Historical Newspapers* database reveal uses of "teen-ager" in newspapers, women's magazines and parenting magazines during the 1930s.
9. "Teen-Age Bill of Rights," *New York Times*, January 7, 1945, p. 16.
10. James Gilbert, *A Cycle of Outrage: America's Reaction to the Juvenile Delinquent in the 1950s* (New York: Oxford University Press, 1986).
11. Lucy Rollin, *Twentieth-Century Teen Culture by the Decades: A Reference Guide* (Westport, CT: Greenwood Press, 1999), p. 189.

12. Alan Betrock, *The I Was a Teenage Juvenile Delinquent Rock 'N' Roll Horror Beach Party Movie Book: A Complete Guide to the Teen Exploitation Film, 1954–1969* (New York: St. Martin's Press, 1986).
13. Orville Prescott, "Books of the Times," *New York Times*, October 8, 1954, p. 21.
14. Grace Palladino, *Teenagers: An American History* (New York: Basic Books, 1996), p. 160.
15. Johnson, *Edward Stratemeyer*, p. 22.
16. David Farah, *Farah's Guide*, 12th printing (self-published by David Farah, 2005), p. 379.
17. Franklin W. Dixon, *The Tower Treasure* (New York: Grosset & Dunlap, 1927), pp. 1, 3.
18. Dixon, *Tower Treasure*, p. 26.
19. Leslie McFarlane, *Ghost of the Hardy Boys* (Toronto: Methuen, 1976), p. 182.
20. *Ibid.*, p. 183.
21. Carolyn Keene, *The Hidden Staircase* (New York: Grosset & Dunlap, 1930), p. 184.
22. *Ibid.*, pp. 186, 187.
23. For interviews with Adams and Wirt Benson, see David Farah and Ilana Nash (eds.), *Series Books and the Media; or, This Isn't All!: An Annotated Bibliography of Secondary Sources* (Rheem Valley, CA: SynSine Press, 1996).
24. Carolyn Keene, *Nancy's Mysterious Letter* (New York: Grosset & Dunlap, 1932), p. 7.
25. Keene, *The Hidden Staircase*, pp. 49–50.
26. Judy Klemesrud, "100 Books – and Not a Hippie in Them," *New York Times*, April 4, 1968, p. 52.

8

DAVID SEED

American spy fiction

Unlike British spy fiction which has tended to concern itself with issues of empire, the spy in American writing initially carried the status of a fighter for independence. James Fenimore Cooper's *The Spy: A Tale of the Neutral Ground* (1821), generally taken as the prototype of the genre, is concerned with distinguishing its protagonist from a "common spy," as Cooper explained in his 1831 introduction. The novel centers on the activities of Harvey Birch, an American who uses his occupation as a peddler to travel between the rival forces during the War of Independence and gather information on the whereabouts of the English soldiers. The prevailing ethic in *The Spy* of military honor is based on overt bravery, in other words on the very quality which Birch's role debars him from showing. Others may declare their loyalty verbally; he has to screen his commitment behind the discourse of trade, even at the risk of being pronounced a traitor. Others wear the uniform of their calling; he goes through a whole series of disguises. Birch performs like an actor within an uncongenial context. Cooper thus, like many succeeding crime and mystery novelists, has to nudge the reader toward revelatory details, but without giving too much away. Throughout the novel he exploits incomplete lighting where figures – especially Birch – cannot be seen clearly; and he draws our attention to dress, especially the clothing which muffles the face of Birch.

Every spy has to have a handler and Birch's is none other than George Washington. In the coda to the novel, during his interview with Birch, Washington spells out the agent's fate: "Remember that the veil which conceals your true character cannot be raised in years – perhaps never."[1] Tropes of masking and veiling persist to the very end, although Birch is firmly placed within the cause of American independence.

Cooper's evocation of the problematic position of the spy makes a striking contrast with that of Jeptha Root Simms, whose 1846 novel *The American Spy* has a clear patriotic purpose in commemorating the sacrifice of Nathan Hale in the "war for American Freedom of thought and act." Conservative in its characterization, the novel laboriously establishes Hale's domestic, romantic and – once hostilities break out – his military credentials prior to his intelligence gathering. Once Hale is arrested, Simms pulls no punches in depicting the barbarism of the English and shows the summary execution as a tableau of pious patriotism from "Liberty's Hero – Freedom's Early Sacrifice!" So ends "our hero," as Simms insistently calls him. But the whole point of the novel is to ensure that his name lives on; the spy as romantic hero was further promoted in this period by works such as Catherine Sedgwick's *The Linwoods*, William Gilmore Simms's *The Partisan* and John Pendleton Kennedy's *Horse-Shoe Robinson* (all 1835), novels working within Cooper's tradition of historical romance. In her survey of nineteenth-century spy fiction, Christine Bold argues that, despite the tension between the figure of the spy and the US ideal of democratic openness, the former was used to explore the nation's cultural anxieties.[2]

A more ironic version of the spy's role is projected in Herman Melville's *Israel Potter* (1855), where his protagonist stumbles from guise to guise depending on situations always beyond his control. For a time, Potter serves as a courier bearing secret messages in the heel of his boot for Benjamin Franklin in Paris, but Melville scarcely allows this role to generate any patriotic force because Potter seems to be maneuvering through situations in a constant masquerade, even at one point pretending to be a madman. Ambrose Bierce included two stories on espionage in his 1891 collection *In the Midst of Life*, which build their darker ironies on the fact that they concern the arbitrary nature of political oppositions in the Civil War. The protagonist of "Parker Adderson, Philosopher" is a Unionist captive who jokes nonchalantly with his captor until he hears he is going to be shot on the spot. In the ensuing fracas the Confederate general is fatally wounded and both captive and captor expire at the same moment. "The Story of a Conscience" reverses the terms of the previous situation: this time the captive spy is a Confederate. The twist comes with him reminding his captor that he knows the other is a turncoat. The spy is led to his execution; the turncoat shoots himself.

Espionage tends to lapse from American fiction until the Cold War, partly because of the USA's policy of isolationism, though there were exceptions. Max Brand, writing as Frederick Frost, published three spy thrillers in 1936–7 dealing with the machinations of the Germans leading up to the war.[3] John P. Marquand's series featuring his Japanese secret agent Mr. Moto started in 1935, and Upton Sinclair's Lanny Budd series started in 1940 with *World's End*. In *Presidential Agent* (1944) Sinclair's plan was that his hero would "fall under his [Roosevelt's] spell, and become a secret agent getting information for him in Europe."[4] He adopts the code name

"Zaharoff" (an echo of the World War I arms dealer) and is paid out of a secret fund. Budd's role here is to give Roosevelt the information that would enable him to end American isolationism. When he is brought out of retirement in *The Return of Lanny Budd* (1953), his role is now more institutionalized and he plays an active part in the central intrigue, namely thwarting a Communist-backed neo-Nazi counterfeiting ring operating in East Germany. Now Budd is invited to work for the US Secret Service against a national enemy which combines fascism with Stalinism.

With the coming of the Cold War the nature of America's enemy became fixed and the protagonists became more explicitly tied to agencies representing the nation. Paul M. A. Linebarger's *Atomsk* (1949) describes the mission of an American agent into a secret Soviet atomic installation in the Far East. Dugan is a master of disguise, but also an expert psychologist (Linebarger himself was a "psy-war" specialist), which gives a sophistication to the action sadly lacking in early Cold War fiction. The narrator of Sterling Noel's *I Killed Stalin* (1951) is commissioned by the elite International Intelligence Agency (Bu-X) to carry out the shooting after being inducted into the American Communist underground. Robert Heinlein's *The Puppet Masters* (also 1951) makes the identification between agency and nation more explicit through the trope of the family. The narrator is once again working for an elite (unnamed) agency, whose director (the "Old Man") has a direct line to the President. As in Noel's novel, the narrative is reactive and defensive, this time to an invasion of the USA by slugs who transform their human victims into unthinking robots, i.e., into the Communist stereotypes of the period. The emphasis in these two novels and in Donald Hamilton's *Death of a Citizen* (1960) is placed on action rather than information. The latter was the first in a long-running series about Matt Helm, special agent in a secret agency which operates outside the law. In *Death of a Citizen* Hamilton coyly leaves the enemy unnamed, merely "them," but the reader is left in no doubt that the targets are Communists. The notion of combat is projected on to civilian life: "the real front lines are located in the laboratories," a character declares.[5] Within this new form of covert warfare Western scientists have become the prime targets.

In the early 1960s the long-serving CIA chief E. Howard Hunt was invited by a New York editor to write an "American counterpart to the popular James Bond series."[6] Hunt had to clear this idea with his superior Richard Helms, who saw the potential for positive publicity and gave his approval. In fact, the former director of the CIA, Allen Dulles, had been a keen reader of the Bond novels as they came out (himself editing a collection of spy stories in 1968) and even wrote a memorial to Fleming on his death in 1964. Hunt composed a series starting with *On Hazardous Duty* (1965) around the CIA operative Peter Ward, and devised an "operational" style which maintained a rapid sequence of events always privileging the technique of his operatives. In *The Kremlin Conspiracy* (1985), Neal Thorpe is ex-CIA, but brought into action to help thwart a Soviet plot. Their malign intrigue involves placing their "agent of influence" in the United Nations, an action which is counterpointed against the benign operation to get a Jewish dissident out of Russia. Hunt's narrative is remarkable in its total skepticism about public gullibility in the face of Soviet disinformation.

From the 1970s onwards in the wake of revelations that, contrary to its charter, the CIA had engaged in domestic intelligence activity, that agency itself became the site of conflict. The title of Aaron Latham's *Orchids for Mother* (1977) disorients the reader with a fabricated nickname for the CIA chief of counter-intelligence, a thinly disguised portrait of James Angleton. Latham depicts administrative rivalry within the CIA against the background of the emerging Watergate crisis (which Latham covered for a New York journal as it unfolded) and devotes considerable space to revealing what was then new information about agency practice. However, one drawback to this otherwise engaging narrative is its unproblematic use of an omniscient narrative method, totally at odds with the novel's subject which is the sheer difficulty of getting definite information. In a similar critical spirit, James Grady's *Six Days of the Condor* (1974) describes the fate of Department 17, an innocuous research section devoted to tracking "all espionage and related acts recorded in literature."[7] A discrepancy in a shipping invoice, reported to a higher level, results in all members of the unit being shot except for one, who then becomes a fugitive. In parallel with this action, events are investigated by an unnamed "old man" within the higher ranks of the CIA, who discovers that a group of renegades have been using the agency as their cover for drug-smuggling from Laos. Grady originally planned a five-novel sequence showing the gradual development of Condor, but rejected the plan when the 1975 film adaptation (*Three Days of the Condor*) was so successful.

William F. Buckley, Jr. began his series of spy novels as a conscious reaction against the negative portrayal of the CIA in films such as *Three Days of the Condor*. Accordingly he planned a "book in which the good guys and the bad guys are actually distinguishable from one another," rejecting the viewpoint of writers like Graham Greene, John Le Carré and Frederick Forsyth.[8] He came up with a hero named Blackford Oakes, partly modeled on himself with some elements of Bond added. As Buckley's biographer John B. Judis points out, *Saving the Queen* (1976) was written out of the Watergate era when the Rockefeller Commission was investigating the CIA.[9] The novel's flashback narrative centers on Oakes's entry into the CIA during the Korean War (Buckley himself served under E. Howard Hunt briefly during 1951) and his subsequent mission to Britain to discover who in the royal family was passing on secrets to the Soviets. Evidently in an attempt to outdo Fleming, Buckley describes Oakes having sex with the Queen and of course revealing the traitor. This fantastically idealized tale suggests a total congruence of British and American interests.

Happily, Buckley's later novels developed more complexity than that shown in *Saving the Queen*. In *Stained Glass* (1978) his loyalties are torn between the CIA and an old school friend who has become a dangerous campaigner for German reunification. Because of the risks involved, Oakes is commissioned to kill his friend and, when he expresses reluctance, the Director explains the higher good: "It is to guard against the high possibility of a world war and the loss of Europe."[10] Each Oakes novel unfolds during a political crisis: *The Story of Henri Tod* (1984) against the building of the Berlin Wall, *Mongoose, R.I.P.* (1987) in the aftermath of the Cuban missile crisis, and so on.[11] In addition, Buckley made it a hallmark of his fiction to include political leaders among his characters. Kennedy, Castro, Reagan and others all play their parts in his narratives, which helps to explain a difference from the Bond novels. Unlike the latter, Oakes is not present throughout and is therefore by no means the main player in the action.

Since the 1960s, espionage has featured regularly in mainstream US fiction. Kurt Vonnegut's *Mother Night* (1962), however, could best be described as an anti-spy novel since it subverts the basic conventions of the genre. The narrative presents the confessions of Howard W. Campbell, Jr., who is awaiting trial as a war criminal in Jerusalem. He was recruited as a secret agent in 1938 to monitor Nazi activity in Germany, but in the process his "cover" has become indistinguishable from actual fascism. Consider also the explanation given by Campbell for why he becomes a spy: "The best reason was that I was a ham ... I would fool everyone with my brilliant interpretation of a Nazi, inside and out."[12] Many spy novels stress the agent's feeling of doubleness in maintaining a cover, but here Campbell predicts his own identification with the target type. Like Ezra Pound in Rome, he has made wartime broadcasts to America ("native white gentiles") from Berlin. The covert patriotism found in most spy novels here collapses into the absurd as Campbell takes on the guilt of the Nazis, as if Vonnegut is hinting that postwar American hostility to Communism amounts to a new fascism. It is significant that in this period only the American Legion hailed Campbell as a national hero.

One of Thomas Pynchon's first stories, "Under the Rose" (1961), is a pastiche episode imitating the scenario of a late nineteenth-century international intrigue. *Gravity's Rainbow* (1973) incorporates espionage within the welter of competing agencies in Western Europe at the end of World War II.

Tyrone Slothrop, the nearest candidate for a protagonist, engages in a search for information about himself, discovering that he had been sold in childhood for a behavioral experiment. Pynchon presents espionage pathologically as a form of paranoia, except that in Slothrop's case his fears are confirmed. John Barth's *Sabbatical: A Romance* (1982), by contrast, describes a cruise around Chesapeake Bay by an ex-CIA agent, Fenwick Turner, and his wife. Turner plans to write, but definitely not "another CIA novel."[13] In fact, *Sabbatical* presents a narrative "shadowed" by CIA activities, some of which are detailed in footnotes. Turner's brother, also a CIA officer, is missing in dubious circumstances, and Turner and his wife ponder news reports of yet another CIA officer found shot and dumped in the bay. Indeed the bay itself is a locus of mystery since the couple find an island strangely missing from the charts. *Sabbatical*, despite its title, proves to be a tense, paranoid narrative full of suspicions about the extent of CIA activities.

Norman Mailer has written: "I've always been fascinated with spies," drawing a double analogy with actors and authors as all temporarily embodying a "false life."[14] In the immediate aftermath of Watergate, he began to pursue this interest by interviewing John Ehrlichman, former counsel to President Nixon, about his 1976 novel *The Company*, which dramatizes the tensions between the CIA and the White House. Mailer praised the book as a "tour-de-force of a novel," partly because it gave a thinly disguised account of recent events and partly because the possibility emerged that Watergate had been a CIA operation.[15] In an essay from the same period, "A Harlot High and Low," Mailer meditated further on cover stories about this event and concluded that "the CIA may be no more than a general locus signifying an unknown factor whose function is intelligence and whose field is the invisible government."[16] Mailer's huge 1991 novel *Harlot's Ghost* substantiates this perception by presenting the agency as a complex web of relations and power centers. It consists of the memoirs of CIA officer Harry Hubbard from the early 1950s up to the assassination of Kennedy. Hubbard is not so much an agent as a witness (or spectator) to history, and an interpreter. Like a surrogate reader, he tries to make sense of the medley of rumors, reports and half-truths he encounters. Like James Ellroy's *American Tabloid* (1995), *Harlot's Ghost* skillfully evokes the tensions between the CIA and rival agencies like the FBI, and also attempts to trace out sexual lines of power linking Kennedy to the CIA and the Mafia. Hubbard becomes convinced that the real motivation for much CIA activity is to secure funds for its extra-legal activities.

To Alan Furst should go the credit of establishing the subgenre of what he himself calls "historical espionage fiction," Furst's chosen mode since the publication of *Night Soldiers* in 1988. Unusually, Furst has taken Europe between 1933 and 1944 for his preferred location and time limits. He has acknowledged the influence of Graham Greene, Joseph Roth and Eric Ambler, and his novels are characteristically full of allusions to their works and also of thick period description, the product of Furst's careful historical research. His novels evoke a world of displaced peoples, of multiple and shifting identities, quite different from the Cold War ethos of his contemporaries. Indeed, he has described the Cold War as "forty-four years of obliquity, treachery, lies, and counterlies."[17] The protagonist of *Kingdom of Shadows* (2000) is Nicolas Murat, an expatriate Hungarian who engages in a series of secret missions across central Europe. He resembles a spy but is not working for any agency. Rather, he is typical of Furst's protagonists in functioning as the confused witness to turbulent events in Europe.

A more startling variation on the theme of espionage was woven by Ingo Swann's 1978 novel *Star Fire*, a cautionary tale about the arms race. Both the USA and the Soviet Union have been developing microwave transmitters which, when directed from satellites, could induce the collapse or even cause the deaths of whole populations. At this point, enter the protagonist, one David Merriweather, a singer gifted with the psychic facility of distant viewing, enabling him to access top-secret computer codes. Merriweather sends a message to the premiers of each superpower warning them to halt their programs. Panic ensues and both countries launch their transmitter satellites "as a precaution," at which point Merriweather has the satellite of one country attack the control facility of the other, destroying two cities. Strange as *Star Fire* sounds, it had a connection with US intelligence, who discovered that from the late 1960s the Soviet Union had been conducting secret research into "psychotronics," i.e., psychic practices with political applications. Swann himself participated in an experiment in 1972 which was supported and developed by the CIA's Directorate of Science and Technology.

One of the most sophisticated current practitioners of spy fiction is the former journalist Robert Littell, whose first novel, *The Defection of A. J. Lewinter* (1973), won the British Crime Writers' Association Golden Dagger award. Littell's choice of subject was strategic because a defection focuses the issue of credibility in one character. Lewinter is an American scientist who attempts to go over to the Soviets, but whose motivation remains an enigma to both sides for most of the novel. *The Tears of Autumn* (1974) shows Littell's CIA agent virtually freelancing in his hunt for evidence that Kennedy's assassination was the result of a conspiracy by the Vietnamese.[18] Littell has acknowledged a debt to John Le Carré, describing him as the "grand master," and has written the latter into his magisterial *The Company: A Novel of the CIA* (2002), which traces out the history of that agency up to the end of the Cold War. Here Littell captures the drama of interpreting partial information where CIA tradecraft and the reader's processing of the narrative both meet. An agency instructor declares at one point: "spies are perfectly sane human beings who become neurotically obsessed with trivia," the classic case in *The Company* being that of James Angleton, who sank into paranoid suspicion after the revelation that his close friend Kim Philby was a Soviet agent.[19] Angleton up to that moment has personified CIA practice in that analysis of tiny snippets of information can have real consequences, sometimes leading to death.

In classic Cold War spy fiction by E. Howard Hunt and others the source of suspense is when and how a project will be realized. In Littell's work, by contrast, the narrative subject has to be actively sought by the reader. In *An Agent in Place* (1991) the protagonist travels to Moscow and tells the authorities he wants to defect, then claims that he is a "sweeper" erasing old records, and only later do we realize that he is a pawn in a disinformation scheme to discredit Gorbachev by officials opposed to *glasnost*. Littell's *Legends* (2005) is even more complex in its application of multiple personalities to espionage. The "legend" of the title refers to the constructed identity an agent lives behind. Robert Ludlum's *The Bourne Identity* (1980), for instance, describes the attempts by "Jason Bourne" to recall his forgotten CIA legend, which has been superimposed on a biographical identity suppressed even deeper in his memory. Littell's novel concerns one Martin Odum, ex-CIA operative turned private eye. When a young Russian woman asks him to find her brother-in-law, the first scenes recall the openings of Hammett and Chandler, but once the action begins Odum finds himself slipping between three quite different identities: CIA agent, IRA explosives specialist and Civil War historian. At one point Odum remarks: "it seems as if every riddle is part of another greater riddle"; and indeed his search for information is as much about his own past as about unfolding events.[20] The action radically disorients the reader because it emerges that every character is living through "legends." Dissimulation has become the norm.

Littell's sophistication is shared by his contemporary Charles McCarry, who himself served as a "deep cover" agent in the CIA from 1958 to 1967 and who has expressed admiration for Eric Ambler, Somerset Maugham's *Ashenden*, and Richard Condon (*The Manchurian Candidate*, 1959). *The Miernik Dossier* (1973), which carried an endorsement by Ambler, ingeniously uses the medium of an official file to narrate the attempts by Polish-Soviet intelligence to orchestrate an Islamist uprising in the Sudan. In spy fiction the provenance of information is always an issue: if something is so secret how can it be disclosed? McCarry ingeniously gets round the problem by presenting the reader with a narrative refracted through a whole medley of documents: diary excerpts, intercepted messages, debriefing notes and so on. The result is to engage the reader's curiosity. In effect, we become proxy case officers. In common with other spy novelists, he used his first novel to launch a series protagonist, the intelligence agent Paul Christopher, but the method of *The Miernik Dossier* prevents him from taking center stage. Instead, he remains one agent among others.

The vast majority of spy novels discussed here concern themselves with the Cold War. Alex Berenson's *The Faithful Spy* (2006), by contrast, moves into the new field of Islamic terrorism by describing the actions of a CIA agent who has penetrated al Qaeda. The novel depicts the severe difficulties of the CIA in uncovering new networks and, in common with many other novels discussed here, describes a loner protagonist who has been out of CIA circulation so long that he is suspected of having gone over. In the event, he helps thwart a conspiracy to detonate a "dirty" bomb in New York and at the end of the novel is welcomed back into the patriotic fold.

NOTES

1. James Fenimore Cooper, *The Spy: A Tale of the Neutral Ground* (Harmondsworth: Penguin, 1997), p. 398.
2. Christine Bold, "Secret Negotiations: The Spy Figure in Nineteenth-Century American Popular Fiction," *Intelligence and National Security*, 5 (4) (1990): 17–29.
3. Max Brand and Frederick Frost were pseudonyms of Frederick Schiller Faust. Frederick Frost, *Secret Agent Number One* (1936), *The Bamboo Whistle* (1937), and *Spy Meets Spy* (1937 [UK title *Phantom Spy*]).
4. Anthony Arthur, *Radical Innocent: Upton Sinclair* (New York: Random House, 2006), pp. 305–6.
5. Donald Hamilton, *Death of a Citizen* (London: Hodder Fawcett, 1966), p. 63.
6. E. Howard Hunt, *Undercover: Memoirs of an American Secret Agent* (New York: G. P. Putnam's Sons, 1974), p. 133.
7. James Grady, *Six Days of the Condor* (London: Hodder & Stoughton, 1975), p. 11.
8. William F. Buckley, Jr., "Introduction," *The Blackford Oakes Reader* (New York: William Morrow, 1994), p. xiii.
9. John B. Judis, *William F. Buckley, Jr.: Patron Saint of the Conservatives* (New York: Simon & Schuster, 1991), p. 374.
10. William F. Buckley, Jr., *Stained Glass* (New York: Doubleday, 1978), p. 91.
11. "Operation Mongoose" was the name of the CIA covert plan to assassinate Castro.
12. Kurt Vonnegut, *Mother Night* (New York: Dell, 1966), p. 41.
13. John Barth, *Sabbatical: A Romance* (London: Secker & Warburg, 1982), p. 144.
14. Norman Mailer, *The Spooky Art: Some Thoughts on Writing* (London: Little, Brown, 2003), p. 117.
15. Norman Mailer, "Interview with Ehrlichman," *The Time of Our Time* (London: Little, Brown, 1998), pp. 858–9.

16. Mailer, "A Harlot High and Low," *The Time of Our Time*, p. 875.
17. Alan Furst (ed.), *The Book of Spies: An Anthology of Literary Espionage* (New York: Modern Library, 2004), p. 181.
18. For a survey of treatments of the Kennedy assassination in fiction, see Donald McCormick and Katy Fletcher, *Spy Fiction: A Connoisseur's Guide* (New York: Facts on File, 1990), pp. 272–8.
19. Robert Littell, *The Company: A Novel of the CIA* (London: Macmillan, 2002), p. 72.
20. Robert Littell, *Legends: A Novel of Dissimulation* (London: Duckworth, 2006), p. 295.

9

EDDY VON MUELLER

The police procedural in literature and on television

"Presence" is an important concept in contemporary urban law enforcement practice. Since the late 1960s, evolving strategies and practices in police departments the world over have emphasized the benefits of increased police presence – putting more officers on the streets, increasing the frequency of car patrols, and so forth. Making the police more present, in practical terms, means making them more visible, the assumption being that the spectacle of police power makes easier and more effective the exercise of that power.[1] In fact, this is not so new a concept. From the beginning, police were meant to have presence. When in 1829 Sir Robert Peel replaced the archaic Watch with London's Metropolitan Police Force, generally considered the first urban institution worthy of the name, he dressed his men to impress. The sight of a tall-bonneted, bright-buttoned "bobby" presumably being more likely to give a malfeasant pause for thought than that of a Watchman looking like every other lad down the pub.[2]

Uniformed police, marked by that garb as privileged members of a government-sanctioned, paramilitary organization with broad discretionary powers, function today as in Peel's time as walking deterrents, visible signs of state power and surveillance. As such, urban police forces have in recent years deployed their officers not so much according to an individual's expertise or affinity with specific neighborhoods and communities, but in response to statistical mappings of criminal behavior, assigning more personnel to areas where the threat to people and to property is perceived to be greatest. Ironically, then, seeing more cops frequently means an area is more dangerous, not less. If assessed by that metric, current popular culture is a mighty perilous place. However fortunately far one might be from the grim realities of urban crime, however mercifully infrequent one's personal encounters with police in their professional capacity might be, we are never more than a click away from cops.

Police have been increasingly prominently featured in all manner of media since the mid nineteenth century. In novels, motion pictures, serials, and particularly in the periodical press, police and police work have been articulated, with widely varying degrees of accuracy, to larger and larger audiences, most of whose members had little or no direct experience of law enforcement. In the wake of the Second World War and the emergence of television as the pre-eminent mass-medium, Americans saw a dramatic increase in police stories, many of which are very different from earlier works in which police appeared primarily as foils or straight-men to assorted amateur crime-fighter savants or private detectives, or as interchangeable bit-players in the endless public drama of crime and punishment in the papers.

Some of these new sagas of the street fall into the mode of the "police procedural." I do not assay here to provide a comprehensive catalogue of the procedural – such an effort would fill volumes, and there are excellent works detailing police in fiction and television, whose catalogues inevitably include procedurals as a matter of course. Rather, it is my intention to isolate and briefly to analyze the particularities of the police procedural as a distinct formal and narrative category within police fiction.

Police work vs. detection: personnel and methodology of the procedural

As the moniker implies, the police procedural, in print or on the screen, organizes its narrative around the execution of a process, an orderly and to some extent standardized set of practices used by law enforcement to detect, deter and investigate criminal activity. Whether set in a crime-ridden Baltimore or crime-ridden Bristol, the procedural is most frequently about the trials, triumphs and occasional travesties of police work as *work*, performed by paid agents of widely varying gifts and aptitudes. Law enforcement in the procedural mode is, moreover, an *industrialized* process: there is a complex division of labor, marked by professional hierarchies and specialized training (in other words, patrol officers gather evidence, they do not test it; a detective in the Stolen Cars Unit brings Homicide in on the case when the recovered limo has a shot-up body in its trunk, etc.), the individual members of the force are mobile, to some extent expendable (like employees in any firm), and like many industrial laborers, police officers are often alienated, both from their constituency (the public they are expected to "serve and protect")[3] and their ostensible masters (legislatures, superiors, judges and so forth; the "authors" of the laws they enforce).[4]

Given the nature of police labor presented in the "procedural" tale, the methods used to confront crime and the men and women who do the confronting are strikingly different from what is found in most detective fiction, which is frequently focused on the work of an exceptional individual, rather than on the operations of an organization or an institution. The "great detectives" of fiction, film and television are nonpareil: the crimes they solve could only be solved by them and only by use of their own idiosyncratic techniques. Not surprisingly, many great detectives have little patience with mere police, viewing them as marginally competent at best and in some cases as a positive impediment to seeing justice done. However, not all fictional super-sleuths share the rich contempt for police work so frequently evinced by the likes of Sherlock Holmes and Nero Wolfe, whose dealings with the LeStrades and Cramers of the world invariably serve to confirm the stunted inadequacy of the latter and the stunning brilliance of the former. And even when ostensibly employed *by* the police, as in the case of Charlie Chan or Adrian Monk, the "great detective" is more likely to be hindered by them than helped.

It is noteworthy, too, that many great detectives are amateurs or, at least, private contractors. Even the hard-boiled sleuths of the American pulps, the Mike Hammers and Sam Spades, though often friendly with individual agents of the police force, view police procedure writ as unwieldy and ineffective. Law is not their business, though some of them may occasionally produce justice as a by-product of their work. All of which is not to say that there are no eccentric geniuses in postwar police fiction. Occasionally, great detectives do wear a badge, giving up their amateur status, so to speak, and going pro. Consider the title character of the *Columbo* franchise, created by Richard Levinson and William Link and most memorably played by Peter Falk. Lieutenant Columbo is a quirky, disheveled, and brilliant homicide detective. A partnerless mumbler who eschews tough talk and investigative routine, Lt. Columbo is also, tell-ingly, a virtual stranger to violence: he even has pals take his firearms tests for him. The denouement of his telefilm mysteries, like those of so many "drawing-room" detectives, is usually a recitation to the killer of his or her actions, frequently astonishing his befuddled fellow officers. In other words, Columbo is a textbook great detective but a highly improbable cop.

The procedural multiplies and disperses its protagonist, or rather the protagonal *function* is served not by an individual, but most often by the combined efforts of a regularly constituted group – a squad, a pair of patrol officers, a task force. And it is seldom by genius alone that killers are caught. Genius, when it appears in the procedural, always needs to call for back-up. Largely on these grounds, I would provisionally bar from procedural rank most of the police dramas or novels centered on such specialized or ex officio operatives as psychopathologists (*Profiler*, *Criminal Minds*), forensics experts (*CSI*, *Quincy*, *Bones*) and consulting amateurs (*Cracker*, *Medium*, *Monk*). While many of the texts agree in some of their particulars with the procedural mode, in most cases the personnel of these stories are presented as anything but typical agents of law enforcement.

We also should set aside the majority of "rogue cop" tales, so dramatically epitomized by Clint Eastwood in Don Siegel's 1971 *Dirty Harry*. The rogue cop is, by definition, an outsider, and difficult to contain within the regulations and routines that delineate the procedural. Many a procedural ensemble, however, includes an unruly cop, or even a rogue, in the same way as a protagonal collective might have a quirky genius numbered with its company. But ultimately, the rogue, like the token great detective, becomes a disruptive force that most often has to be tamed or driven out in order for the integrity of the police unit as a whole to be maintained.

The overall ordinariness of individual police workers is fundamental to the procedural's representation of law enforcement as the bureaucratic, industrialized enterprise it has become. If the "thin blue line" between the commonweal and the looming threat of crime and disorder relies on Titans, then we have cause to worry, should ever the Titans fall (and in procedurals, they often do). Luckily, or so civic logic would have it, there will always be another ordinary officer walking the beat, studying for a sergeant's exam, making detective, climbing the ranks and gaining the expertise necessary to hold the line, even as in Ed McBain's 87th Precinct novels or Dick Wolf's interminable iterations of *Law & Order* individual agents of the system may come and go, retiring or losing their lives in the line of duty (or extra-textually losing the favor of fans or holding the network's feet to the flames for too robust a raise). Still, the vast and frequently dysfunctional machine of which they are one small part continues to grind away apace.

The long arm of Joe Friday: mass media and the procedural mode

By centralizing the collective labor of professional agents of the state – specifically, police workers – the police procedural ultimately validates the practices of an industrialized, bureaucratic apparatus for the prevention of crime, the pursuit and capture of offenders, and the (attempted) maintenance of public order. The fact that the procedural mode is so late appearing on the popular culture scene may have something to do with the fact that, for much of the late nineteenth and early twentieth centuries, the actual police, especially in the United States, were not particularly well known for fulfilling any of those functions.

Historically, police enjoyed wide discretionary power. Individual police agents were at liberty to decide, in all but the most exigent circumstances, what if any action to take in response to a particular situation. As a result of this freedom of action, the police were (and some would say *are*) anything but even-handed in their administration of the law, their actions frequently reflecting their personal political, ethnic or economic interests. Police misconduct and corruption became a major concern in communities large and small. Since officers were free to choose whether to haul a panderer or a pickpocket to jail, why make such a decision for free?

In the 1920s, however, the clamor for police reform, which had been a steady drumbeat for decades, grew to deafening cadence. This is not least because Prohibition had created a huge increase in criminal activity by illegalizing in the United States something that virtually everyone did anyway, and thereby making police discretion a far more conspicuous issue. But the increased agitation was due as well to the existence of radio. Leaping over the literacy gap as easily as over state lines, radio proved to be a medium of extraordinary persuasive powers. Police corruption in Brooklyn or Los Angeles might not mean much to citizens of Ithaca or Bakersfield, the latter communities being too far from it to be touched much by it, but the radio collapsed distance and brought reports of graft and of the efforts of anti-corruption crusaders into the homes of millions of listeners.

Mass media revolutionized public awareness of police activity, both scandalous and heroic. Once familiar to the public anecdotally or through the jaundiced lens of journalism, if at all,[5] and then principally as a body of corrupt, cronyish partisans or club-swinging ward heelers, the police began to gain a kind of presence very different from that generated by helmets and pseudo-soldierly uniforms. The radio began to give the police a heightened media presence, first through reportage, then through ostensibly fact-based dramatic series like Phillips Lord's 1935 *Gang-Busters*, based on FBI activities, and Ed Byron's 1939 *Mr. District Attorney*. Shows like these, while hardly devoid of sensationalism, made much of "modern" investigative techniques. Both series featured teams of specialists, some of them former police officers, both had episodes focused on cleaning up police corruption, and both eventually moved, like so much radio fare, to television. When the police procedural made its initial appearance in prose in 1945, the reading public had already undergone an extensive re-education in terms of who the police were, and what they did.

LeRoy Lad Panek, whose *The American Police Novel* surveys police literature in the United States dating to the 1880s, marks the emergence of the procedural with the 1945 publication of Lawrence Treat's *V as in Victim*. "Granted, the book had a prominent detective theme," Panek notes, ". . . Treat's innovation was his heroes. They are cops."[6] Specifically, they are typical rank-and-file cops: career officers, not incompetent, not blunderers, but also by no means particularly passionate or prodigally gifted. He goes on to enumerate some thirteen features, found in *V as in Victim*, that he identifies as the distinguishing features of American police fiction. Not all of these are necessarily typical of what will become the procedural mode of police storytelling. Some of these, such as "copspeak," the specialized jargon of the law enforcement trade, and the partnership as an emotional core – Panek's numbers two and seven – are found in any number of narratives featuring crimes and crime-fighting, from psychological thrillers to cop comedies. More important to the procedurals that will follow are the kinds of cops that people Treat's novel, and the methods they employ in the pursuit of their occupation.

Mitch Taylor, the ostensible protagonist of Treat's novel, is incapable on his own of solving the murder case he inadvertently catches. It is only by teaming up with Jub Freeman, a dubiously dashing lab-rat, that the culprit is caught: Mitch doggedly digging up evidence, Jub subjecting it to then cutting-edge scientific analysis. Neither man has a monopoly of the means of solving the mystery, and both of them arrive at a successful resolution primarily by doing their jobs. Indeed, *V as in Victim* is in part the story of a worker's reformation, Mitch maturing over the somewhat convoluted course of the book from a lackadaisical, indifferent cop trying to collect his paycheck while expending the least possible effort, to a dedicated team player keen on fighting crime.

While *V as in Victim* demonstrates the central features of the police procedural, it did little to launch the procedural as a viable commercial form. Lawrence Treat was an established author (under that name, Lawrence Arthur Goldstone had already published seven mystery novels), but it was not a bestseller. It was published only in soft-cover, in a compact edition made for portability and pitched to an audience looking for a brisk, uncomplicated read. The "pocket edition," the post-Depression world's answer to the penny dreadfuls of an earlier century, was conceived for a public on the move, for a commuter culture.[7] It was the form many a crime story and many a procedural would take, another part of the mediascape that in 1945 was still dominated by radio and which would soon fall under the sway of television.

The police procedural came to television in 1951, by way both of radio, which was typical of early TV, and of cinema, which was not. Now cherished as something of a classic, at the time of its production in 1948 *He Walked by Night* was, like *V as in Victim*, very much just product. A postwar slump in the picture business, occasioned by the end of wartime price controls and the Consent Decrees which broke up Hollywood's vertically integrated studios, created an environment which favored films that could be swiftly sold and cheaply made. Helmed by Alfred Werker and Anthony Mann, the film cribbed freely (as in "free source material" and "free advertising") from the innumerable press accounts of the exploits and pursuit of Erwin "Machine-Gun" Walker, a well-educated California veteran who turned to larceny and was later apprehended in Los Angeles after two gun-battles with police and an extensive manhunt. It was a story that presented plenty of exploitable material for postwar popular culture – violence, suspense, a soldier-turned-sociopath – as well as being a topical, real-world prototype of successful, "scientific" police work.

Often described as "semi-documentary" (most of the film was shot on location, though that is a choice far more financial than aesthetic), *He Walked by Night* fits relatively comfortably into the postwar cinematic trend identified after the fact as film noir, but, like *V as in Victim*, it serves up a twist. Rather than presenting a typical noir narrative about a lone hard-boiled hero (specifically or symbolically a war veteran) pitted against a mob of shady operators, it concerns a lone hard-boiled *villain* (here a war veteran, trained in electronics and demolition) pitted against an organized army of police operatives. After he executes a patrolman who interrupts one of his heists, Roy (played against type by "poverty row" heart-throb, Richard Basehart) finds himself the target of the entire police force.

The protagonal collective, the emphasis on process, the reliance of justice on both science and the totality of police efforts rather than on the gifts of a singular, exceptional individual, all mark *He Walked by Night* as a fully fledged police procedural, the first ever made for the big screen. That alone would merit its inclusion here, but the film also introduced a national audience to an actor and writer named Jack Webb, and it introduced Jack Webb to the procedural, a form Webb would go on to make uniquely his own. Webb appears, briefly but memorably, in *He Walked by Night* as a white-coated, quietly strange criminologist. While making the film, Webb met and befriended Marty Wynn, a Los Angeles police detective who had worked the Walker case and had been hired as a consultant. Inspired by the film and his friend, Webb conceived of a radio series that would chronicle as faithfully as possible the "real" crime-fighting that was being done every day by America's police. The show found a home on the NBC radio network in 1940 as *Dragnet*.

He Walked by Night is now mostly remembered because of its link to *Dragnet*, a sire recalled only by the deeds of his son. No doubt the very nature of television helped fix *Dragnet* in the firmament. Films, especially low-budget B-movie fare like *He Walked by Night*, remained essentially ephemeral well into the 1950s – until a market for movies was established on television, the vast majority of motion pictures were available to the public only once, during their theatrical release, and then seldom if ever seen again. A similar brand of oblivion waited for many a hard-boiled pocket-sized paperback, itself another example of mass-culture ephemera; industrial culture is all too often disposable culture. Many works of police and procedural fiction published as pocket-editions or in pulps or gazettes have not seen reissue.

Thanks to re-runs, programs recorded on film, like *Dragnet*, gained access to a theoretically limitless aftermarket – the media equivalent of immortality.

Dragnet remains in active syndication today. Popular with critics and audiences alike, the show ran until 1959, spawned a 1954 feature, won four Emmys, and was nominated for three more. The series was briefly resuscitated in 1967 and again in 1989. *Dragnet* became both a classic and a cliché: a big-budget Hollywood send-up was made in 1987, and a rather belabored hour-long dramatic series of the same name was floated by veteran procedural producer Dick Wolf for NBC in 2003.

In many ways, then, *Dragnet* is *the* cop show, and therefore the image of urban crime, urban police and law enforcement procedure, with which millions of Americans (or millions of Americans lucky enough to avoid first-hand experience of the Real Thing) were familiar. While antiquarians of the procedural must look to *V as in Victim* as to Gilgamesh, Webb's *Dragnet* is our *Odyssey* and our *Metamorphoses*. For decades to come, authors and television scribes alike will take cues from *Dragnet*. Ed McBain, the policeman turned author whose 87th Precinct series has long been held to be the cornerstone of procedural fiction (he both outlasted and outsold Treat), acknowledged the show's influence on his work,[8] and references to the program, its theme, or to Webb's Joe Friday appear in virtually every made-for-television cop show in the US or the UK since.

Consistent with the procedural's emphasis on process, even though Webb's iconic, deadpan Joe Friday is undoubtedly the series' focal character, *Dragnet* is never *about* Joe Friday. Each episode instead centers on a single investigation, measured by the methodical efforts of Friday and his various partners as they examine crime scenes, interview witnesses and gather evidence, which is then dutifully handed over to experts for interpretation. "In fact, Joe Friday could hardly be described as a protagonist at all," notes Jarret S. Lovell, "his character was merely a stand-in for the entire Los Angeles Police Department (LAPD) and a proxy for all of American policing."[9] His proxy status was more or less official, too. Webb's alliance with the LAPD went well beyond collaboration with Wynn. The Department collaborated extensively with the production with the blessing of no less an authority than Chief William H. Parker, who ran the LAPD until 1966 and who receives screen credit in *Dragnet*'s titles.

Not surprisingly, the cooperation of the police was implicitly and explicitly contingent on the program promoting a positive image of the force, or at least not doing anything to promote a negative one. "Neutrality" seems to be the creator's top priority, not in the sense of *balance* – there is no attempt to depict the "other" side of the story, the crook's – but in depicting the police as having an almost clinical objectivity. There is an androidal quality to Webb's performance of Friday, and to Friday's performance of his duties; he is a well-oiled policing machine, always observant, never vindictive or vengeful. If he killed people instead of arresting them, he would be the Terminator in a gray flannel suit. Friday and the LAPD in *Dragnet* are not overly concerned with the prevention of crimes, or with the rectification of any of their root causes (poverty, racism, etc.), though Friday and his cohorts will sometimes editorialize on both subjects. Nor does it fall to Friday to punish. Instead, he is an embodiment of the black letter of the California Penal Code, essentially a pair of lidless eyes and a pair of tireless legs geared exclusively for collection of information necessary to the smooth functioning of the other professionals through whose collective efforts alone the streets can be made safe.

Thus, it is never Joe Friday, the man, who triumphs against crime in *Dragnet*. Each episode presents an epilogue describing the fate of the perpetrators the detectives have tracked down, all of whom end in some stage of digestion by the courts. In *Dragnet* it is always the system that wins.

Ripped from the headlines: topicality and procedural "realism"

We have already seen how those responsible for policing the perilous terrain of postwar urban America helped to give rise to the new wave in police storytelling that became the procedural. It is but one of many ways that the procedural mode in print and screen fiction displays a pronounced preoccupation with "authenticity" and "realism." Procedurals are not the only kind of postwar cultural production to show such tendencies. Many artists and audiences of the period had a passion for the "authentic" – witness the fleeting vogue in the United States and elsewhere for the work of the Italian "neorealists," or the "social consciousness" phase in American fiction and film. But while other manifestations of these realist tendencies were temporary, or at least waxed and waned, an over-determined, almost journalistic realism is graven into the very foundations of the police procedural, and hewing to high standard of authenticity remains a prerequisite for any potential contribution to the canon.

While detective stories often delight in the macabre and exotic, the extremes of both criminal enterprise and detective virtuosity (one need only glance at Professor Moriarty, bizarre poisons, trained apes, and fortune-cookie-tongued Asian super-sleuths to see this principle in vigorous operation), the procedural usually presents us with the mechanisms of presumably standard crimes confronted by typical investigators. The procedural is therefore always at pains to establish its bona fides. The resumé of the author of a book, for example, or the creator of or consultant to a television program might become an important watermark. In the print arena, both McBain and Wambaugh worked as policemen; as did many police fiction authors including Bill Kelly, John Westermann, Robert Sims Reid and Michael Grant (not all ex-cops work in the procedural mode, and this roll-call is by no means comprehensive; Panek again provides the best bibliography). Other procedurals have been penned by FBI agents, lawyers, criminologists and, in the case of the pioneering African-American proceduralist Chester Himes, by an ex-convict.

Needless to say, cop stories told by cops or other parties to the operations of law enforcement have a potent claim to realism, if eye-witness testimony is to be trusted. First-hand observation of another kind bolsters the credentials of police novels penned by journalists with a background in hard news or crime reporting. The oft-adapted David Simon, formerly of the *Baltimore Sun*, now of a veritable dynasty of Home Box Office *vérité* dramas including *The Corner* and *The Wire* (both written in collaboration with retired Baltimore detective Ed Burns, giving the team a two- or, rather, a four-fisted grip on the real), is probably the best known of these, but his is not a solitary truth-claim. Like the policeman-turned-author, reporters writing crime and police fiction evoke the power of proximity. The crime-reporter and the cop have, we assume, seen the bodies, literally and figuratively, and borne witness to the quotidian atrocities of the urban underworld. Like the characters they write about, these chroniclers assert membership in what Christopher P. Wilson calls the "secret, sometimes dark, unchanging fraternity of knowing."[10]

Beyond the truth-claims of the authors, Realism is inscribed in the formal execution of the police procedural. McBain bolsters the credibility of his precinct novels by providing dummy documents in facsimile – a reproduction of an official NYPD "conviction card" in *Cop Hater* (1956) and a hand-gun license complete with a fictional signature in *The Killer's Payoff* (1958). *Dragnet* is moored to reality fore and aft, each episode punctuated with a kind of time-stamp, identifying the spatial and temporal coordinates of the story, and ending with the vital statistics of the criminals' come-uppance in court. *The Corner* and *The Wire* and others occasionally observe a downright Greek sense of dramatic unity, presenting episodes that take place entirely within the narrow confines of a single day, or a single shift. And in every case, the *language* of the procedural leaps out. Indeed, the procedural voice is unmistakable and essential, a vernacular of the station and the street that as much as anything establishes the immediacy and authenticity of the work.

In police procedurals, "copspeak" and adherence to the minutest details of literal law enforcement procedure – the use of appropriate dispatch calls, identifying particular streets and makes of cars and such – function as more than local color. They frequently operate as a code, one which goes undecrypted, and which serves thereby to isolate the reader from a circuit linking the fictional police, the actual police and the framer of that fiction. In other words, the receiver of the text is persuaded that there is some extratextual "reality" known to the author, but from which the reader remains, fascinated, ever excluded. It is as if the procedural offers a window – dim, perhaps, grimed and with a bullet-hole or two in it – into a parallel universe of disillusioned and desperately outnumbered cops, and robbers who seem to spring, as if from sown dragon's teeth, from the very fabric of our existence, from the cities we live in, the trains we ride, the prosperity we enjoy and the poverty that inevitably counterpoises it. Except this parallel universe is supposed to be an indexical replica of a "real" world, the knowledge of which much of middle-class culture is designed to protect us from. In other words, the world of the procedural is not perceived as fictional in the same way as, say, the story worlds of a Harry Potter or a *Battlestar Galactica* are. The world of the procedural is supposed to be the real world – if not, mercifully, *our* real world – with only the names changed (more echoes of *Dragnet*) to protect the innocent. Except when some actual trauma or tragedy thrusts us through the looking-glass, we the innocent know this violent, heartrending world mostly from a distance, glancing over the shoulders of the police and proceduralists paid to stand watch at its borders.

Police omnipresence: procedural cop-opera and the tragic detective

Of course, the "fraternity of knowing" has become a lot less exclusive of late, if, arguably, no less dark. There are an awful lot of procedurals in circulation these days. Watch enough of them, and you have the lingo and the law so cold one starts to feel like a vicarious veteran of the Force. Given the form's generally meticulous and frequently ballyhooed "realism," and the tens of millions of people – virtually all of whom must live beyond the "thin blue line" – who have tuned in to or turned the pages of more recent, more cynical procedurals, it is almost comical to encounter in them, again and again, so many laments, litanies, rants and riffs on the fact that civilians "don't know what it's like to be a cop."

While the procedural as a literary form remains vigorous, the television procedural would appear to be in a Golden Age. Not only are procedurals abundant on the small screen, many of them are also excellent. Since the stunning success of *Hill Street Blues* in the early 1980s, the procedural has been established as one of the broadcast medium's premier genres, garnering critical plaudits, top-name talent, and prime prime-time real estate. The growth of DVD and video aftermarkets has offered a new means by which such programming can be disseminated to its fans.

While things might look rosy for the police procedural as a genre or as a narrative mode, looking at these shows for insight into our collective assessment of the state of law and order and its agents in the twenty-first century yields a very different view. The procedural's personnel, from the beat cops to the dicks to the brass, are variously depicted as frustrated, over-worked and psychologically traumatized. Among TV cops, substance abuse is rampant (especially alcohol abuse, a major theme in police culture, police storytelling and the history of police reform), divorce, infidelity, questionable parenting routines, and acts of brutality or inappropriate use of lethal force not infrequent. Many police agents are contemptuous of civil and state authority, and are willing to bend or break the law in pursuit of justice, even "good" (read "effective") cops – *especially* effective cops. The team of LAPD detectives at the center of cable television FOX's long-running and acclaimed Copocalypse *The Shield*, for instance, are – almost to a man – multiple felons; their leader, Vic Mackey, is consistently singled out as an exemplary urban crime-fighter, despite his incessant drug-peddling, racketeer-ing, beat-downs and executions.

Even those police whose professional conduct does not rise to the Mafioso standards seen in *The Shield*, such as *Prime Suspect*'s Jane Tennison, or *NYPD Blue*'s good-heartedly trollish Andy Sipowicz, are emotionally savaged by their experiences. They are not "great detectives," but tragic ones: borrowing a contemporary policing military motif, they are soldiers in a war, the "war on crime," that they have learned can never be won. There will always be another killer, another rapist, another pimp, another child abuser. If crime prevention is to be a police function, then the TV cop's fight is not merely futile, but absurd, since every week demands new corpses, new cons. Like Sisyphus with a shield, the TV's tragic detectives keep pursuing crooks and making cases, knowing that their efforts, even when successful in the short term, are ultimately meaningless. Small wonder so many of them end their fictional careers like far too many police end their actual ones: in suicide, in drink, in despair.

A similar tone pervades Wambaugh's work, whose procedurals look long and hard at the psychological burdens borne by police agents. His novels are a combination of nostalgic admiration for the men and women (but, really, still mostly men) willing to try to protect society from itself and horror at what that society is capable of and the emotional, physical and moral peril it poses its wage-slave guardians. Often depicting compromised and conflicted cops as buffeted as much by ideological and existential crises as by thuggish felons, many procedurals become melancholic "cop-operas," in which the perpetual demands and disappointments of "the job" continually erode the foundations of order by gnawing away at the unfortunate enforcers of the law. Interestingly, while a number of Wambaugh's novels highlight the experi-ences of uniformed officers, most of the prime-time procedurals are centered on non-uniformed police persons – detectives, undercovers, "white-collar" cops, if you will. Dressed down to permit penetration of the community, the inverse of the logic that promoted paramilitary regalia for urban police in the nineteenth century, this suit-and-tie class of cops is, to some extent, an invisible host, its functions and dysfunctions camouflaged in civilian clothes, hidden in plain clothes, if not in plain sight.

Television serials disrupt this camouflage, revealing (and occasionally reveling in) the voyeuristic peek at the guts of the machine. Our contemporary gaze, however, is neither wholly salacious (as is the case in some more exploitative modes of crime fiction) nor dispassionate (as is the perspective of early procedurals of the *Dragnet* school). The cop-opera's keening duets of grotesque criminal pathology and bleak crime-fighter futility present us with a different kind of spectacle than that provided by the sight of uniformed police charged with patrolling against "the dangerous classes."[11] Watching contemporary policemen and women at work, we are not so much in awe at their cudgels, helmets or badges, but in awe of their suffering, their endless, pyrrhic struggle – an odd sympathy, since for so many the police represent an authority that remains singularly unsympathetic to *them*. Wilson notes, "The procedural would ultimately reinforce not the faith of midcentury, but police fatalism about a public stirred to cycles of outrage and then indifference."[12] For TV crime and disorder, like the real kind, can only be confronted, never eradicated, and the fictional battle for "law and order," like the real one, must be fought without any reassurance whatsoever from history, human nature or television that it can ever be won.

NOTES

1. Alfred Blumstein and Joel Wallman (eds.), *The Crime Drop in America*, rev. edn. (Cambridge University Press, 2006), p. 336.
2. Wilbur R. Miller, *Cops and Bobbies: Police Authority in New York and London, 1830–1870*, 2nd edn. (Columbus, OH: Ohio State University Press, 1997), pp. 32–4.
3. John Raymond Cook, *Asphalt Justice: A Critique of the Criminal Justice System in America* (Westport, CT: Praeger, 2001), p. 40.
4. Samuel Walker, "Historical Roots of the Legal Control of Police Behavior," in *Police Innovation and the Control of the Police: Problems of Law, Order, and Community*, ed. David Weisburd, Craig Uchida and Lorraine Green (New York: Springer-Verlag, 1993), p. 38.
5. Jarret S. Lovell, *Good Cop/Bad Cop: Mass Media and the Cycle of Police Reform* (Monsey, NY: Willow Tree Press, 2003), p. 57.
6. LeRoy Lad Panek, *The American Police Novel: A History* (Jefferson, NC: McFarland & Company, 2003), p. 35.
7. Geoffrey O'Brien, *Hardboiled America: The Lurid Years of Paperbacks* (New York: Van Nostrand Reinhold, 1981), pp. 33–8.

8. Interestingly, McBain's procedural prose first appeared under the noble kangaroo ensign of Pocket Books, the pioneer publisher of the compact paperback. He cites the significance of *Dragnet* in his introduction to the 1989 reprinting of *Cop Hater*, the first of his 87th Precinct novels; see McBain (ed.), *Cop Hater* (New York: Pocket Books, 1989), p. xi.
9. Lovell, *Good Cop/Bad Cop*, p. 102.
10. Christopher P. Wilson, *Cop Knowledge: Police Power and Cultural Narrative in Twentieth-Century America* (University of Chicago Press, 2000), p. 92.
11. Eric H. Monkkonen, *Police in Urban America, 1860–1920* (London: Cambridge University Press, 1981), p. 42.
12. Wilson, *Cop Knowledge*, p. 92.

10

FRED L. GARDAPHE

Mafia stories and the American gangster

Before the word "mafia" entered the American vocabulary, the bad guy portrayed in literature, dramas, radio programs, film and television was more often than not a bandit, a thief, a thug, or some other version of an outlaw who did bad deeds in dastardly ways that were more often than not discovered and punished by traditional social powers. The word "gangster" came to be used to represent the urban version of such a bad guy who worked with a band of criminals. The gangster as we know him today is a mix of fact and fiction. First appearing in the newspapers and newsreels of the 1920s, the gangster figure has grown to heroic proportions. Disseminated through powerful mass media exposure, the gangster subliminally serves as a cultural icon, reflecting changing notions of masculinity and socio-economic class in the United States.

The gangster, typically represented by a male figure, emerged in response to the evolution of corporate capitalism in the early twentieth century. Although criminal gangs had long occupied American cities, Prohibition and the desperate poverty brought on by the Great Depression in the 1930s provided opportunities for individual crime leaders to emerge and thrive. During the late 1920s and early 1930s, the exploits of gangsters such as Al Capone, John Dillinger, "Baby Face" Nelson and "Pretty Boy" Floyd became national news, fueled fictional accounts and captured the popular imagination. These real-life gangsters became more than ordinary criminals by committing their crimes with dashing and daring bravado; they were all blatant transgressors of the boundaries between good and evil, right and wrong, and rich and poor. As corporate capitalism promoted consumerism and widened the gap between rich and poor, Americans became infatuated with the gangster, whose stylish dress and fancy cars yet humble origins defied the boundaries separating social classes.

These increasingly fascinating characters began to appear in American films during the late 1920s and early 1930s that often portrayed gangsters as degenerate and overly feminized men losing their independence in the new capitalist society. Later films recast them as men who wielded power through sexuality and guns. Films such as *Little Caesar* (1930) and *Scarface* (1932) established a lasting association in popular culture between the gangster and particular ethnic groups, including Jewish, Irish, African, Asian and – especially – Italian Americans. The cinematic images of masculinity associated with these ethnicities served to stereotype and marginalize these groups. This marginalization was amplified in the 1950s through the 1970s when, amid growing feminist criticism of conventional understandings of manhood, the ethnic gangster embodied the masculine qualities under attack.

During this period, the word "mafia" began to be used to refer to the Italian presence in organized crime. The origins of the word are debated, but most sources agree that the word "mafioso" preceded "mafia" and referred to a "tough-guy" presentation of masculinity. Some have speculated that "mafia" came from Arabic and referred to those natives of Sicily who hid in the hills during Arab occupation and rebelled against Arab powers. Others have suggested that the word began as a graffiti acronym that protested the occupation of Sicily by the French, "Morte ai Francesi Italia Anela," which means "Italy wishes death to the French," or it might have come from a cry in dialect when a parent saw his/her daughter being attacked by a French soldier, "Ma Fia," or "Mia figilia" ("My daughter!"). These latter uses are pretty much accepted as more mythic than real, and the agreement is that the word refers to Sicilian groups or "cosche" who took the law into their own hands as a way of dealing with the problems arising when a weak government did not attend to the needs of the Sicilian people, enabling local families to rise to power as they fulfilled the needs of the Sicilians. The word became a part of American culture during the early immigration of Italians to the United States and grew to refer to any organized crime activity.

Since the 1960s, the mafia gangster in literature, theater and film has more often than not been the product of Italian American writers and film-makers. Mario Puzo, Francis Ford Coppola, Martin Scorsese, Brian De Palma, Gay Talese, Michael Cimino, Abel Ferrara, Giose Rimanelli, Frank Lentricchia, Louisa Ermelino, Anthony Valerio, Don DeLillo, and Tony Ardizzone are some of the major artists who have been drawn to the figure of the gangster. In their hands, the mafia gangster has become a cultural figure of mythic proportions. It might have been the news media and the televised Congressional investigations into organized crime through the Kefauver hearings (1950–51) that put the word "mafia" into the minds of US Americans, but it would not be until the publication of Mario Puzo's novel *The Godfather* in 1969 that the mafia entered their hearts and souls. With the publication of *The Godfather*, Mario Puzo was instantly promoted to celebrity status. Not since the publication of Pietro di Donato's *Christ in Concrete*

(1939) had an American author of Italian descent been thrust into the national spotlight on such a grand scale. The timing of *The Godfather*'s publication had much to do with its rapid climb to number one and its sixty-seven-week stay on the *New York Times* bestseller list. The novel came off the press in the middle of the ethnic revival period of the 1960s. It also followed the Congressional hearings on organized crime and the publication of Peter Maas's non-fictional bestseller, *The Valachi Papers*, through which mobster-turned-informer Joe Valachi described his activities inside organized crime.

In *The Godfather*, mafia is seen as a natural force in the Sicilian world from which Vito Corleone comes, a world which he attempts to recreate in his new home in America. In this world, Don and his family are portrayed as the "good guys" and the American establishment with which they struggle, that is, the institutions of law and business, are set up as the "bad guys." In this novel Puzo presents the hypothesis which in effect is the real Italian American dream: what if America assimilated to our ways? The world that Don Vito Corleone replicates in America is built on the solid foundations of a centuries-old social order in which fate or destiny, more often than not through birth, determined the life an individual would lead. In the feudal-like system of Sicily and southern Italy, the peasant could not hope to aspire to a better life by challenging the forces that controlled his life. The result of this would be that attention was focused on what *could* be controlled – the family unit. This is the reason so many emigrated to other lands. The world to which so many immigrants came was one built on the myth that through freedom each person could become whatever they wanted if they worked hard enough. This Puritanical work ethic and the built-in reward system did not require that the family stick together and often led to the break-up of the nuclear family. The Don's Old-World notion of a work ethic requires that the family stick together, and any attempt by an individual to leave it threatens the livelihood of the entire family. In fact, for a family to survive with its Old-World values intact, it must work against assimilation and strive to have its surrounding environment conform to their way of life. Thus, the central conflict of this novel is how to keep the family together for its own good in a land that has lost its dependence on the family unit for survival.

The mafia that Puzo romanticized in his fiction became a subject to be realized in the writings of Gay Talese and Ben Morreale, and in the Martin Scorsese films *Mean Streets* (1973), *Goodfellas* (1990) and *Casino* (1995) – the latter two films based on books by Nicholas Pileggi. To better understand Talese's contribution to the American gangster story, we need to remember that most, if not all, of the reporting on the gangster from his earliest media appearance through Al Capone had been done from the outside looking in. Since the 1920s Americans have been fed stories third- and, rarely, second-hand through reporters such as Ben Hecht, who doubled as a journalist and dramatist for the screenplays for *Underworld* (1927) and *Scarface*, for example.

When Talese sees the young Bill Bonanno in the federal court building in Manhattan on January 7, 1965, he sees, not a gangster, but a guy who could easily have been his friend. "I wondered, not for the first time, what it must be like to be a young man in the Mafia."[1] *Honor Thy Father* (1971) is Talese's personal tour of the mafia. Most people looked at the Bill Bonanno of the 1970s and saw a mafioso. When Talese looked at him he saw a family man. The same way that Mario Puzo saw his own family in the Corleones, Talese saw his in the Bonannos. This is dangerous stuff, especially for journalists, who are expected to uncover and uphold the truth. There are critics who believe that he dressed his subject up and whitewashed characters that all others had dismissed as hopeless criminals. But Talese, being Italian American, could see something that other writers could not.

At the same time that Puzo is creating the fictional Corleones and Talese is writing about the real Bonanno family, Ben Morreale is creating a realistic fiction of the "mafioso." Unlike Mario Puzo's romantic depictions of the gangster, the mafiosi of Ben Morreale's novels come from his observations of Sicilian life. In *A Few Virtuous Men (Li cornuti)* (1973), Morreale creates a gangster unlike any seen in US culture. Morreale has often complained that Puzo had no idea what he was writing about and that, in fact, Puzo's mafia was nothing like the real thing.

Morreale shows his version of the mafia through the eyes of a priest. Fr. Buffa, who is given the *injuria* or nickname "Juffa," after the great Sicilian fool of folklore, is set up as a reliable, if not pathetic, narrator. In Racalmora, a fictional name given to Racalmuto, Morreale's ancestral home-land, the Mafiosi are known by various names – "the men with moustaches," "the virtuous men." And in the town there is order; everything is *sistemato*, well arranged, in its place. A character named Pantaleone, a local writer/historian, based on the real Sicilian writer Leonardo Sciascia, explains that "*sistemato*" comes from the Greek, meaning "ensemble, together, a state of relationships."[2] Bill Bonanno echoes this years later when he writes his own story in *Bound by Honor* (1999): "Mafioso is, first and last, about the nature of relationships. Unless this most essential and traditional point is under-stood, nothing else about who we are and where we come from, what we have done and what has eventually become of us here in America is any way comprehensible."[3]

Many Italians, even Sicilians, in the United States had never heard of the word "mafia" until it became immortalized by the US news media. Morreale reflects this reality in his novel when he writes:

Every once in a while a son of these immigrants would return and ask, "Tell me, what sort of thing is this Mafia?" Most people shrugged their shoulders honestly, for they knew nothing about it although they understood things. But the questions continued.[4]

The villagers eventually get to the point where they begin to see there are benefits in encouraging the proliferation of the idea of mafia.

So many of these questions were asked by such rich and intelligent people who could read and write, who indeed wrote in magazines and books about this mafia – some even said that Racalmora was a town of "Mafiosi" ... Eeh. One had to take a certain pride in all this. One was spoken of in America.[5]

Even Don Taralla sees it as bait for tourists and does nothing to stop it all. Morreale offers an apology through the character Pantaleone:

These virtuous and virile men became "more virulent" as Pantaleone said. He reasoned that the mafia was a state of mind in Sicily that had been fed by the imperialism of Greece, Rome and the Normans, but most of all by the colonialism of the Spaniards ... Taralla was the answer to a thousand years of colonialism.[6]

Pantaleone goes on to write:

Certainly, for the historian this Mafia does not exist because there are no documents, no witnesses, no records of any kind that can be nailed down by footnotes. Therefore, for the historian, the scholar, the Mafia is something beside time, that runs parallel to history. In a hundred years there will be no bibliography on the Mafia ... And yet actions take place, things happen. What are we to make of them?[7]

The true mafia exists only in the United States, says Pantaleone. "Is it an accident that of all the countries where Sicilians have gone, only in America has this Mafia taken hold?"[8] He goes on to compare Richard Nixon to the mafiosi of Sicily, finding them all to be virtuous men. He comments that "It was a stroke of genius when Fellini in his Satyricon went out of his way to choose a face to play the role of Trimalchio who was Richard Nixon as an old man."[9] It is interesting to note here that Trimalchio, a character from Petronius's *Satyricon*, was the original title of F. Scott Fitzgerald's *The Great Gatsby*. What characterizes Trimalchio is that he is fat, showy and given to great excess, very unlike the slim, wiry Sicilian gangsters of Morreale. The real gangster, as portrayed by Morreale, is the epitome of a gentleman on the surface, no matter what violence he has been accused of conducting. And indeed, when Taralla dies in a car explosion, his *figura* is preserved when above his coffin is a black banner upon which are the words "He Was a Gentleman."

The mafia continued to be a major subject in fiction produced by later writers of Italian American origins, and the most significant publications reinvent the figure of the mafioso in interesting ways. Giose Rimanelli and Frank Lentricchia use sexuality to undermine the power of the traditional gangster and turn the signs of traditional masculine strength into weakness. In this way, these two writers reinvent the gangster figure to function as a criticism of American and Italian American cultures. I have paired these two authors because I believe that they both employ a sense of irony – with which, as scholars and artists, they are very familiar – in their depictions of the gangster. They both, in different ways, set up the figure of the gangster not only as a target of cultural criticism, but as a subject who criticizes the very culture that surrounds him. Thus, the gangster becomes a critic of culture as the author, or cultural critic, criticizes the culture of the gangster. Both authors debunk the myths created around the mafia in the United States. In his novel *Benedetta in Guysterland* (1993) Rimanelli plays around with and mocks outright the facts that were recorded by Talese and romanticized by Puzo. Through parody, he enables us to examine historical "mafia truths" for the fictions that they really are. Much of what has come to be known as "mafia" or mafia-related could easily have been fiction. As Jerre Mangione and Ben Morreale suggest in their historical study *La Storia: Five Centuries of the Italian American Experience* (1993), the power of the mafia in Sicily was exaggerated by the Italian government, which sought popular support to eliminate this powerful opposition force. In his novel *Music of the Inferno* (1999) Lentricchia debunks traditional mafia myths by having the protagonist "out" a fictional gangster as a homosexual within an old-fashioned Italian American community. He turns what is stereotypically portrayed as a homosocial community into a critique of traditional notions of masculinity through the figure of a homosexual gangster. Until Rimanelli's and Lentricchia's fiction, the gangster was never represented as a homosexual. By queering the mafia, they challenge narrow definitions of masculinity defined by earlier gangster figures. Both novelists use the gangster's sexuality to draw attention to the absurdity of having their behavior represent an ethnicized version of the John Wayne big man. Both of these authors indict such portrayals through their uncovering of the secret world behind the gangsters they have found in their fictions.

A completely different take on the mafia comes to us in the writings of Louisa Ermelino who creates new notions of masculinity, first in a male character in her novel *Joey Dee Gets Wise* (1991), and then through the female characters of her novel *The Sisters Malone* (2002). Ermelino takes on the stereotypical notions of masculinity and transforms our way of seeing them, giving us a good sense of how gender lines have always been blurred. From her first novel, *Joey Dee Gets Wise: A Story of Little Italy*, to *The Black Madonna* (2001), to her latest, *The Sisters Mallone: Una Storia di Famiglia* (2003), Ermelino has been exploring and explaining the places where much power lies in Italian American culture – with the mothers. What earlier male writers have suppressed in their creation of father/son stories, Ermelino uncovers and exploits.

Ultimately, Ermelino's reinvention of the gangster through female characters opens up possibilities for the gangster figure to continue to serve Italian American storytellers in new ways. In *The Sisters Mallone*, Ermelino takes us deep into Italian American culture through three sisters whose immigrant grandfather, born Malloni, finds himself surrounded by the Irish in New York City and does what he can to fit in, even if it means changing his name to Mallone. But as the surface hides the danger of depth, these Irish-looking girls are Italian through and through and capable of any number of heroic acts.

The reinvention of the mafia gangster continues in the work of Anthony Valerio. In *Lefty and the Button Men* (2000), originally published as *Conversation with Johnny* (1997), Valerio presents an entertaining and sometimes parodic, sometimes sardonic look at crime and culture.[10] He attempts a literary hit on two stereotypes that have plagued Italian Americans: the gangster and the lover. While he does not eliminate them, he certainly paralyzes both of them long enough for us to see that the cult of *The Godfather* is over. The seed of this novel is a short story Valerio published back in 1990, in the first issue of *Voices in Italian Americana*. "The Last Godfather," which appears as a chapter in *Lefty*, sounds the death knell for the gangster as representative of Italian America and resurrects the Italian American writer as a hero in its place. *Lefty* wraps that story in a context that leaps the ghetto boundaries of Italian American storytelling to create a balance between history and imagination so that a culture's history can be used to create art.

Don DeLillo, a major contemporary American writer, not known for his portrayals of Italian American characters, uses the gangster figure in a number of his novels. The first appearance in his work of a DeLillo gangster is Arondella, a mysterious character from his first novel *Americana* (1971). The gangster figure reappears in DeLillo's *Running Dog* (1978) in the form of Vincent "The Eye" Talerico, a minor character who is in charge of acquiring first-run films for a New York mafia family. Another DeLillo gangster comes to us right out of the pages of US history in the novel *Libra* (1988). The character of Carmine Latta is a fictional representation of Carlo Marcello, the

New Orleans mob chieftain supposedly connected to the John F. Kennedy assassination. We do not get much more than this in the novel regarding the gangster figure. There is a bit about the Chicago gangster, Sam "Momo" Giancana, whose mistress was sleeping with John Kennedy. In *Libra*, even though DeLillo plays with many of the facts in order to create his drama, he seems to have his hands tied by history concerning how much play he can give the gangster figure, especially when so little is told from the gangster's point of view. Yet, the figure of the gangster serves as a critic of the WASP world in which the conspiracy of a president's assassination involves players from a variety of cultures. It is in his novel *Underworld* (1997) – the title echoing the famous 1927 gangster film – that DeLillo makes his most pronounced statements about the gangster through his protagonist, Nick Shay.

A novel rich in many of the stories that have become American history and legend, *Underworld* takes us under the world as we know it to where bookie-fathers disappear, to where nuclear weapons are turned into hazardous waste eliminators, and to where the dead get resurrected. Nick Shay's father, Jimmy Costanza, was a bookie who disappeared one day. Nick tells his brother Matt that their father "did the unthinkable Italian crime. He walked out on his family. They don't even have a name for this."[11] That is why Nick's mother legally arranged for Nick to keep her last name. The ability to care for one's family is one of the key factors in determining one's masculinity in Italian American culture. Matt believes his father was abducted by the mob, but Nick believes he did in fact run away, abandoning those family responsibilities. Nick relates to the gangster in terms of solitude. "I've always been a country of one. There's a certain distance in my makeup, a measured separation like my old man's."[12] He presents an Italian word – *lontananza* – that explains it, a word that interestingly connects the artist to the gangster:

> Distance or remoteness, sure. But as I used the word, as I interpret it, hard-edged and fine-grained, it's the perfected distance of the gangster, the syndicate mobster – the made man. Once you're a made man, you don't need the constant living influence of sources outside your self. You're all there. You're made. You're handmade. You're a sturdy Roman wall.[13]

DeLillo has actually taken the quality of the gangster and turned it into something to be emulated by those who want to achieve, if not independence, then certainly a sense of the ability to survive without much dependence on others. When the professional man takes on the gangster he becomes a rebel public intellectual who can mock the very society in which he thrives.

The influence of the greats of magical realism, such as Gabriel García Márquez, Ben Okri and Toni Morrison, are apparent as Tony Ardizzone creates a different sense of reality to show how the mafioso/gangster is created by society and how that figure evolves into and out of the figure in his novel *In the Garden of Papa Santuzzu* (1999). Papa Santuzzu believes that *La Merica* (America) holds a fortune for his family. Unwilling to leave the land where he was born, he sends off child after child, until he is left alone with his visions and his memories. Twelve stories, each presented in the voice of a different child or relative of Santuzzu, tell of the trials of traveling across the ocean; one is dedicated to explaining how the mafia came to be.

Luigi Girgenti was one of Santuzzu's sons, and his tale tells of how Luigi was transformed into a mafioso one restless night when he heard the wolves up in the hills calling for him. Luigi sneaks out of his Sicilian village home and calls out, "Hey wolves, why don't you come out and play / Or else shut up so I can sleep! / I'm a village boy who's roamed this way / To romp and frolic, gambol and leap."[14] In his midnight ramblings he comes upon the wolves' campsite; he steals food and eats until his stomach is full for the first time in his life. He then notices a bag of gold, and after snatching a few of the coins he gets hit by lightning "right through the crack of my culu [ass]."[15] In no time, he is transformed into a wolf and begins to run with the pack.

Luigi's adventures as a wolf teach him that he can achieve justice in a world where the power is held by the *baruni* or barons (who were often absentee landlords) and administered by the *gabbilloti* or the henchmen who worked for the barons. Ardizzone presents the social structure of much of Sicily during the nineteenth and early twentieth centuries out of which it is believed that the mafia evolved. His wolves are presented as Robin Hood-like bands that are out to balance the scales of justice for the *campagnoli* or the country folk. The wolves transformed from men because when a man witnesses others starving, "How can he remain a man? Thus wolf packs formed in the Sicilian forests and hills and commenced to rob the robbers, taking back a small portion of what was rightfully ours."[16] The wolves embody many of the characteristics associated with the mafioso: loyalty, success, perseverance, intuition, community, intelligence and sometimes the shadow. While this is a minor appearance of the gangster figure, it represents an advance in that Ardizzone returns to the origins of the Sicilian mafioso to show that there are two sides to the figure: the repressive, represented by the *gabbilloti*, and the revolutionary, represented by the wolves.

The most recent images of the mafia in America come through David Chase's television series *The Sopranos* (1999–2007). Like many male baby-boomers in the throes of middle age, Tony Soprano is trying to figure out who he is and why he does what he does. He has come to realize that he is not the man his father was, and that his son will not be able to carry on the family tradition. Trapped between the past and the present with an unimaginable future, he begins to feel weak and visits a doctor after a couple of fainting spells. When his doctor suggests he visit a psychologist to help him deal with stress, he stumbles upon a way of feeling better, but for Tony Soprano it comes with a cost, and that cost is betraying the tribal code of keeping silent, especially to strangers. Tony begins to lose a traditional sense of manhood by first talking about his work, and second by talking about it with a woman. Hesitant at first, he finds that as he continues to talk he begins to question the traditional order of things, which leads him to question his role as husband, father, son and gangster. After Tony Soprano there can be no mafia, in the traditional sense. When Tony breaks *omerta*, he is no longer behaving the way a traditional mafioso should.

The Soprano family functions in the everyday world of middle-class America, but maintains an old-world sense of structure and obligation that separates them from their neighbors. And while the patriarchal mode of that world is weakening, its matriarchal foundation is surfacing. Whether it is through Tony's wife, his mother or his psychiatrist, the power of women to change the world is featured as never before. Whether Tony Soprano represents a degeneration or a regeneration of the gangster remains to be seen, and actually is not as important as the fact that he has come to signify the postmodern American who struggles to fashion an identity that reconciles an ethnic past with a multicultural present.

Mario Puzo's version of the gangster in *The Godfather* served to humanize the gangster figure as no one had done previously. Puzo's novel and Coppola's subsequent films changed the way the world viewed Italian Americans. More attention was paid to Italian Americans through increased surveillance of Italian Americans by government agencies such as the FBI, and new public expectations arose for how Italian American men should behave. Martin Scorsese's gangsters reinforced this notion and firmly established the Italian American gangster as the prototype for a post-feminism masculinity that remained untouched by social and political developments. Both the romanticization and the realization of the gangster in American literature and cinema worked to set up the Italian American male as the last survivor of good old-fashioned macho masculinity, the kind that John Wayne used to represent. The strong, silent type, who settled scores with fists instead of diplomacy, started to become politically incorrect. When Tony Soprano asks his psychiatrist, "Whatever happened to the strong silent type played by Gary Cooper?" in the first episode of *The Sopranos*, he is asking a question that his very presence in the media answers. It is through the reinvention of the gangsters created by the likes of Mario Puzo, Gay Talese, Ben Morreale, Giose Rimanelli, Frank Lentricchia, Louisa Ermelino, Anthony Valerio, Don DeLillo and David Chase that we begin to see new possibilities through the old images. Whether the writer romanticizes, realizes or reinvents the mafioso, he or she places mafia stories firmly at the center of US American culture.

NOTES

1. Gay Talese, *Honor Thy Father* (New York: Fawcett Crest, 1971), p. 447.
2. Ben Morreale, *A Few Virtuous Men (Li cornuti): A Novel of Sicily* (Plattsburgh, NY: Tundra Books, 1973), p. 11.
3. Bill Bonanno, *Bound by Honor: A Mafioso's Story* (New York: St. Martin's Paperbacks, 2000), p. xv.
4. Morreale, *A Few Virtuous Men*, p. 80.
5. *Ibid.*, p. 81.
6. *Ibid.*, p. 81.
7. *Ibid.*, p. 159.
8. *Ibid.*, p. 160.
9. *Ibid.*, p. 162.
10. Anthony Valerio, *Lefty and the Button Men* (Xlibris Corporation, 2000).
11. Don DeLillo, *Underworld* (New York: Scribner, 1997), p. 204.
12. *Ibid.*, p. 275.
13. *Ibid.*, p. 275.
14. Tony Ardizzone, *In the Garden of Papa Santuzzu* (New York: Picador USA, 1999), p. 75.
15. *Ibid.*, p. 76.
16. *Ibid.*, p. 79.

I I

LAURA BROWDER

True crime

Over forty-two years ago, Truman Capote wrote a bestselling book, *In Cold Blood*, and loudly proclaimed that he had invented a new art form. As Capote told George Plimpton in a long interview: "journalism, reportage, could be forced to yield a serious new art form: the 'nonfiction novel,'" and that "a crime, the study of one such, might provide the broad scope I needed to write the kind of book I wanted to write. Moreover, the human heart being what it is, murder was a theme not likely to darken and yellow with time."[1]

Whether or not Capote invented something called the "nonfiction novel," he ushered in the serious, extensive, non-fiction treatment of murder. In the years since *In Cold Blood* appeared, the genre of true crime regularly appears on the bestseller list. It is related to crime fiction, certainly – but it might equally well be grouped with documentary or read alongside romance fiction. And while its readers have a deep engagement with the genre that is very different from the engagement of readers of crime fiction, its writers are often forced to occupy a position – in relation to victims, criminals and police – that is complex and contradictory.[2] In this essay I will be tracing the history and development of this hybrid genre, as well as examining some of the tensions – between reader, writer, criminal and cops – that are at its heart.

In Cold Blood made reading about gory crime – in this case, the random murder of a farm family in Holcomb, Kansas – respectable. Moreover, despite its French epigraph it insisted on the Americanness of the victims – and the killers. It ushered in a theme which has since been richly mined by true crime authors: that violent crime is an act that can fundamentally reshape a community and create or lay bare the unspoken fears between members of that community. As Capote wrote, the murders "stimulated fires of mistrust in the glare of which many old neighbors viewed each other strangely, and as strangers."[3] The victims – Nancy Clutter, who recently starred in a high-school production of Tom Sawyer; her father, Herbert, who regards the land on which he lives as nearly "paradise – Eden on earth" – are quaintly American. So, in a different vein, are their killers – the first, the "chunky, misshapen child-man," Perry Smith, who could change his expression so that "the corrupt gypsy became the gentle romantic," whose mother is Cherokee, who wets his bed, sucks his thumb, and could slide into a fury "quicker than ten drunk Indians," and Dick Hickock, with his "venomous, sickly-blue squint" and prison tattoos. When the book ends, it does so with the detective who solved the crime walking away from the Clutter graves, "leaving behind him the big sky, the whisper of wind voices in the wind-bent wheat" – an evocation of the prairie that seems almost straight out of "America the Beautiful."[4]

In Cold Blood, with its self-conscious turns of phrase, portrayed cherry-pie-baking, 4-H club-attending, churchgoing characters who lived at a great, even nostalgic remove from the urban readers of *The New Yorker*, where *In Cold Blood* was originally published in installments. Capote invited readers not only to get to know the dreams of the victims – marriage, agricultural success – but also the visions of the killers, like the dreams Perry Smith had had since childhood: "the yellow bird, huge and parrot-faced, had soared across Perry's dreams, an avenging angel who savaged his enemies or, as now, rescued him in moments of mortal danger."[5] Everything about the book screamed its importance.

Forty years earlier, Theodore Dreiser had demonstrated in *An American Tragedy* – his novel about a young, overly ambitious poor boy, Clyde Griffiths, who kills his pregnant girlfriend in a desperate attempt to keep pursuing his climb up the social ladder, and then is executed for the crime – that an individual, sordid crime could become a metaphor for the American condition. Holcomb's residents, with their "narrow frontier trousers, Stetsons, and high-heeled boots with pointed toes," are iconically American.[6] And indeed, readers picked up on the insistent Americana in which the book was steeped: Capote estimated that, of the letters he had received from readers, "about 70 percent . . . think of the book as a reflection on American life, this collision between the desperate, ruthless, wandering, savage part of American life, and the other, which is insular and safe, more or less."[7] Reading the book could be a safe, yet thrilling way of experiencing this collision.

Though Capote's treatment of violent crime may have taken a new form, non-fiction accounts of gory crimes have long been a marketplace staple. Documentary treatments of violence have been popular in the United States for close to 200 years, as witnessed by the violent ballads and broadsides dating back to the early nineteenth century, and, at the end of that century, the enormous interest in true crime sparked on both sides of the Atlantic by the Jack the Ripper case.

True crime literature first flourished during the Elizabethan era in the form of simple pamphlets detailing the exploits of local murderers. In 1735, John

Osborn published his three-volume set, *Lives of Remarkable Criminals*. George Wilkinson's *Newgate Calendar*, published in 1775, included for the first time the details of everyday life – drink, food, clothing – and thus provided true crime as a form of social history. As Thomas Byrnes points out, by the end of the nineteenth century, the nature of the crimes documented had begun to change, away from crimes that were economic in origin, and towards more complex crimes: "Highway robberies were rampant, police corruption was not uncommon, innocent people were framed, tales of cannibalism were drifting in from the colonies, and sex crimes (mostly rape) were starting to appear with frightening regularity."[8] These crimes were not only more complex, but often more lurid – and increasingly morally ambiguous.

Karen Halttunen has documented the intense interest that late seventeenth-century colonists in the United States demonstrated in execution sermons – and that mid nineteenth-century readers evinced in the biographies of killers, newspaper accounts and printed transcripts of murder trials. She argues that these narratives reconstructed

> the criminal transgressor: from common sinner with whom the larger community of sinners were urged to identify in the service of their own salvation, into moral monster from whom readers were instructed to shrink . . . The new Gothic murderer – like the villain in Gothic fiction – was first and last a moral monster, between whom and the normal majority yawned an impassable gulf.[9]

The Jack the Ripper case was as fascinating to Americans as to the British, it seemed, and its coverage emphasized, for the first time, forensics as an important element in the narrative. However, it was not until the appearance of Thomas Duke's 1910 *Celebrated Criminal Cases of America* that the United States witnessed a similar explosion in true crime as a national genre. In some respects, the formula for true crime has not changed since Duke's day. In his preface, Duke, the captain of police in San Francisco, assured readers that, "While this volume will show that in some instances fabulous amounts of money have been unlawfully obtained, it will also show that retribution invariably overtakes the professional criminal and brings with it untold misery and degradation."[10] And, pursuing a theme that still holds a prominent place in contemporary true crime books, Duke notes that a "perusal of this volume will show that, while many of the most desperate characters have inherited their criminal tendencies, environment frequently transforms an ideal youth into a veritable fiend."[11] Then, as now, readers were able both to participate vicariously in the horrible crime and to pronounce moral judgment upon it.

Duke provided true crime as a lens through which to view United States history. The cases which he covered, and which he listed geographically as

San Francisco cases, celebrated cases on the Pacific Coast, and celebrated cases east of the Pacific Coast, including such events as the assassinations of Presidents Lincoln, Garfield and McKinley; the killing by a mob of Mormon leader Joseph Smith; the Haymarket riots of Chicago; the draft riots in New York City during the Civil War; the Jesse James Gang. Of course, the book also contains such true crime staples as fill the pages of today's books, such as "Cordelia Botkin, who Murdered Mrs. Dunning and Mrs. Deane in Delaware with Poisoned Candy Sent Through the Mail," "Adolph Weber, Who Murdered His Father, Mother, Sister and Brother in Auburn, Cal.," and "Jesse Pomeroy of Boston, a Fourteen-year-old Fiend." Yet where the book departs from today's true crime books is in its at least partial focus on criminals of color and foreign criminals – Australians, Mexican bandits and Chinese killers. Even more unusual is its coverage of crimes in which people of color were the victims, such as the New York draft riots (as Duke writes, "The following is a list of colored people who were murdered by the mobs in a particularly atrocious manner") or the case of Captain Nathaniel Gordon, who in 1860 "seized and shipped 897 Africans from the Congo River, and was captured and subsequently executed in New York. Eighteen victims died from suffocation."[12] Today, one would be hard-pressed to find a true crime book in which both victims and killers are not white.[13]

By the 1920s, lurid true crime magazines had emerged, a form that continues to flourish, as do Sunday supplement treatments of true crimes and the ubiquitous documentary cop shows on television. While true crime books may be formulaic, that formula is constantly evolving. And just as the form of true crime literature has changed over time, so, too, is there a true crime to suit every decade: the twenties had Leopold and Loeb, the gay lovers who killed a child for thrills – their "depraved," sexually transgressive behavior serving, in the popular press, as the explanation for their brutality. The thirties were the decade of the gangsters, figures who were sympathetically glossed in the mass media as anti-government folk heroes: from that period we have Bonnie and Clyde and Al Capone. And then by the mid-sixties we were given the drifters Smith and Hickock, who brutally slaughtered the Clutters. Like Leopold and Loeb, these killers were other, deviant – men whose lives seemed remote from those of most middle-class readers. Most of the books dating from this era feature lone drifters who preyed upon strangers, such as the Boston Strangler.

Most of all, *In Cold Blood* led to the development of what we now know as true crime books – paperbacks thick enough to function as doorstoppers and featuring the inevitable photo insert. These books have a number of features in common: they are generally hefty – between 400 and 800 pages long – and thus demand a significant investment of time on the part of their readers.

Almost always, the victims are female; most of the time, the killer or killers are male. True crime books generally contain a multi-page insert of what are usually described as dramatic, shocking, or chilling photographs of the killer and the victims. As one true crime editor says:

> pictures are at least 60 percent of the initial draw and you can't sell a paperback if you don't have solid pictures. This may seem trivial, but it is a key issue because what makes a book different is that it delivers the things you can't get anywhere else. This includes things like the autopsy pictures, the severed breasts of prostitutes, the slashed throats – things you'll never see on TV or in the newspaper or anywhere else.[14]

These photographs heighten the aura of reality so important to true crime readers. Yet many of these photos are not gory at all: they also portray the killer and victim in happier circumstances, as well as in their roles as corpse and apprehended criminal; they document the police officers and lawyers involved in the case, and they nearly always feature a picture of the convicted killer being led away to a lifetime in prison.

In other words, the plot of a true crime can easily be gleaned from a quick ruffle through the photo insert, or even a glance at the back cover. These are books read not for plot, but for detailed description, and for their linear analyses of what went wrong. For even as these books posit the existence of socially inexplicable deviance – pure evil, in short – they also reaffirm notions of causality, by encouraging the reader to participate in a voyeuristic dissection of the victim's mistakes, her failure to read obvious clues. As true crime writer Jack Olsen, author of *Son: A Psychopath and His Victims* (1983) and *"Doc": The Rape of the Town of Lovell* (1989), says, "it's what people have come to expect from the genre, an explanation of the criminal mind, of criminal behavior, and how to avoid people like that."[15]

True crime books are very different from detective stories, with their contract with the reader of fictionality – it is impossible to imagine a true crime variant of the "English cozy," as one subgenre of detective stories is called. The label of "true" crime gives the material in these books the aura of fact – an air of authority enhanced by the journalistic, "non-literary" style in which they are written, by the thick description of events, and by the inclusion of supporting photographic and other documentary evidence. This perceived factuality removes the responsibility for aestheticizing violence from both the writer and the reader of such works.

While true crime may be a form of documentary, it is a dystopian version. Whereas the traditional documentary is generally designed to raise people's consciousness about terrible conditions in order to effect change, true crime presents a picture of problems that are insoluble, because they are rooted within the individual psyche and often have no apparent roots in social conditions. We are in the realm of the psychopath or, more frequently, of the sociopath, whose evil has no visible cause: legislation cannot remove the source of the problem.

True crime is a politically slippery genre. On the one hand, true crime books uphold conservative values – policemen are heroes, criminals are punished, sometimes by death. True crime writers are often affiliated with victims' rights groups, and some, like former policewoman Ann Rule, work with law enforcement agencies. While Capote treated the events he described as an American tragedy, and described criminals and victims in novelistic, rather than moralistic terms, some of the most successful true crime writers who followed him have framed their stories as morality tales – and gave themselves starring roles in the narrative. The bestselling true crime book of all time, *Helter Skelter* (1974), which dealt with the Manson family murders, was written by Vincent Bugliosi, the prosecutor who tried the case. Bugliosi's job both made it easy for him to gain access to insider information, since he was the ultimate insider, and made his own stance in regard to the killers unambiguous: his job was to put them in prison for life or to get them the death penalty.

Yet true crime books are also subversive, in that they tend to question the very foundations of patriarchal culture – the family in true crime is often a poisonous unit. This focus on the family has not always been a trait of the genre. The first true crime books in the 1960s generally presented violence and evil as a threat from without, rather than within, the family. In Capote's *In Cold Blood*, the nice middle-class Clutter family was brutally slaughtered by a pair of gay drifters. These killers were other, deviant – men whose lives seemed remote from those of most middle-class readers. Late in the decade, we would get the Manson family – middle-class children who seemed to have been infected with a kind of sixties craziness, who claimed their inspiration for mass murder was drawn from a Beatles album.

While the 1960s saw the first "modern" true crime books appear, it was not until the seventies, and the rise of the women's movement, that the genre gained dramatically in popularity, and that a new type of true crime book began to appear – one focusing on horrendous murders committed within the family setting, usually by respectable men, pillars of society. While the true crime books of the sixties tended to focus on the dangers from without – men who broke into houses to kill single women, or peripatetic psychopaths far removed from the main currents of American society – the new true crime books emphasized the danger from within the nuclear family.

Since the seventies, it has been the case that while some true crime books detail the ravages wrought by crazed strangers, a greater number concern murders committed by those men who are entrusted with protecting and caring for women. There are rogue policemen, such as LAPD officer William "Mild Bill" Leasure, the protagonist of Edward Humes's 1992 work, *Murderer with a Badge*. There are bad FBI agents. As the jacket copy for Aphrodite Jones's 1992 book *The FBI Killer* attests:

> Susan Daniel Smith, 27, prayed for a handsome Prince Charming who would take her away from the squalor of her rural Kentucky community to live in romance and luxury. When a good-looking, big city FBI agent named Mark Putnam entered her life, Susan thought her prayers were answered. She was dead wrong.

There are bad doctors: the villain of Jack Olsen's *"Doc"* is a trusted family doctor, a Mormon, in a small town, who for twenty-five years had been raping and molesting his women and children patients. Dr. Jeffrey MacDonald, of Joe McGinniss's bestselling *Fatal Vision*, was a former Green Beret who was convicted of murdering his wife and two young children. Dale Cavaness, the protagonist of Darcy O'Brien's *Murder in Little Egypt*, was a respected Illinois doctor who beat his wife, and ultimately murdered his two sons. There are rotten kids, such as Chris Pritchard, the North Carolina teenager who bludgeoned and stabbed his mother and step-father, and was the focus of Joe McGinniss's *Cruel Doubt* (1991) and Jerry Bledsoe's *Blood Games* (1991). There are parents who kill their children, like Marie – Hilley in Philip E. Ginsburg's *Poisoned Blood* (1987) – who poisoned her mother-in-law, mother, husband and daughter, then "duped a man into marriage, faked her own death, and came back to him – as her long-lost twin!" In true crime books, fathers, and sometimes mothers, kill their children, and children kill their parents. Most of all, women who are duped by the promise of romance are killed by their erstwhile lovers.

True crime books are a popular arena for metaphysical discussions about the nature of evil, the meaning of retribution, and the impossibility of knowing another. The nineteenth-century anxiety about confidence men and painted women is sustained in the popularity of true crime books. In Thomas French's *Unanswered Cries*, it is the helpful next-door neighbor who is the killer: though he saves lives as a firefighter, he butchers his neighbor in her own home. As *The Stranger Beside Me* (1980), Ann Rule's account of her relationship with Ted Bundy, evidences, one's friend and co-worker could turn out to be a killer.

Because of this perceived factuality, the true crime writer occupies an uneasy place. Ann Rule's *The Stranger Beside Me* is a great example of this; because Rule, who is one of the most popular writers in the genre, has such a powerful personal presence in the narrative, these problems are highlighted.

In a sense, *The Stranger Beside Me* tells two integrally related stories: the fall of serial killer Ted Bundy, and the rise of true crime writer Ann Rule.

When Rule and Bundy meet, it is Rule who appears to be in the worse position: "On the surface, at least, it seemed I had more problems than Ted did . . . My marriage was in deep trouble, and I was again trying to cope with guilt. Bill and I had agreed to a divorce only weeks before he had been diagnosed with melanoma, the deadliest of skin cancers." While she at first finds Bundy attractive – "almost the perfect man" – the middle-aged Rule, struggling to support her four children through writing stories for *True Detective* magazine, spends many of her working hours with the Seattle homicide detectives, whom she finds to be "highly sensitive men – men who understood that if I didn't find enough cases to write up, my kids might not eat."[16] For Rule, an important part of being a good mother is writing true crime.

However, as the tally of murdered young women grows in Seattle – including an acquaintance of one of Rule's daughters – and Rule worries about her daughters' safety, she finds herself in a double bind that is an exaggerated version of the one many true crime writers face: she is torn between her dependence for income on the goodwill of the police, who grant her access to information; between her identification with the victims of these terrible rape/murders; and finally, upon the necessity of treating Bundy as though he is an innocent friend, although she herself suspects that the handsome subject, who introduces himself to women as "Ted," and who has a faint English accent, may be a killer. Rule even calls a police detective friend of hers early on to see if Bundy owns a VW Bug similar to the one used by the killer – and finds that he does. However, Rule has just signed a contract to write a book about the string of brutal murders. Given her suspicions – and the fact that thirteen months after she gives his name to the police, they begin the process of subpoenas and arrests that will lead to his eventual downfall – she is caught between seemingly irreconcilable goals. To make her book work, she needs the confidence both of the police and of the killer. And yet, as the mother of teenaged daughters, and as someone who identifies with the victims of violent crime, how can she justify her continued protestations of friendship to Bundy – the money she sends him while he is in prison, the long, boozy lunches she shares with him when he is out on bail, the phone calls and the letters?

"When I began writing fact-detective stories," Rule tells us, "I promised myself that I would always remember I was writing about the loss of human beings, that I was never to forget that. I hoped that the work I did might somehow save other victims, might warn them of the danger." She reminds the reader of her membership, by invitation, in the Committee of Friends and

Families of Missing Persons and Victims of Violent Crimes, and offers the reader her own exoneration:

> I have met many parents of victims, cried with them, and yet I have somehow felt guilty – because I make my living from other people's tragedies. When I told the Committee how I felt, they put their arms around me and said, "No. Keep on writing. Let the public know how it is for us. Let them know how we hurt, and how we try to save other parents' children by working for new legislation that requires mandatory sentencing and the death penalty for killers."[17]

In her allegiance to the victims' families, Rule compares herself favorably to the reporters, with their "ugly and cruel" techniques, whose "dogged pursuit ... of something new to write was going to interfere mightily with the police investigation," while "Frantic families of the missing girls ... were besieged by some of the most coercive tactics any reporter can use."[18] These reporters re-injure the families of victims; Rule herself helps heal families.

While distancing herself from journalists, Rule also draws a distinction between the "real" world she and the cops inhabit, and the world of crime fiction: as she lists over forty links between Bundy and the crimes, she concludes that:

> For a fiction writer, it would have been enough. For an actual criminal investigation, it was circumstantial evidence, block upon block piled up until there was no doubt in the Washington detectives' minds that Theodore Robert Bundy was the "Ted" they had sought for so long.

Yet this stance is problematic: on the one hand, Rule concedes that

> I was still walking a tightrope between Ted and the detectives, a rope that seemed to wend over higher and higher precipices. It was imperative that I continue to write fact-detective stories, and any breach of faith with a police agency would mean the end of that. Neither did I want to be disloyal to Ted, although it was becoming more and more difficult not to believe that Ted was the man the police sought.[19]

This admission takes place shortly after Rule writes to Ted in prison, discussing her book contract with W. W. Norton: "I offered to share my profits with him, gauged by the number of chapters he might write in his own words." For even after Bundy has been convicted and sentenced for the kidnapping of a woman who managed to escape before he killed her, "there were still so many facets of the story that were hidden from me, and still that chance that Ted was being railroaded." Rule identifies herself as another woman manipulated by Bundy: "Because he could control women, balance us carefully in the tightly structured world he had created, we were important to him."[20]

Meanwhile, Rule's fortunes rise as Bundy's sink: while Bundy is on the road following a successful escape from prison, Rule is finally making it: "All of it was unreal. Only a few years before, I had been – if there is such a creature – a typical housewife, a Brownie leader. Now I was off to Hollywood to write a movie, with the FBI waiting for me." This disconnect grows stronger as the book wears on, until finally we arrive, in Rule's afterword, at the point of Bundy's execution, a time when, Rule tells us, "First, I was going to do the Larry King show ... A limousine met me at the airport and delivered me to a skyscraper." The time of the execution draws closer: "The limo driver took me to the best hotel in town, where the 20/20 staff was waiting for me. There were also thirty-four phone messages marked 'Urgent.'"[21] Just as *In Cold Blood* echoed one Theodore Dreiser novel, *The Stranger Beside Me* seemed to echo another: it recalls nothing so much as Sister Carrie rocking in her chair, a wealthy celebrity, while in another part of the city the man whom she had looked up to and adored turns on the gas in his flophouse room and quietly expires. Yet in some minor sense Bundy had the last laugh: in his final, videotaped interview with James Dobson (who has since achieved prominence as the head of the conservative Christian group Focus on the Family), Bundy attributed his lethal fantasies to ... reading detective magazines.

Two recent works have put something of an uncomfortable spotlight on the relationship between true crime writers and the events and people they document. The 2005 film *Capote*, directed by Bennett Miller and starring Philip Seymour Hoffman and Catherine Keener, focused on the moral compromise at the heart of *In Cold Blood*. Capote, too, found himself in a fraught position: his book could not succeed without the death of the two killers – and to get his intimate portrait of them, he had befriended them over the years. Indeed, the two men believed (probably incorrectly) that Capote had the power to gain them another stay of execution. Their last days, in which Capote dodged their desperate telegrams and then declined to visit them on the day of their execution, laid bare the essential falsity of their relationship. When composer Ned Rorem heard Capote, at a dinner party, remark that "it can't be published until they're executed, so I can hardly wait," he was outraged enough to write a letter to the *Saturday Review of Literature*, which he started by noting that "Capote got his two million and his heroes got the rope." Kathleen Tynan recalled that her husband, the critic Kenneth Tynan, overheard Capote receiving the news of the impending execution, "and Truman, according to Ken, hopped up and down with glee, clapping his hands, saying, 'I'm beside myself! Beside myself! Beside myself with joy!'"[22] Kenneth Tynan was similarly moved to write a negative review of the book for the *Observer*.

Yet the controversy in which Capote found himself embroiled was nothing compared to the lawsuit for libel, settled for $325,000, filed by convicted killer Jeffrey MacDonald for fraud and breach of contract against Joe McGinniss, the author who had written a true crime bestseller, *Fatal Vision*, about his case. MacDonald, a Green Beret doctor, had been tried and convicted of killing his pregnant wife and two small daughters, and sentenced to life in prison. In his defense, he had claimed that the crime had been committed by drug-crazed hippies who broke into his house chanting "Acid is groovy" and "Kill the pigs," before they savagely attacked him and bludgeoned and stabbed his family to death. Despite the presence of the word "pig" written in blood on the premises, his claim was undercut not only by his own relatively minor wounds, but by the presence of a recent, blood-soaked copy of *Esquire* magazine on the coffee table, featuring an article about the Manson murders – crimes strikingly similar to the one he described. Glibly put, one could say that MacDonald wanted the jurors to accept an older true crime model – the deviant, crazed outsiders committing senseless murder – and they had opted instead for a seventies-style explanation that highlighted the guilt of the super-masculine patriarchal figure in the family.

Before the murder trial, MacDonald contacted McGinniss and asked him to write about the case in exchange for a share of the book's proceeds – an offer he had made to several other authors, including prominent true crime writer Joseph Wambaugh, author of *The Onion Field* (1973). Yet Wambaugh had written MacDonald a strongly cautionary letter about the "truth" in true crime:

> You should understand that I would not think of writing *your* story. It would be *my* story. Just as *The Onion Field* was *my* story and *In Cold Blood* is Capote's story ... I suspect that you may want a writer who would tell *your* story, and indeed your version may very well be the truth as I would see it. But you'd have no guarantee.[23]

McGinniss, by contrast, took the bait – and agreed to give MacDonald a generous share of his advance and royalties in exchange for the privilege of living with MacDonald and his defense team during the trial, and being privy to all of their deliberations. While McGinniss quotes one of the psychiatrists testifying at trial that "this is a guy ... who would be appalled at the thought of women's lib," and cites MacDonald's promiscuity as evidence of his personality disorder, he and MacDonald, according to members of the defense team, spent hours together discussing their many relationships with women and classifying women on the basis of their looks.[24] For four years after the trial ended, McGinniss continued to write to MacDonald in prison, professing his friendship and his belief in MacDonald's innocence. Since McGinniss refused to show him the galleys of the book before it came out, MacDonald's first inkling that McGinniss had, instead, portrayed him as a psychopathic killer in the hyper-masculine mode came when Mike Wallace, during a taping of "60 Minutes" in MacDonald's prison, read him some of the harshest passages out loud.

Just as McGinniss's MacDonald was a deceptive creature, one who hid his psychopathology behind the mask of a warm, caring doctor, MacDonald's McGinniss was a figure in a funhouse mirror: the writer who pretends to be a mirror of his subject, but is in fact his own person. McGinniss offered himself as mirror when he wrote to MacDonald, "let's face it, early marriage is no picnic for anyone. It sure as hell wasn't for me," and goes on to confess his own infidelities to his pregnant wife before concluding:

> Having gone through that sort of experience myself, I think I might be more attuned than most people to the possibility that you shared some of these reactions in your own life . . . There is enough already known in terms of your extracurricular life to demonstrate that you were at least as promiscuous as I was.[25]

In his comparison of himself to MacDonald, as in the activities he shared with MacDonald – checking out women, drinking beer and watching sports – McGinniss invites his subject to see him as not just sympathetic, but deeply similar.

In MacDonald's view, McGinniss was incapable of seeing him clearly, intent as he was on fitting MacDonald into a preconceived model of the psychopathic killer. After the book was published, McGinniss told reporter Bob Keeler, who was interviewing him for *Newsday*, that MacDonald "is so different from what he appears to be. I feel very sad that he didn't turn out to be who he wanted me to think he was. Because that would have been a whole lot easier."[26] Yet an innocent MacDonald would have presented the same problems for McGinniss that a successful appeal on the part of Perry Smith and Dick Hickock would have done for Capote.

Finally, the portrayal that McGinniss offered of MacDonald – of a selfish beast masquerading as a caring man – was perfectly analogous to the portrait of McGinniss that MacDonald was able to construct successfully for the jury at the fraud trial. At that trial, MacDonald's lawyers released letters that McGinniss had written to him shortly after MacDonald's incarceration, in which he asks "What the fuck were those [twelve] people thinking of?" and tells him that "total strangers can recognize within five minutes that you did not receive a fair trial," and that "there are too many people who care too much about you" to let him be forgotten. To the jurors in that trial, one of whom reportedly said that she would have awarded "millions and millions of dollars to set an example for all authors to show they can't tell an untruth," the journalist was in this case no better than the murderer – and MacDonald, like Ted Bundy before him, had gotten his revenge on the author who had so successfully packaged him for mass consumption.[27]

In his letter to Jeffrey MacDonald, what Joseph Wambaugh did not note, perhaps out of delicacy, is that, as one editor observed, book contracts for true crime writers often contain a "conviction clause that states if the guy is not convicted of the crime, then we have the choice to cancel the book. This is for legal reasons because you can't have someone killing someone only to get away."[28] And that, finally, is what most throws into question the truth in true crime, and renders the genre an uneasy blend of reportage and moralism – because the veracity that it promises is incompatible with the rigid demands of its formula.

NOTES

1. George Plimpton, "The Story Behind a Nonfiction Novel," *New York Times*, January 16, 1966, pp. 2–3, 38–43, reprinted in Thomas Inge, *Truman Capote: Conversations* (Jackson, MS: Mississippi University Press, 1987), pp. 47–68.
2. For a discussion of true crime readers, see Laura Browder, "Dystopian Romance: True Crime and the Female Reader," *Journal of Popular Culture*, 39.6 (December 2006): 928–53.
3. Truman Capote, *In Cold Blood* (1965; repr. New York: Signet, 1980), p. 15.
4. *Ibid.*, pp. 23, 254, 26, 128, 43, 384.
5. *Ibid.*, p. 299.
6. *Ibid.*, p. 13.
7. Plimpton, "The Story Behind a Nonfiction Novel," p. 67.
8. Thomas Byrnes (ed.), *Writing Bestselling True Crime and Suspense* (Rocklin, CA: Prima Publications, 1997), p. 4.
9. Karen Halttunen, *Murder Most Foul: The Killer and the American Gothic Imagination* (Cambridge, MA: Harvard University Press, 1998), pp. 4–5.
10. Thomas Duke, *Celebrated Criminal Cases of America* (San Francisco: James Barry, 1910), p. iii.
11. *Ibid.*, p. iv.
12. *Ibid.*, pp. 600, 602.
13. Among the exceptions to this is Jack Olsen's *Charmer* (1994), about a black psychopath who preyed on white victims.
14. Paul Dinas, in *Writing True Crime*, ed. Byrnes, p. 257.
15. Interview, in *Writing True Crime*, ed. Byrnes, p. 230.
16. Ann Rule, *The Stranger Beside Me* (1980; repr. New York: Signet Books, 1989), pp. 29, 48.
17. *Ibid.*, pp. 72, 73.
18. *Ibid.*, p. 88.
19. *Ibid.*, pp. 174, 212.
20. *Ibid.*, pp. 192, 210, 398.
21. *Ibid.*, pp. 257, 489, 490.
22. Gerald Clarke, *Capote: A Biography* (New York: Simon & Schuster, 1988), pp. 354, 216.

23. Quoted in Janet Malcom, *The Journalist and the Murderer* (New York: Alfred A. Knopf, 1990), p. 29.
24. Joe McGinniss, *Fatal Vision* (New York: Putnam, 1983), p. 432. On their putative friendship, see Malcolm, *Journalist*, pp. 21–2, 140.
25. Malcolm, *Journalist*, pp. 121–2, 35–6, 6.
26. *Ibid.*, p. 25.
27. *Ibid.*, p. 45.
28. Paul Dinas, *Writing Bestselling True Crime*, p. 256.

12

MAUREEN T. REDDY

Race and American crime fiction

Race is ubiquitous and powerful in American crime fiction, as central in the genre as it is in American society; however, in fiction as in life, race matters are frequently denied, displaced, or otherwise so thoroughly disguised that many readers overlook them. Despite the tremendous expansion of serious critical interest in popular fiction generally and in crime fiction in particular during the final decades of the twentieth century and the first decade of the twenty-first, few critics have examined the workings of race in crime fiction, with most critical attention to race limited to examining texts by writers of color with detectives of color.[1] While such analyses have been helpful to the larger critical project of comprehensively mapping the genre, limiting discussion of race to texts in which race is directly addressed and in which the race at issue is not white serves to disguise further the actual roles of race in American crime fiction. Whiteness – its boundaries, its value, its meanings and perceived threats to its dominance – has been a primary concern of crime fiction throughout its history in the US.

Although even sketchily tracing the evolution of American crime fiction is beyond the scope of this essay, it is worth remembering that crime fiction grew out of mass fascination with true crime narratives and that in the US the popular appetite for crime stories was fed partly by newspapers' crime reporting, especially their police report columns. The *New York Sun*'s "Police Office" column, begun in 1833, is widely regarded as the origin of crime reporting in the US.[2] In a study of constructions of gender, race and class in episodic crime reportage of the 1830s, journalism professor Carole Stabile notes that race was the single most salient fact about any black criminal or victim, as race was usually the sole identity category mentioned in reports about any crime involving a black person.[3] Further, almost all mentions of black women in these reports presented them as criminals, not victims (indeed, not a single account of an offense by a white man against a black woman appeared in a decade of crime reports in the *New York Sun* and the *New York Herald*), whereas white women frequently appeared as victims.[4] Significantly, the category "white" was featured only by implication in these reports, as white victims and criminals were often multiply identified – by social class, by ethnicity and so on – but never by race. Whiteness, then, was the default position in these crime stories, assumed and therefore not requiring mention. That whiteness is the invisible, silent norm is now old news, but the effect of multiple mentions of blackness in each story in which the perpetrator is black – Stabile offers several examples in which race is mentioned three times in a single sentence – likely had some impact on "threat construction," as through sheer force of repetition the supposed connection between blackness and criminality was reinforced for readers.[5]

Throughout the nineteenth century, the racial ideology of the US held whiteness to be both the *sine qua non* of true Americanness and the essential qualification for citizenship in a participatory democracy. Since crime fiction, like other popular art forms, tends more frequently to reflect dominant beliefs than it does to challenge them, it is unsurprising to find whiteness treated as both a norm and an ideal in early crime fiction. That most distinctively American of crime genres – the hard-boiled – came into being at a time when anxieties about race and about the role of race in Americanness were matters of public debate.[6] The hard-boiled and the "classic" or "golden age" mystery are contemporaries. That many people believe the hard-boiled came into being solely in reaction against the classic mystery points to the anachronistic qualities of the latter, which indeed seems to be of an earlier time and a distant place. In fact, though, S. S. Van Dine's (pen name of Willard Huntington Wright) *The Benson Murder Case*, widely acknowledged as the first American clue-puzzle mystery, was published in 1927, a year *after* new editor Joseph Shaw changed *Black Mask* magazine to focus on crime fiction and just two years before Dashiell Hammett's *Red Harvest*, widely acknowledged as the first hard-boiled novel, appeared. The racial anxieties so important to the hard-boiled may seem absent from classic mysteries of the same period, but that very lack of direct engagement with critical issues of the day is an important component of these fictions' appeal to readers, as they tend to reassure readers that the status quo, including a firmly established racial hierarchy with whiteness at its pinnacle, is under no serious threat. These novels are urbane, but not urban, despite their usual setting of New York. Their upper-middle-class worlds – of Philo Vance, of Nero Wolfe – gesture more toward Europe than toward actual American cities, and the threats to those fairly rarefied financial and social worlds generally come from other (white) insiders.[7] In relying on a plot structure that ignores race, the golden age novels are of course always about whiteness, but a whiteness that need not speak its name because its dominance is secure and in no need of defense. In contrast, the hard-boiled is urban, not urbane, and whiteness is always in need of protection in the gritty, newer cities of the west.

The first hard-boiled writers saw themselves as engaging in an anti-elitist social critique meant to expose and to stand against the rampant corruption and downright decadence of the established social order, yet their fiction consistently reinscribes a conventional racial hierarchy. In his summary of post-Civil War economic and social factors, the confluence of which eventually gave rise to the hard-boiled, Dennis Porter stresses the dominance of monopoly capitalism and the resulting class conflict as well as the shift from an agrarian to an industrial, urban economy, but says nothing about immigration or black migration.[8] Porter sees the Nineteenth Amendment (Prohibition) as also important, in that it made ordinary people into lawbreakers and spawned a whole new class of criminal syndicates, and notes that in Jazz Age America,

> the time was ripe for the emergence in a popular literary genre of a disabused, anti-authoritarian, muckraking hero, who, instead of fleeing to Europe, like the sophisticates of lost generation fiction, stayed at home to confront crime and corruption on the increasingly unlovely streets of modern urban America.[9]

That summary takes the hard-boiled writers at their own estimation, ignoring the role of racial anxiety in inspiring their work.

Among the other factors that should be included in any survey of the conditions from which the hard-boiled arose is the fraught racial situation nationally. There were twenty-five race riots in US cities in the first half of 1919, riots that historians attribute to the dashing of black hopes for full citizenship that had been raised by black participation in the US war effort.[10] Although the number of lynchings peaked in the last decades of the nineteenth century, at least seventy black people were lynched in that first year after the war's end.[11] In 1922, the US House of Representatives finally passed the Dyer Anti-Lynching Bill, which had been introduced in 1918, but the US Senate failed to approve it, its passage stopped by Southern Democrats (all white).

In addition, a number of cases challenging race-based restrictions on immigration and citizenship came before the Supreme Court in the period following World War I, with two of the most far-reaching in their effects brought by immigrants claiming the right to be considered white and therefore eligible for citizenship. In *Ozawa* v. *US*, decided in 1922, a Japanese man argued that he was entitled to citizenship under the 1906 Naturalization Act. In delivering the opinion of the court, Justice George Sutherland asserted that from the beginning of Congressional attention to immigration,

[t]he intention was to confer the privilege of citizenship upon that class of persons whom the fathers knew as white, and to deny it to all who could not be so classified. It is not enough to say that the framers did not have in mind the brown or yellow races of Asia. It is necessary to go farther and be able to say that had these particular races been suggested the language of the act would have been so varied as to include them within its privileges.[12]

The decision goes on to specify that "the words 'white person' are synonymous with the words 'a person of the Caucasian race.'" Within a few months, the Supreme Court dealt with another case, US v. *Bhagat Singh Thind*, in which a South Asian man claimed the right to citizenship because he was Caucasian and therefore white. In this case, the Supreme Court decided that not all Caucasians are white (although one must be Caucasian to be white) and attempted to end similar future claims by referring to ordinary usage in daily life: "What we now hold is that the words 'free white persons' are words of common speech, to be interpreted in accordance with the understanding of the common man, synonymous with the word 'Caucasian' only as that word is popularly understood."

Who can be counted as white is the chief question for the court in both of these cases. Whereas the court is clear in its decision that both Ozawa and Thind cannot be so counted, it is much fuzzier on the general question, whose answer turns the decision-making over to the "common man," who is evidently white himself. But was the common man certain he could decide correctly? In California, in particular, racial anxiety seems to have been focused primarily on Asians, particularly Chinese, whose immigration was limited by the Chinese Exclusion Act of 1882 and its various extensions, which prevented Chinese from becoming American until 1942. Asians are often the villains in early hard-boiled fiction, which frequently incorporated a "yellow peril" theme. In several of Dashiell Hammett's Continental Op stories, for example, Asians pose a threat to whiteness both through their supposedly ruthless high intelligence and through a type of undecidability, moving in and out of whiteness by tricking the "common man."[13] Many of the villains in Hammett's stories are at the margins of whiteness, with their liminality figured as one element of the corrupt, decadent environment the detective must navigate.

An essential part of the hard-boiled detective's heroism is his own unquestionable whiteness, a factor often overlooked by critics who emphasize the importance of the detective's masculinity but fail to note that it is a specifically *white* masculinity. When the villains of the hard-boiled are white men, their whiteness is always in some way compromised, usually by their greed, which leads them to collaborate with racial others. In Raymond Chandler's stories, the detective's adversaries are often white women and various non-white men. Occasionally, the white female villains get away, but the non-white men are always completely destroyed by fiction's end. None of this is to suggest that early hard-boiled writers deliberately set out to valorize whiteness or to reinforce anti-Asian immigration policies, but instead it is intended to identify the racial codes that operate in these fictions even when the authors consciously set out to do something else. So, for instance, Chandler's "Red Wind" includes a subplot about two police officers, one white and one Mexican-American, that evidently is meant to take a swipe at racism, but ends up reinforcing racist ideology by treating both the decent Mexican-American cop (he is a "Mexican of the nice sort") and the racist, stupid white one as exceptions.[14]

The urban settings of the hard-boiled are intimately intertwined with racial codes, as cities are where one finds large minority and immigrant populations. Writing not long after the race riots of 1919 and focused on exactly the "mean streets" where these riots erupted, the early hard-boiled writers show their detectives to be the sole white men tough enough to confront the lawlessness of mobs of racial others. That the detectives mostly work alone is part of their appeal, and in the early days differentiated them from the white mobs that portrayed themselves as defenders of the American way, notably the Ku Klux Klan. In 1923, several years before *Black Mask* changed editors and began to focus exclusively on crime fiction, the magazine ran a special issue on the Klan and followed with a "Klan Forum" for several months, with readers writing in to debate the KKK. Sean McCann notes that Carroll John Daly's first story about Race Williams – the first hard-boiled detective, now mostly forgotten – appeared in that special issue, with Williams an opponent of the Klan.[15] McCann details the highly ambivalent opposition to KKK ideology in hard-boiled fiction, describing the "emotional core of Klan rhetoric" as an ideal of community and showing how the hard-boiled detectives, loners all, defined themselves against such an ideal.[16] However, the populist roots of both ideologies (the hard-boiled and the KKK) result in an overlapping understanding of whiteness as essential to Americanness, an understanding the traces of which remain legible even in those fictions by Daly and Hammett that, according to McCann, directly reject a "dream of common inheritance" and instead consistently offer "modes of action and affiliation that had nothing to do with inheritance."[17] For instance, McCann points to Hammett's *The Maltese Falcon* to illustrate his claim that, in the hard-boiled, criminality and corruption are not connected to culture or race; *Falcon*'s criminals "make this point most immediately since their crucial feature – that they are so cosmopolitan – works to underscore the fact that their association is based not on inheritance, but on shared criminal interests."[18] However cosmopolitan these criminals may be, what they have in common is being shut out of white masculinity: Brigid by gender and ethnicity, Joel Cairo by race and sexuality, and Caspar Gutman by ethnicity. In short, their very cosmopolitanism stands in opposition to Sam Spade's inheritance as a white man, with crime and criminality associated with the not-white, not-masculine. Later versions of the hard-boiled, particularly Mickey Spillane's brutal, crude fictions, often more directly centralize racial division, but the valorization of the detective's white masculinity is encoded in the genre from the beginning. Ross Macdonald, probably the most important and accomplished of the second generation of hard-boiled writers, set his novels away from the multiracial, class-stratified cities of the genre's origins, placing his detective, Lew Archer, in virtually all-white, fairly wealthy Santa Barbara. Absence of racial difference does not equate to absence of race, and indeed whiteness remains important in Macdonald's novels, perhaps all the more so for its silent, normative invisibility.

Given the historical context and the centrality of white masculinity to the genre, it would have been impossible to have a hard-boiled novel with a man of color or a woman of any race as the detective in the first- or second-generation novels. Rudolph Fisher's *The Conjure-Man Dies* (1932) is generally considered to be the first crime novel by a writer of color, although it is not the first to feature a detective of color. That distinction belongs to *The House Without a Key*, which introduces Charlie Chan, created by Earl Derr Biggers in 1925 specifically to counter widespread "yellow peril" racism. Significantly, both Charlie Chan and Fisher's detective Perry Dart are police officers (Fisher's other detective in *Conjure-Man* is a physician), although their books are not police procedurals, but instead hark back to very early versions of the mystery, such as Charles Dickens's *Bleak House* (1853). That is, these novels display little interest in the teamwork of police detection, the narrative focus of a subgenre that developed in post-World War II America; instead, the police detective in each operates substantially alone, like a private eye, or else in collaboration with amateurs. Taking into account the paucity of men of color on actual police forces prior to the 1964 Civil Rights Act and the crime novel's dependence on verisimilitude, it is unsurprising that the black police detectives we encounter in mid-twentieth-century crime fiction are assigned to majority-black areas.

When Chester Himes set out to write detective fiction, he at first was stymied, later telling an interviewer that "I had started out to write a detective story ... but I couldn't name the white man who was guilty because all white men were guilty."[19] A decade later, though, Himes returned to the detective story idea – suggested by an editor, who recommended that he read Hammett and others and then follow their lead – and began his Harlem detective series, featuring Coffin Ed Johnson and Grave Digger Jones. Reflecting on this speedily written series of eight novels, Himes said he had not done anything new, but instead had merely "made the faces black."[20] However, Himes's novels have little in common with their hard-boiled models beyond attention to an urban milieu, a focus on crime, and highly detailed descriptions of (often extreme) violence. Most obviously, Himes has two detectives, partners, not the loner figure of the hard-boiled, and those detectives work for the police. Coffin Ed and Grave Digger are both less isolated than their white predecessors (that is, they have each other) and more isolated, as they are seen as the enemy by the (white) rest of the police force because they are black, and by Harlemites because they are police officers. Perhaps because of this racially caused isolation, Himes's work had little influence on the police procedural, which was slowly developing while he was writing the Harlem detectives series, but it certainly influenced later creators of black private detectives, such as Walter Mosley and Gar Anthony Haywood.

The first major revision of the hard-boiled, and of American crime fiction in general, arrived in 1977, when Marcia Muller challenged the genre's insistence on masculinity as one of the detective's most important attributes with *Edwin of the Iron Shoes*. By the late 1980s, Muller's Sharon McCone was at the center of a feminist counter-tradition in American crime fiction. In what may seem a curious critical oversight, barely noticed at the time the McCone series began in earnest in the early 1980s or even later, as Muller achieved wide recognition as the creator of the first feminist private detective, was Sharon's doubled outsider status as a woman of color. Until the mid-1990s, when several women of color detectives created by authors of color finally appeared in print, Muller remained a lonely pioneer, with Sharon McCone the sole female private eye who was not white. The lack of critical attention to Sharon's race may be related to Muller's own downplaying of race in the novels. Throughout the series, Sharon's racial identity seems generally far less significant in her work as a detective than does her gender, a pattern that is common for *white* women (fictional) detectives but not for detectives of color created by authors of color. Further, until *Listen to the Silence* (2000), Sharon's Indian appearance makes no difference in her life except when others comment upon it or it is otherwise drawn to her attention, usually by racist whites. Before that novel, her Indianness is *wholly* a matter of appearance, as she has no tribal affiliation or social/cultural connection to Indians.

For nearly a quarter-century, Muller seems not to have known what to do with her detective's race beyond using it as one among many characteristics and experiences that individualize Sharon, such as her love of her cats or her pursuit of a pilot's license, or as a quick way to place other characters beyond the pale of progressive social attitudes. Muller's McCone novels, in short, offer sporadic critiques of the centrality of whiteness in crime fiction but do not challenge that centrality in either structure or theme. Similar critiques tend to appear as set pieces in various white feminist series, where overt white racism briefly disrupts a novel's action and provides an occasion for the detective to express outrage at racism, which is typically portrayed as personal prejudice. That uncertainty and awkwardness in relation to race are shared by many white crime writers in the post-Civil Rights era, as we find fewer instances of people of color automatically cast as villains, some detectives who are people of color, and occasional direct commentary about racism, but also the persistence of normative whiteness. That is, race remains invisible except when the race is not white and when the author intends to criticize racism.

Only with the emergence of black-authored hard-boiled detectives in the 1990s was the centrality of whiteness to the genre called into question, a challenge that then extended into examining the meanings of whiteness in other crime genres, as fiction by writers of color came into print in substantial numbers. Series by Walter Mosley, Gary Phillips and Gar Anthony Haywood, all featuring black private detectives, attempt to revise the codes of the hard-boiled by addressing race and simultaneously challenging (to some degree) the traditional linkages of masculinity, violence and (hetero)sexual power. All three modify the conventional solitariness of the detective by embedding the black detective in a community and, in two cases, in a family. However, they also incorporate similar versions of black masculinity that seem designed as correctives to dominant, racist stereotypes of black men as violent, dangerous, over-sexed predators unfit for civilized society, absent from their children, lazy, unwilling to work hard at anything. Mark Anthony Neal, in *New Black Man*, argues that the ideal of the "Strong Black Man" championed by generations of black leaders and of course rooted in a desire to counter dominant negative representations of black men has now become its own major problem for black men, insisting as it does on hypermasculinity.[21]

The Mosley and Phillips series in particular counter white supremacist stereotypes with black male detectives who are masculine in the "Strong Black Man" model, but also fairly close to constructions of white masculinity: reasonable, intelligent, hard-working, protectors of women and children, heterosexual, and so on. The familiarity of these conceptions of masculinity helps to explain both the popularity of the three series and the dead end that each has seemed to reach. Of the three, only Mosley's Easy Rawlins series continues regularly with new installments, most recently *Blonde Faith* (2007). Gary Phillips's Ivan Monk series has not had a new entry since 2000, when he published *Only the Wicked*; Phillips has, however, continued to publish non-Monk mysteries and a book of short stories featuring Monk (*Monkology*). Similarly, Gar Anthony Haywood's Aaron Gunner series has evidently stalled with *All the Lucky Ones Are Dead*, which came out in 1999, although Haywood has published other books under the pen name Ray Shannon.

These three series are distinguished not so much by how the detectives are characterized or by the crimes investigated as they are by the ideological framework of the questions they ask. Those questions are all rooted in the complexities of race, which is generally at the center of these series' plots. If the foundational but often covert premise of the traditional hard-boiled is that the core US value – whiteness – is under siege and requires defense, then, conversely, the premise of each of these three series is that blackness is *always* under siege by whiteness.

In these series, violence is depicted as specifically racial in a direct reversal of the traditional hard-boiled's use of violence: in the Phillips and Mosley novels, in particular, the detective's violence is generally a response to threats from whiteness. However, the detectives do not exactly prove their blackness via violence as their predecessors prove their own whiteness, but instead they perform a reactive version of blackness – of Strong Black Maleness – that they are depicted as being trapped into by whiteness and that of course they would prefer to resist. For instance, in an early scene in *Little Scarlet* – set in Los Angeles in 1965, in the wake of the Watts riots – Easy defends his white shoemaker friend from an angry black customer. Easy says to the threatening customer, "I been in the house for some time now, trying not to break out and start doin' wrong," and warns him that he is just about out of self-control. The man nearly begins to cry in frustration, and Easy thinks,

> I heard his cracked tone. I knew he was just as crazy as I was at that moment. We were both black men filled with a passionate rage that was too big to be held in. I didn't want to fight but I knew that once I started, the only thing that would stop me would be his lifeless throat crushed by my hand.[22]

Similarly, in a later scene, when accused by another black man of lying, Easy responds with an insult and reflects, "That was the only choice I had. Either we were going to fight or we weren't. If we went at it either he was going to win or I was. That was the way it was on the street corners in Watts in 1965 – riot or no riot."[23] They do indeed end up fighting, and Easy wins, knocking his opponent to the ground. "In my youth," Easy remarks, "that would have been the moment for me to say something insulting about Newell's manhood but I was past that kind of behavior."[24] In both of these examples, the actual or potential violence is between black men, but the clearly established context is a white-controlled world that pushes black men into misdirected violence against each other.

Phillips's *Only the Wicked* offers a similar pattern. At one point, Monk is racially harassed by several white men and answers them back, but then thinks he has left his good sense back at his motel.[25] No fight ensues, but the pattern is similar to that in *Little Scarlet*, as we see that the violence is initiated by whites, with black men left to decide how to respond. Neither Easy nor Monk ever succumbs to the temptation of the extreme violence typical of the (white) hard-boiled, nor is violence ever represented as a proof of manliness. The most violent character in Mosley's series is Mouse, who serves as a kind of repository of all basic urges (sex, violence, etc.) that Easy controls in himself; Mouse is not more masculine than Easy, just more dangerous and unpredictable. *Surviving* violence, however, is depicted in both novels as a mark of black manhood. Both Monk and Easy reflect on the scars they carry and the punishments their bodies have borne. Repeatedly, both Phillips's and Mosley's novels stress the social context of undiminished white power. In *Only the Wicked*, the crimes are ordered by a powerful white supremacist who never dirties his own hands but who pays others to aid in his determination to maintain the status quo. The hierarchical relation of white men and black men structures ideas of black masculinity in *Little Scarlet*. A white police detective's decent behavior toward him is Easy's "first piece of solid evidence I had that the white man's grip on my throat was losing strength."[26] Later, when that same detective lets Easy "do [his] business without interference or condescension," Easy thinks, "It was as if I'd died and gone to another man's heaven. This man whose soul I inhabited had been white, and his heaven was filled with ordinary things that were like magic to me."[27]

Critic Cynthia S. Hamilton argues that the traditional positioning of the detective as an "outsider witness whose very marginality reveals the compromised honor of those in power, socially, politically, and/or economically," makes crime fiction especially attractive to black writers, to whom it presents a "ready made opportunity to explore the dynamics of racism and double consciousness."[28] Hamilton's view suggests the genre is more flexible, more capable of accommodating even radical shifts in perspective, than close readings of these series support. Mosley and Phillips, and to a lesser degree Haywood, end up deconstructing hard-boiled ideology in their novels, not merely tinkering with it a bit. Making the faces black does indeed require a reconsideration of what constitutes masculinity and how one performs black masculinity. That performance seems still largely an improvisation in these novels, with the detectives working out through trial and error those "ordinary things" that are taken for granted in the white man's heaven of the hard-boiled.

Although a number of black women writers began publishing crime fiction at about the same time as the black male writers considered here, only one series features a black female private eye, Valerie Wilson Wesley's detective Tamara Hayle, who has appeared in eight novels, beginning in 1994 with

When Death Comes Stealing. The other dozen series by black women that began in the 1990s include three with police officer protagonists, eight with amateur detectives, and one team of a white police officer and a black news reporter.[29] These series – including those with police officer protagonists – take the distrust of the police and the critique of widespread social corruption typical of American hard-boiled fiction much further than do most other crime novels, suggesting a systemic opposition of law and justice. However, arguably their most important collective intervention in the form is the shift they perform in assumed audience, as all of these series address black women as their primary audiences, while also including direct commentary on race matters clearly aimed at a white, secondary audience. In placing a black female consciousness at the center of their texts, writers such as Barbara Neely (author of the Blanche White series, focused on a domestic worker/ amateur detective) and Paula Woods (author of the Charlotte Justice series, about a police officer) disrupt and thereby make visible the white (and usually male) bonding that presumably is one of the pleasures of traditional crime fiction for its majority audience. These writers' interpellation of the reader *as* a black woman is an even more radical revision of the genre than is making the detective black and female.

If the 1980s were the decade in which feminist writers with female prota- gonists remade crime fiction by breaking forever the genre's assumption that detection is "an unsuitable job for a woman," to borrow P. D. James's resonant title, then the 1990s may well have been the decade that undid the grip that whiteness had so long maintained on the genre. That decade saw the literary debuts – and, often, both critical and popular successes – of not only a considerable number of black American crime writers, but also the begin- nings of series by and about other racialized groups, including Japanese Americans (e.g., Dale Furutani's Ken Tanaka series) and Latinos, especially Chicanos. Ralph E. Rodriguez's study of Chicano/a crime fiction, *Brown Gumshoes*, shows that the detective novel provided a congenial medium for working out issues of identity and culture in the aftermath of the Chicano/a movement of the 1960s and 1970s.[30] The plots of Manuel Ramos's Luis Montez series, for example, frequently turn on internalized racism and on divisions among Chicanos rooted in the nationalist movement. At the same time – and in response to the same cultural/historical conditions, as well as in all likelihood to the success of writers of color – white writers began to create protagonists of color, perhaps most notably Barbara Hambly's Benjamin January, a free man of color in nineteenth-century New Orleans.

Beginning also in the 1990s, some white writers with white protagonists addressed race directly in crime fiction, with mixed results. The interracial buddy relationship common in action films such as the *Lethal Weapon* movies had its analogues in crime fiction well before this period, as for instance in Robert B. Parker's Spenser series. Parker's character Hawk generally operates as an almost superhuman (and therefore not quite human) violence machine, stepping in to assist Spenser in tough situations. Other such sidekicks tend to serve as evidence of the white protagonists' absence of racism in several series, resulting in a racial dynamic no more progressive than the old Lone Ranger/Tonto pairing. Several white writers in the 1990s tried something considerably different, however, including in their crime fiction people of color who are neither hyper-violent nor subservient sidekicks nor villains symbolizing threats to US whiteness. Among the most interesting and successful of these writers are Sara Paretsky and Dennis Lehane, who both consistently incorporate consideration of race issues in their fiction in relation not only to people of color – who also feature in important roles in both series – but also to their white protagonists. In contrast to the many white writers who include characters of color primarily to offer evidence of their detectives' freedom from racism, Lehane and Paretsky invent plots that turn on race and allow their protagonists to consider the many ways in which they are implicated in racism. In Lehane's *A Drink Before the War*, for instance, detective Patrick Kenzie reflects searchingly on the deep racial divisions in Boston and concludes that racism created and maintained those divisions, without exempting himself from the category of those who benefit from racism. Similarly, in Paretsky's *Total Recall*, detective V. I. Warshawski's investigation embroils her in the tension between blacks and Jews that has grown in the post-Civil Rights era, with V. I. frequently having cause to think about her own racial assumptions. Even these writers, however, both clearly interested in race issues and committed to racial understanding, shy away from serious attention to whiteness itself apart from people of color.

In sum, race remains central to crime fiction in the twenty-first century, although precisely how it operates in that fiction has changed significantly, especially in the past two decades. Whether crime fiction is able finally to break with its continuing thematization of whiteness as the core American value remains to be seen. That break, or the lack of it, could stand as a useful measure of whiteness's position in reality, not solely in fiction.

NOTES

1. Two examples are Kathleen Gregory Klein (ed.), *Diversity and Detective Fiction* (Bowling Green, OH: Bowling Green State University Popular Press, 1999), and Stephen F. Soitos, *The Blues Detective: A Study of African American Detective Fiction* (Amherst: University of Massachusetts Press, 1996).

2. Carole A. Stabile, "'The Most Disgusting Objects of Both Sexes': Gender and Race in the Episodic Crime News of the 1830s," *Journalism*, 6.4 (2005): 404.
3. *Ibid*.: 411.
4. *Ibid*.: 409.
5. *Ibid*.: 411.
6. For a more detailed version of this argument, see Maureen T. Reddy, *Traces, Codes, and Clues: Reading Race in Crime Fiction* (New Brunswick, NJ: Rutgers University Press, 2003), pp. 6–40.
7. Stephen Knight's essay, "The Golden Age," offers a concise and persuasive reading of the genre. In *The Cambridge Companion to Crime Fiction*, ed. Martin Priestman (Cambridge University Press, 2003), pp. 77–94.
8. Dennis Porter, "The Private Eye," in *The Cambridge Companion to Crime Fiction*, p. 96.
9. *Ibid*., p. 96.
10. C. Vann Woodward, *The Strange Career of Jim Crow*, 2nd edn. (New York: Oxford University Press, 1966), pp. 114–15.
11. *Ibid*., p. 115.
12. FindLaw website, www.findlaw.com/casecode/index (accessed July 30, 2008). All quotes from Supreme Court decisions come from this site.
13. See Reddy, *Traces, Codes, and Clues*, pp. 21–4.
14. Raymond Chandler, "Red Wind," *Trouble Is My Business* (New York: Random House, 1992), p. 213. Discussed in more detail in Reddy, *Traces, Codes, and Clues*, pp. 31–2.
15. Sean McCann, "Constructing Race Williams: The Klan and the Making of Hard-Boiled Crime Fiction," *American Quarterly*, 49.4 (1997): 678.
16. *Ibid*.: 682.
17. *Ibid*.: 711.
18. *Ibid*.: 700.
19. Quoted in Soitos, *The Blues Detective*, p. 137.
20. John A. Williams, "My Man Himes: An Interview with Chester Himes," in *Amistad I*, ed. John A. Williams and Charles F. Harris (New York: Random House, 1970), p. 49.
21. Mark Anthony Neal, *New Black Man* (New York: Routledge, 2005), pp. 25–8.
22. Walter Mosley, *Little Scarlet* (New York: Little, Brown, 2004), p. 7.
23. *Ibid*., p. 58.
24. *Ibid*., p. 59.
25. Gary Phillips, *Only the Wicked* (Walnut Creek, CA: Write Way Publishing, 2000), p. 230.
26. Mosley, *Little Scarlet*, p. 17.
27. *Ibid*., p. 274.
28. Cynthia S. Hamilton, "The Signifying Monkey and the Colloquial Detective: Reading African American Detective Fiction," *Forecast*, 15 (2005): 226–7.
29. For details on these series see Reddy, *Traces, Codes, and Clues*, p. 51.
30. Ralph E. Rodriguez, *Brown Gumshoes: Detective Fiction and the Search for Chicana/o Identity* (Austin, TX: University of Texas Press, 2005).

13

MARGARET KINSMAN

Feminist crime fiction

"For women to find a voice, a voice telling them that they may have adventures, that action is a woman's appropriate sphere, has been the difficult task of the last several centuries."[1]

This is the story of a feminist counter-tradition in the crime and mystery fiction genre, and the story of that counter-tradition's impact. The late 1970s and early 1980s saw American writers Marcia Muller, Sue Grafton and Sara Paretsky, independently of each other, each creating a female private eye/ investigator character; all three novelists subsequently developed commercially successful and popular series based on their mold-breaking female private eye creations. Positioned at the center of the narrative, in the familiar first-person voice of the hard-boiled tradition embodied by Chandler's Philip Marlowe, characters such as Sharon McCone, Kinsey Millhone, and V. I. Warshawski were allowed agency, intelligence and action. These were pioneering constructions of the modern female detective figure; as more women writers featuring strong central women characters came on board throughout the 1980s and 1990s, from both the USA and the UK, a range of feminist sensibilities came to bear on the genre, and it has never looked back. Now, at the end of the first decade of the twenty-first century, it is not only safe to say, but perhaps imperative to understand, that crime and mystery fiction really has not been the same since the birth of these three gumshoes, and many more like them. John Clarke describes these "deviant" ground-breaking detectives, as "one of the focal points around which new forms of generic differentiation are constructed ... Where the PI was quintessentially 'everyman' in his white, male heterosexuality, the development of the detective story genre during the 1970s and 1980s saw the 'eye' change ... [T]he detective has changed gender, 'race' and sexuality ... [T]hese 'deviant' detectives involve claims about alternative, ignored or suppressed 'realities.'"[2]

While obviously drawing inspiration from the hard-boiled blueprint as consolidated between 1920 and the 1940s by writers such as Dashiell Hammett and Raymond Chandler, the oeuvre of Paretsky and others has a breadth and a depth that goes beyond simple imitation of the male tradition. As Paretsky herself noted, in a 1994 interview about the process of creating V. I., "I didn't want Philip Marlowe in drag. What I really wanted was a woman who was like me and my friends ... The difference is that she didn't pull her punches. She didn't feel like she had to make nice."[3] This is not to claim, however, that the development from a Chandler version of hard-boiled to contemporary mainstream re-negotiations of hard-boiled was a seamless one; as Gill Plain notes in a recent theoretical discussion of gender and genre, the particular attempt to form the hard-boiled mode into a feminist narrative that still pays homage to tough-guy fiction is a project "riven with contradictions."[4]

The generic attachment to the romantic man of genius, positioned in lonely splendor on the Great Detective Pedestal, has, however, clearly been open to dismantling, to configurations of other kinds of knowing and being and figuring it out. A brief comparison of two sets of extracts from the prominent authors Chandler and Paretsky is instructive in illustrating key features of the hard-boiled mode as it was expressed by Chandler and as it is being revisited by many women writers. The first set is from concluding sections in two novels.

At the close of Chandler's *The High Window* (1943), private eye Philip Marlowe is pictured in classic loner, laconic mode:

> It was night. I went home and put my old house clothes on and set the chessmen out and mixed a drink and played over another Capablanca. It went fifty-nine moves. Beautiful, cold, remorseless chess, almost creepy in its silent implacability.
>
> When it was done I listened at the open window for a while and smelled the night. Then I carried my glass out to the kitchen and rinsed it and filled it with ice water and stood at the sink sipping it and looking at my face in the mirror.
>
> "You and Capablanca," I said. [5]

Paretsky's recent novel, *Fire Sale* (2005), closes with her detective, V. I., positioned rather differently:

> I had dinner with Lotty the day after the Lady Tigers' season ended, and told her how discouraged I felt. She frowned in disapproval, or disagreement.
>
> "Victoria, you know my grandfather, my father's father, was a very obser-vant Jew ...
>
> "Me, I don't believe in God, let alone the coming of the Messiah. But I did learn from my zeyde that you must live in hope, the hope that your work can make a difference in the world. Yours does, Victoria ... If a Messiah ever does come, it will only be because of people like you, doing these small, hard jobs, making small changes in this hard world."
>
> It was a small comfort, and that night at dinner it felt like a cold one. But as the Chicago winter lingered, I found myself warmed by her grandfather's hope.[6]

The Chandler extract contains a number of motifs and characteristics indelibly identified with the hard-boiled form: the first-person narrative voice; the night-time temporality; the solitude of the protagonist, drinking and playing chess alone; the "[b]eautiful, cold, remorseless" antagonist (whether the Capablanca chessboard, the city, or corruption), with "its silent implacability"; and the implication of putting past experience behind and living to fight another day in the imagery of listening at the open window and smelling the night. The Paretsky extract also identifies with the hard-boiled mode, most obviously in her use of the first-person narrative voice (now gendered as female) and the night-time urban setting. But there are some salient differences to take account of. Chicago's wintry landscape may be "lingering" but it is not menacing, and the text moves both V. I. and the winter towards warmth; a contrast to Marlowe's distant eavesdropping activities, before he turns away from his window, to his own reflection in the mirror. V. I.'s physical solitude is mediated by Lotty's companionship and their reflective conversation is anchored in the normal domesticity of dinner time. Marlowe's companions are a drink and a chessboard. V. I.'s existential solitude is "warmed" by Lotty's refusal to let her friend wallow in feelings of despair and discouragement, while Marlowe talks to himself, conjuring up the ghost of Jose Capablanca, the Cuban chess prodigy – another man of genius. Both texts signal that the detectives' crusades will continue, in spite of existential angst; but the characters of Marlowe and V. I. are informed and motivated by different subjectivities, perspectives and codes of ethics. Paretsky's concluding section suggests that V. I. is engaged in a collective enterprise, in contrast to Marlowe's solitary pursuits. Her text signals links, across differences of age, gender and ethnicity, between the living and the dead; the past and the present; the hard-boiled form as it was, and as it is now.

The second set of extracts shows the detectives positioned in relation to their offices and their clients. Again, salient contrasts present themselves. Marlowe, in *The High Window*, meets a prospective client:

> I had an office in the Cahuenga Building, sixth floor, two small rooms at the back . . .
>
> Three hard chairs and a swivel chair, flat desk with a glass top, five green filing-cases, three of them full of nothing, a calendar and a framed licence bond on the wall, a phone, a washbowl in a stained wood cupboard, a hat-rack, a carpet that was just something on the floor . . .
>
> I hung my hat and coat on the hat-rack, washed my face and hands in cold water, lit a cigarette and hoisted the phone book on to the desk . . . Somebody had just opened the door of the outer office . . .
>
> He looked me over without haste and without much pleasure . . .
>
> "You're Marlowe?"
>
> I nodded.
>
> "I'm a little disappointed," he said. "I rather expected something with dirty fingernails."

"Come inside," I said, "and you can be witty sitting down." . . .

"A private detective," he said. "I never met one. A shifty business, one gathers. Keyhole peeping, raking up scandal, that sort of thing."

"You here on business," I asked him, "or just slumming?"

"Marlowe," he said . . . "I'll try hard, but I don't think I am going to like you."

"I'm screaming," I said. "With rage and pain."

"And if you will pardon a homely phrase, your tough guy act stinks."[7]

Paretsky's first novel, *Indemnity Only*, introduces V. I. thus:

The night air was thick and damp . . .

I got off Lake Shore Drive at Randolph Street and swung down Wabash under the iron arches of the elevated tracks. At Monroe I stopped the car and got out.

Away from the lake the city was quieter. The South Loop, with no entertainment beyond a few peepshows and the city lockup, was deserted – a drunk weaving uncertainly down the street was my only companion. I crossed Wabash and went into the Pulteney Building next to the Monroe Street Tobacco Store. At night it looked like a terrible place to have an office . . .

I shoved open the heavy stairwell door, climbing slowly to the fourth floor . . . In the dim light I could read the inscription on the door: "V. I. Warshawski. Private Investigator."

. . .

With the lights on my office looked spartan but not unpleasant . . . I'd bought the big wooden desk at a police auction. The little Olivetti portable had been my mother's, as well as a reproduction of the Uffizi hanging over my green filing cabinet. That was supposed to make visitors realize that mine was a high-class operation. Two straight-backed chairs for clients completed the furniture . . .

I could hear a heavy tread . . . and guessed it was my anonymous visitor . . .

"Yes, Mr. Thayer. Now what seems to be the problem?"

"You know, I don't mean any offense, but I'm not sure I should talk to you after all. Not unless you've got a partner or something . . . this really isn't a job for a girl to take on alone."

"I'm a woman, Mr. Thayer, and I can look out for myself. If I couldn't, I wouldn't be in this kind of business. If things get heavy, I'll figure out a way to handle them – or go down trying. That's my problem, not yours . . ."[8]

Again, the extracts are linked by the first-person narrative voice, the urban location, the detective figure on the move, in a car or on foot, doing their job. Both detectives have an acerbic tone in conversation. While Marlowe's office is austere and impersonal, V. I.'s space is evoked through a link to her mother. Marlowe the male detective and V. I. the female detective are both marked by what John Cawelti explains as "[t]he marginal social position, the ambiguous relationship to the social elite, and the mood of failure and frustration that characterize the hard-boiled detective."⁹ Marlowe is marginalized by his profession, whereas V. I. is marginalized by her gender, to which her client repeatedly calls attention. V. I. and Marlowe both occupy resistant speaking positions, thus inviting a resisting readerly position in relation to the clients who try to patronize them; significantly, in V. I.'s case, her resisting subjectivity takes the reader further. This female detective is isolated and distanced, not from other people or society as Marlowe is, but from what society dictates is a woman's place. The female detective is not disinterested and aloof (again, characteristics of Marlowe), or without ideology; rather she functions to detect ideology; to name it / expose it / call it to account as she does with Mr. Thayer's assumptions.

V. I. is "out of place" in her narrative in other respects. Not only is a woman a challenge to Mr. Thayer's idea of who should be a private detective, V. I.'s presence in Chicago interferes with the patriarchal notion that the night-time city streets pose danger for women, and that there are places where women may not / should not go. Paretsky's opening paragraphs serve to normalize V. I.'s presence by evoking the dark landscape through which the detective drives in terms of the lake and the parks where "people [are] seeking relief from the sultry air." In the more isolated Loop area, where V. I. parks in order to visit her office, the "drunk weaving uncertainly" is there not to unnerve V. I., but as an unthreatening "only companion" in the deserted area. The certainty with which V. I. claims and occupies her subjectivity and her spaces in this first novel has reverberated throughout the Paretsky oeuvre, as well as providing a blueprint for many other women writers who have put the woman detective in the driver's seat.

Several questions then present themselves: How (and why?) did this shift evolve from the hard-boiled man to the hard-boiled woman? What else, in generic terms, has shifted as a result of the intervention? What was feminist about the intervention? At its most critical and subversive, what has the appropriation achieved or contributed? Where is this "counter-tradition" positioned now, in the early twenty-first century? These questions and debates are still being answered, of course, but we can begin to trace a history and a set of responses by returning to the 1970s.

The female private eye

Genre historians generally agree that Marcia Muller created the first American female private eye, when she introduced All Souls Legal Coop investigator Sharon McCone (whose ethnicity includes Shoshone forebears), in *Edwin of the Iron Shoes* (1977). This series is still running, over thirty years later. The year 1977 also saw the appearance of M. F. Beal's *Angel Dance* featuring

the bi-sexual private detective Kat Guerrera. These singular novels and characters were ground-breaking constructions, though not understood as such
until a critical mass of similarly inspired characters began to appear throughout the 1980s. The year 1982 saw the debut of Sara Paretsky's now-legendary
private eye V. I. Warshawski in the novel *Indemnity Only*. In the same year,
Sue Grafton published *A is for Alibi*, featuring the equally legendary private
detective Kinsey Millhone; and in 1981, in the UK, Liza Cody published *Dupe*
with security agency investigator Anna Lee. Paretsky and Grafton were the
first contemporary American writers to introduce independent, self-employed
female private eyes. (Muller's Sharon McCone operates as a member of a legal
cooperative.) These writers launched a new direction in the subgeneric mode
of the hard-boiled, which has subsequently come to be described by John
Scaggs as an example of successful appropriation and reformulation; and as
transformative, according to Scott Christianson, providing "a place from
which a woman can exercise language as power."[10] In an early critical
essay, Maureen Reddy identifies the emerging "feminist counter-tradition in
crime"; the 1980s, she claims, is the decade in which "Feminist literary
criticism, feminism as a social movement, and feminist crime novels have
grown up together."[11]

Signals of the counter-tradition were emerging as early, some would argue,
as 1930, with the Nancy Drew girl-detective series. The teenage Nancy,
independent and capable, proved an enduring and popular literary creation;
generations of young readers loved her and then grew up. There were very few
grown-up Nancy-type sleuths, however, for adult readers who might have
welcomed more female characters like her in the American world of crime and
mystery fiction. (In contrast, British golden age writers Margery Allingham
and Dorothy Sayers, among others, were writing some very "modern" female
characters such as Amanda Fitton and Harriet Vane.) In 1964, Amanda Cross
[Carolyn Heilbrun] created Kate Fansler, an outspoken English professor and
amateur detective who appeared in an increasingly feminist-inflected series
throughout the 1970s, 1980s and 1990s. While Fansler's debut did not go
unnoticed (the first novel, *In the Last Analysis*, won the MWA Edgar Award),
it was not until the third Kate Fansler novel that Cross's novels began
to embrace explicitly feminist themes and feminist sensibilities, with
Fansler's increasingly sophisticated understanding of gender politics in the
academy and the devastating effects on female professors and students.
Although Cross is far from being a hard-boiled writer, it is the case, as
Reddy observes, that "Cross's interventions in the genre laid the groundwork
for the female detectives who have forever changed the world of mystery
fiction."[12] Certainly, Heilbrun/Cross's series is an important marker in the
project of re-imagining the narrative roles open to women in this historically

masculinist genre with its canonical tradition of confining women to the roles of victim, vamp, villain or sidekick. Great Britain provided another early marker for the appropriations to come, in the shape of P. D. James's 1972 *An Unsuitable Job for a Woman*. Although the novel owes more to the British golden age tradition than to the American hard-boiled, it is important to note that Cordelia Grey, the protagonist, is a private detective. As the central figure, she is an early demonstration that the role of private investigator is indeed a suitable job for a woman; again, she resists the stereotypes of the passive woman, dependent on male protection; or of the sexually predatory woman, threatening to masculine identity.

Gathering ever more critical mass throughout the 1980s, novels featuring strong women characters (which by now included private eyes, police detectives and amateur detective figures who were also inflected by different ethnicities, sexualities and class origins) had become a publishing phenomenon, helped in no small part by the independent women's presses of the 1980s (Virago, The Women's Press, Naiad, Pandora Crime Writers, among others). American writers such as Linda Barnes, Katherine V. Forrest, Barbara Wilson, Karen Kijewski, Janet Dawson, Mary Wings, Julie Smith, Sarah Dreher, and Valerie Miner were all publishing detective series with women characters who were, in varying degrees, expressive of feminist sensibilities. Detectives such as Barnes's Carlotta Carlyle, Forrest's lesbian police detective Kate Delafield, and Smith's Skip Langdon, were portrayed as living unconventional lives, choosing destinies other than marriage as their goal in life; choosing not to conform to what was expected or required of them in their role as "woman"; choosing action and adventure over passivity and dependence; and being willing to take risks. Writers used their novels as spaces in which to explore the dilemmas germane to real women's lives, such as the conflicts that arise from gendered codes of value about work, home, kinship networks, success. Issues such as homelessness and poverty, homophobia, sexism and racism, domestic abuse, incest, pornography were taken up by many writers, bringing to the center what has often been marginalized or treated in stereotypical ways.

The story of the counter-tradition includes important contributions from outside the USA. In the UK during the 1980s, Liza Cody continued the Anna Lee series, and introduced the harder-edged Eva Wylie (aka, in the wrestling world, the London Lassassin), triply marginalized by gender, class and poverty. Joan Smith started the university academic Loretta Lawson series and Gillian Slovo produced the private eye Kate Baier series. Val McDermid wrote two successful series characters, the lesbian journalist Lindsey Gordon and Manchester-based investigator Kate Brannigan. The 1990s saw UK writers such as Michelle Spring, Manda Scott, Nicola Williams, Denise Mina and

Stella Duffy come on board with a variety of female detectives; a burgeoning Australian crime and mystery scene was developing, with writers such as Marele Day and her detective Claudia Valentine. Throughout the 1990s in the USA, Laura Lippmann, Nikki Baker, Carol Smith, Carol O'Connell, Edna Buchanan, Dana Stabenow, Valerie Wilson Wesley, Barbara Neely, Laurie King, Margaret Maron, Caroline Garcia-Aquilera and many others were also creating more women detectives with varying sexual, ethnic and class identities. What these series have in common is a capable, independent, and effective female detective figure (many of them private eyes and others given professions in journalism, education, the law, domestic labor) at the center of the narrative, good sales figures, literary prestige and recognition, and a wide readership which includes male readers. In the same manner as their predecessor, Nancy Drew, these characters are portrayed as people who can have adventures, take care of themselves and who are not easily intimidated or deterred. As modern adult women, they exercise varying degrees of professional, economic, social and sexual autonomy. With very few parents, spouses or children in the picture, the literary creations are answerable first to themselves (perhaps the ultimate feminist act), and then to their clients and to their communities of neighbors, friends and relations. The placement of these fictional female detectives within solid and dynamic communities of other women friends, relatives and associates (who are older, younger, businesswomen, students, working, parenting) is one of the most significant markers of the counter-tradition. First, the community involvement provides an abiding contrast to the loner figure of the earlier male detective; and second, it is testament to the importance of female solidarities in the history of feminist action, analysis and vision. The earlier mode of hard-boiled excluded such networks, as it excluded challenges to the endemic racism and sexism of mid-twentieth-century culture and society. The new generation of women writers, particularly those who self-identify with second-wave feminism, are including what was absent from the genre.

In 1981, Dennis Porter's discussion of art and ideology in detective fiction pointed out that

> no other genre is more conscious of the models from which it borrows and from which it knowingly departs. From Wilkie Collins and Conan Doyle down to Raymond Chandler, Georges Simenon, and Ian Fleming, the most interesting detective fiction is read in large measure for its differences, for its capacity to remain faithful to a tradition at the same time that it reinvents it in unexpected ways.[13]

Porter rightly draws attention to the historic flexibility of the genre and its capacity to re-invent itself. Had Porter's book appeared a decade later, the list of touchstone authors would necessarily have included the names of Muller, Paretsky, Grafton and others, all of whose woman-centered novels were, individually and collectively, to have such an impact on readers, publishers, scholars, and other writers throughout the 1980s and continuing to the present. Not all of these writers of the 1980s and the 1990s, or their main characters, were consciously or avowedly feminist, but many were clearly influenced by the Women's Liberation Movement of the 1960s, the emerging feminisms (inflected by race and class) of the 1970s, and the very real changes in women's lives and expectations that resulted from, among other factors, federal legislation in the 1960s and 1970s. Early concerns of the women's movement (e.g. equal opportunities in the workplace) surface in, for example, Amanda Cross's first few novels, with university professor Kate Fansler insisting on the importance of meaningful work to both men and women. The initial critical excitement about the advent of the female private-eye figure in particular, which rather assumed that because the detective was a woman the character, novel and novelist could be claimed as feminist, has given way to more complex and contested discussions about the range and diversity of new formulations and interventions which dominated the genre throughout the 1980s and 1990s. Recent debate about fiction of the mean streets has centered, according to Lee Horsley, "on the question of whether the hard-boiled sub-genre possesses genuinely radical potential."[14]

Hard-boiled style

Leaving aside the question of "genuinely radical" for the moment, what was it about the hard-boiled style in particular that proved so receptive to feminist appropriation? First of all, the notion of appropriation takes us beyond the simple updating or imitating of a tradition, to include gestures which can be understood to be questioning the politics and ideology of, in this case, gender and subgenre. Appropriation suggests more than a surface change (the feminist private eye is more than a surrogate man), and implies that the intervention functions to expand both the canon and scholarly commonplaces about the private-eye, hard-boiled convention. What are those conventions?

The hard-boiled style is made up in equal measures of the romantic hard-boiled detective figure and what could be described as a melodramatic form, which treats serious themes. In a recent discussion of genre, John Scaggs offers this definition of hard-boiled:

> A type of fiction whose style is derived from the tough-guy prose associated with Ernest Hemingway, and which was developed in the pulp fiction of the 1920s and 1930s in America. The hard-boiled style is terse, tough, and cynical, like the

hard-boiled detectives it features, and the typical hard-boiled story is one of violence, sex, and betrayal.[15]

The hard-boiled school is urban in location, masculine in point of view, fast-paced and frequently violent in word and action. Iconographic features of the hard-boiled form include the cynical tough-talking central detective figure, a terse prose style, a bottle in the bottom drawer, and a city landscape which reeks of menace and corruption from top to bottom, thereby inviting the social criticism which also marks the form. From the beginning, the form was used to expose the materialistic nature of twentieth-century society, with its focus on wealth and power. Physical and verbal violence, in the hard-boiled tradition, is often an expression of the detective figure's hostility to the evil he perceives in his commodified, self-absorbed culture.

The hard-boiled tradition, historically, has been reliant on its attachment to the solitary (and sentimental) "man of honor" private-eye figure described by Chandler in his 1944 essay "The Simple Art of Murder," and demonstrated by Chandler in Philip Marlowe, who was partly inspired by Dashiell Hammett's earlier Continental Op detective. This type of fiction also demonstrates a powerful attachment to the femme fatale figure, one of the stereotypical roles to which female characters were confined. The fiction of this period is marked by predictable assumptions about, for instance, men as active agents and women as passive victims, or betraying vamps, or sacrificing helpmeets. The politics of race and class were increasingly fiercely contested in the 1930s; hierarchies of gender were also open to challenge, but hard-boiled fiction seemed to function as a vehicle for advancing stereotypical views in the face of potential interrogation, as Cawelti's discussion of formula fiction suggests: "the intense masculinity of the hard-boiled detective is in part a symbolic denial and protective coloration against complex sexual and status anxieties focusing on women."[16] This implies that the masculinist nature of the hard-boiled makes it inhospitable to unconventional female characters who are challenging the status quo.

However, it would appear from the record that the first-person narrative voice, the professional role of the private eye, and the city landscape are generic features which have lent themselves with remarkable success to more than one generation of women writers interested in telling stories about "women like us," providing the authors and their protagonists with a narrative and psychic space which they have claimed with enthusiasm and creativity. Linda Barnes's detective Carlotta Carlyle, for example, roams her Boston streets with the confidence and knowledge gained in her part-time job as a cabbie; she lives alone, but is located within the affiliations of an assembled "family," consisting of an on-again, off-again lover, a "little sister" she mentors, an eccentric lodger, and a deceased grandmother who converses with Carlotta from beyond the grave. While critics and theorists vary in their assessments of how successful these interventions are in variously feminist, literary, and genre terms, it cannot be disputed that independent female detective figures are inscribed into crime and mystery fiction in no uncertain terms. It is generally agreed, by genre historians and critics alike, that, in particular, the modern female private eye has proved to be, not only "solidly entrenched in the genre"[17] as one publisher noted, but transformative of the genre. The new generation of female writers and their smart, capable, skillful, witty and resilient detectives seem to have opened up the form, particularly the hard-boiled tradition, by their acknowledgment (both implicit and explicit) of the ideological codes which inform and control the form. For example, writers such as Sarah Dunant, Val McDermid, Sue Grafton and Linda Barnes have discussed, in non-fiction and in interviews, how they have negotiated different kinds of fictional engagement with the question of physical violence, which comes with the territory of hard-boiled, but has a different inflection when the private eye is a woman. As a result, the hard-boiled tradition has been invigorated and renovated by writers who have been influenced by recent decades of feminist activity.

Feminism(s)

Throughout the 1970s, the feminist agenda was gathering pace. Second-wave feminism emerged out of the Women's Liberation Movement of the 1960s and books such as Betty Friedan's *The Feminine Mystique* (1963), which chronicled the frustration many women experienced when they felt forced to return to and stay at home after the war. Other seminal publications included Mary McCarthy's 1963 novel *The Group*, and Marilyn French's *The Women's Room*, novels which were interested in women's friendships and in the progress being made in the contemporary female sphere. Legislative progress was made in terms of equal pay and sex discrimination issues; feminist theater was flourishing; feminist publishers were active; gender politics began to enter the picture. By the 1990s, popular culture had entered the higher education curriculum, alongside Gender Studies and Women's Studies programs which formed in the 1980s. Previously marginalized subjects and histories were being taken seriously as appropriate for study and analysis. Partly in response to the emerging academic forum, feminist analysis began to be about more than equal opportunities and women's rights. Feminist action moved on from creating spaces in a male world for women, to working to create a world that more fully reflected the traditional priorities given by women to caring roles, to relationships, to emotional needs and expression.

For many women, second-wave feminism provided a new way of seeing and understanding the world, overturning all the old certainties. Out of often fiercely contested conflicts between different strands (e.g. socialist feminist versus radical feminist) there gradually emerged more nuanced forms of feminism, which recognized that women are differently placed (in terms of sexuality, or motherhood, or racial identity, or class identity), and that women may choose different, but equally feminist, paths. The crucial understanding that the category of "woman" is not a fixed or unified position led to more thoughtful expressions of feminist analysis and action. This created the possibility for feminist hard-boiled fiction to act not as a flag-waver for feminist identity, but as a vehicle for feminist debate. Carmen Callil, founding member of the important feminist press Virago, discusses women writers of popular fiction as "subversive sybils [who] used their power and influence to change the way women view themselves, and live their lives in the late twentieth century."[18] Callil's claim that "popular women's fiction has always been a way of encouraging women to behave badly"[19] is made primarily in reference to the genres of romance and chick lit, though it could equally be applied to the feminist private-eye novel. Younger generations of readers picking up a Muller or a Paretsky today are introduced to feminism through the experiences and views of female characters whose own values and beliefs were formed by the promises of the women's and the civil rights movements of the 1960s. As these detectives age in "real" time (though Grafton has frozen Kinsey Millhone in a pre-internet/Blackberry era), they find their youthful idealism, activism and risk-taking has not resulted in all the changes they desired then, or now. V. I. in particular comes to an accommodation with the realities of her position as a woman whose actions and beliefs will not change the world, but who continues to try to make a difference with what Walton and Jones describe as a "*working* feminism that seems to reconcile feminist theory and everyday practice" (emphasis in original). The figure of V. I. (and other similar literary constructions) thus "dramatizes ... the hope that ... there might be a space for feminist agency,"[20] even as these characters register for us that the battle is not won and that many of the freedoms and equalities gained for and by women since the 1960s are still quite fragile.

Critical / theoretical perspectives

Feminist criticism / theoretical perspective on the genre was relatively slow to establish itself as a debate, with arguments over the conservative ideology of the genre dominating in the 1980s. As Merja Makinen points out, in her thorough overview of popular fiction and the critical debate, it is "the canon created from within that genre [which] is conservative because, like most academic canons until the 1970s, it privileges conservative and phallologo-centric values in its choice of favoured texts."[21] Reddy's early discussions are alert to the transformative potential of these new directions in the genre, understanding that the project was about more than simply looking for strong women characters, and that there was more to a definition of "feminist" than a central female protagonist. Key discussions from the 1990s include Sally Munt's *Murder by the Book?* (1994) which offers an overview of the 1980s and identifies several key feminist positions/strands/ideologies in use (e.g. liberal, socialist, psychoanalytic, postmodern, identity politics of race, class and sexuality) which Munt applies to different writers' attempts to produce feminist crime fiction, and Walton and Jones's *Detective Agency: Women Rewriting the Hard-Boiled Tradition*, which offers a sophisticated analysis of the mainstream, contemporary hard-boiled tradition at the end of the twentieth century. Both Munt and Walton and Jones argue for the potential subversive capabilities of contemporary interventions, seeing both genre and canon as fluid and open to change, as do discussions by Stephen Knight, Rosalind Coward and Linda Semple, John Scaggs, Susan Rowland and others. Clearly then, feminism(s) and the crime and mystery genre prove to be places where meanings are, to paraphrase Emily Dickinson, and where meaning can be contested.

V. I., Kinsey and Sharon have, from the beginning of all three series, been characters willing, indeed eager, to address cases of social injustice, particularly those persistent ones resulting from gender imbalance. Today's forms of feminism still address persistent social imbalances, but the "space for feminist agency" that the feminist hard-boiled style currently dramatizes is now also concerned with a more open expression of female frustration and doubt, sexuality and desire, and with subjects not often addressed in mainstream popular culture, such as abortion, the pain of desertion, and physical and emotional abuse. Such concerns continue to surface in the counter-tradition, as feminist fictions now grapple with the bitter truth that women's freedom to choose is only as liberating as the choices on offer.

In the recent *Total Recall*, Paretsky alternates the first-person voice of V. I. with her beloved older friend Lotty's voice, allowing Lotty to tell the harrowing story of her abandonment as a young child caught up in the maelstrom of the Holocaust. The insertion of Lotty's voice, and the stories of her own illegitimate origins and the baby she gave away as a young un-wed mother, into the traditional first-person narrative hard-boiled form, are significant illustrations of *shared* female agency and the limiting options that often circumscribe women's lives. Lotty's narrative opens and closes the novel, simultaneously pre-empting the "singular" importance of the private-eye figure, while also consolidating the larger significance of her bond with V. I., a reminder that there is another way of investigating and understanding things, both inside and outside the hard-boiled tradition.

Conclusion

The contemporary female detective figure, whether hard-boiled, soft-boiled, police force member or amateur investigator, demonstrates that the genre can continue to flourish with women as active, intelligent agents of their own (and others') destiny. The early pioneering writers of the feminist private-eye mode were successful in attracting and keeping a wide readership; their novels, some initially circulated by small feminist presses, sell well from within mainstream publishing houses. These women authors, and many who followed, have garnered a wide range of literary awards, both from within the genre (Mystery Writers of America, the UK Crime Writers Association, the Canadian Arthur Ellis Award), and from wider scholarly associations and organizations. They have also made an impact on male writers working within the crime and mystery genre. Largely because of the feminist writers discussed here, many contemporary writers (such as Ian Rankin, Robert Crais, Lee Child) have opened up the emotional and domestic lives of their tough cops and private eyes; and their novels now include interesting women characters who range well beyond the old stereotypes. Virginia Woolf argued persuasively in her essay "Modern Fiction" that fiction "bid[s] us break her and bully her, as well as honour and love her, for so her youth is renewed and her sovereignty assured."[22] The feminist counter-tradition in the hard-boiled style has broken and bullied, honored and loved, in the service of renewing and assuring the form.

NOTES

1. Sara Paretsky, "Sexy, Moral, and Packing a Pistol," *Independent*, June 18, 1997, p. 22.
2. John Clarke, "The Pleasures of Crime: Interrogating the Detective Story," in *The Problem of Crime*, ed. John Muncie and Eugene McLaughlin, 2nd edn. (London: Sage Publications, 2001), pp. 86, 90.
3. Felicia Gresette, "Mystery Women," *Miami Herald*, April 24, 1994, pp. 1J, 41.
4. Gill Plain, *Twentieth-Century Crime Fiction: Gender, Sexuality and the Body* (Edinburgh University Press, 2001), p. 142.
5. Raymond Chandler, *The High Window* (1943; repr. Harmondsworth: Penguin, 1973), p. 221.
6. Sara Paretsky, *Fire Sale* (London: Hodder & Stoughton, 2005), pp. 401–2.

7. Chandler, *The High Window*, pp. 22–4.

8. Sara Paretsky, *Indemnity Only* (1982; repr. London: Penguin, 1987), pp. 5–9.

9. John G. Cawelti, *Adventure, Mystery, and Romance: Formula Stories as Art and Popular Culture* (University of Chicago Press, 1976), p. 160.

10. Scott Christianson, "Talkin' Trash and Kickin' Butt: Sue Grafton's Hard-boiled Feminism," in *Feminism in Women's Detective Fiction*, ed. Glennwood Irons (University of Toronto Press, 1995), pp. 128–9.

11. Maureen Reddy, "The Feminist Counter-Tradition in Crime: Cross, Grafton, Paretsky and Wilson," in *The Cunning Craft: Original Essays on Detective Fiction and Contemporary Literary Theory*, ed. Ronald G. Walker and June M. Frazer (Macomb, IL: Western Illinois University Press, 1990), p. 174.

12. Maureen Reddy, "The Female Detective from Nancy Drew to Sue Grafton," in *Mystery and Suspense Writers: The Literature of Crime, Detection, and Espionage*, vol. II, ed. Robin W. Winks (New York: Charles Scribner's Sons, 1998), p. 1051.

13. Dennis Porter, *The Pursuit of Crime: Art and Ideology in Detective Fiction* (New Haven, CT: Yale University Press, 1981), pp. 54–5.

14. Lee Horsley, *Twentieth-Century Crime Fiction* (Oxford University Press, 2005), p. 9.

15. John Scaggs, *Crime Fiction* (Abingdon: Routledge, 2005), p. 145.

16. Cawelti, *Adventure, Mystery, and Romance*, p. 154.

17. Priscilla L. Walton and Manina Jones, *Detective Agency: Women Rewriting the Hard-Boiled Tradition* (Berkeley, CA: University of California Press, 1999), p. 39.

18. Carmen Callil, *Subversive Sybils: Women's Popular Fiction this Century* (Bury St Edmonds: St Edmundsbury Press Ltd., 1996), p. 15.

19. *Ibid.*, p. 6.

20. Walton and Jones, *Detective Agency*, p. 37.

21. Merja Makinen, *Feminist Popular Fiction* (Basingstoke: Palgrave, 2001), p. 1.

22. Virginia Woolf, "Modern Fiction," in *The Crowded Dance of Modern Life: Selected Essays*, vol. II ed. Rachel Bowlby (London: Penguin, 1993), p. 12.

14

SUSAN ELIZABETH SWEENEY

Crime in postmodernist fiction

"The cheaper the crook, the gaudier the patter, eh?" Sam Spade remarks in *The Maltese Falcon*.[1] "Gaudy" describes something excessively garish or showy, and "gaudier," of course, even more so; although "patter" connotes the smooth, practiced speech used by hucksters to attract customers or by magicians to distract audiences, its primary meaning, according to the *Oxford English Dictionary*, is "thieves' lingo." This word choice suggests that Spade – a modernist private eye attuned to social façades – thinks of being a crook as a performance, even a crudely exaggerated one.

For postmodernist novelists, too, crime is largely a matter of appearances. Indeed, the generic elements linked to solving the mystery in a detective story – observing ambiguous signs and constructing a possible narrative from them – characterize postmodernist fiction in general.[2] Some novels emphasize these hermeneutic and epistemological aspects so markedly that they have been labeled "anti-detective fiction," "postmodern mysteries," "deconstructive mysteries," or "metaphysical detective stories."[3] Investigation is so overdetermined, one might say, that in some instances – like William Hjortsberg's novel *Falling Angel* or Christopher Nolan's film *Memento* – the private eye himself turns out to be the criminal he pursues.[4] Accordingly, numerous critics have analyzed the literary, hermeneutic, semiotic and philosophical significance of detection in these works. Crime seems less important, and has received less critical attention. I want to suggest, however, that many postmodernist novels represent crime – the mystery to be solved – as a kind of gaudy patter: a secret, profane, artificial, imitative, uncanny or incoherent discourse.

Of course, crime was linked to such speech from the detective genre's inception, thanks to those overheard but utterly incomprehensible words accompanying the slayings in the very first detective story, Poe's "The Murders in the Rue Morgue."[5] Witnesses cannot identify the language in which the words were spoken, or rather mistake it for other languages they do not know. Reading their conflicting accounts, Poe's sleuth deduces that the utterances were in no human tongue; therefore, the criminal is not human, but animal. In this instance, as in so much else, Poe anticipated later developments. Many postmodernist novels feature similarly excessive, incomprehensible speech. Its source may be animal, too, as shown by the perplexing numbers that a parrot recites in Michael Chabon's *The Final Solution*; or mechanical, as in the sirens and loudspeakers in Don DeLillo's *White Noise*; or extraterrestrial, such as the radio emissions recorded by characters in DeLillo's *Ratner's Star* and Thomas Pynchon's *Gravity's Rainbow*.[6] It may be human speech disrupted by drugs (in Jack O'Connell's *Box Nine*), cognitive disorder (in Jonathan Lethem's *Motherless Brooklyn*), or cybernetic enhancement (in George Effinger's *When Gravity Fails*).[7] Its effects may evoke ventriloquism, Tourette's syndrome, or the Tower of Babel. It can infect not only dialogue but also narration. Like the orang-utan's utterances in "Murders in the Rue Morgue," then, enigmatic discourse in postmodernist fiction raises profound questions about identity, intention and meaning. But whereas Poe's detective seems to dispense with such questions easily and definitively, they remain unresolved in novels by Pynchon, DeLillo and Auster, among others. Indeed, this contrast – between Dupin's confident linguistic analysis and the noisy, repetitive utterances that persist in later works – epitomizes the shift from the earlier stories' positivistic detection to the sense, in postmodernism, that all one can hope for in response to mystery is "an illusion of meaningfulness."[8]

Silence and noise

Postmodernist crime novels inevitably hark back to Hawthorne's and Melville's dark romances as well as Poe's self-reflexive tales of ratiocination. They also reflect the modern, pessimistic glamor of hard-boiled detective fiction: a distinctively American genre developed by Hammett and Chandler, among others, and further delineated by the stark shadows of film noir. They reveal the influence of international espionage fiction, too – including the adventures of secret agent James Bond – as well as non-fiction accounts of mayhem and murder, from true crime to such classics of new journalism as Truman Capote's *In Cold Blood* or Norman Mailer's *The Executioner's Song*.[9] They allude to history and to other art forms, as in Ishmael Reed's *Mumbo Jumbo*, which recounts an epidemic of exuberant Jes Grew music and dance that afflicts America in the 1920s, illustrated by drawings, photographs and documents.[10] They even incorporate science fiction. But American postmodernism is also shaped by the inverted mysteries of non-native writers such as Vladimir Nabokov – who wrote *Despair* and *The Real Life of Sebastian Knight* before coming to the United States, then left once *Lolita* took flight – and Borges, whose *Ficciones* (including "The Garden of Forking Paths" and "Death and the Compass") was not translated into English until 1962, after which it inspired a new kind of American literature.[11] Later, Umberto Eco's international bestseller *The Name of the Rose* made the metaphysical detective story an even more popular and influential genre, while reinforcing its relevance to poststructuralist literary theory and reader-response criticism.[12] *The Name of the Rose* reveals the influence of "The Murders in the Rue Morgue," in fact – among many other detective stories – by distinguishing between an oral discourse and a written text, describing odd nocturnal sounds, and musing upon the speech of one particular suspect: Salvatore, a monstrously deformed "creature," whose utterances, ignoring linguistic rules and combining elements from many tongues, evoke "the Babelish language of the first day after the divine chastisement, the language of primeval confusion."[13]

If these assorted predecessors and pretexts contributed to the rise of postmodernist crime fiction, then its first important American authors were Thomas Pynchon and Don DeLillo. Although their style and tone are different – and have become more so – Pynchon and DeLillo both draw on themes of conspiracy, paranoia and societal malaise, while deploying actual historical incidents so deftly that history itself becomes another crime story. Pynchon's most accessible and exemplary novel is *The Crying of Lot 49*, a parody of detective fiction that appeared over forty years ago. Although it embeds a series of purloined letters – from plagiarized texts to forged postage stamps – the actual mystery originates in a prank call. When Pynchon's detective, Oedipa Maas, discovers that an old boyfriend made her his executor before his death, she remembers that a year earlier

> at three or so in the morning there had come this long-distance call, from where she would never know (unless now he'd left a diary) by a voice beginning in heavy Slavic tones as second secretary at the Transylvanian Consulate, looking for an escaped bat; modulated to comic-Negro, then on into hostile Pachuco dialect, full of chingas and maricones; then a Gestapo officer asking her in shrieks did she have relatives in Germany and finally his Lamont Cranston voice ... "But Margo," earnestly, "I've just come from Commissioner Weston, and that old man in the fun house was murdered by the same blowgun that killed Professor Quackenbush," or something.[14]

These comic renditions of various characters, roles and ethnicities anticipate the manic digressions, outrageous puns, parodies, jokes and songs that decorate *The Crying of Lot 49*. Oedipa's ex concludes by impersonating Lamont Cranston, an alter ego of The Shadow – a superhero who began as narrator of a 1930 radio show, *The Detective Story Hour*, and eventually appeared in radio dramas, comics, pulp novels and movies, always accompanied by the signature tag, "Who knows what evil lurks in the hearts of men? The Shadow knows!" The allusion to Lamont Cranston introduces the novel's parody of positivist detection; indeed, Oedipa later chides herself for acting "like the private eye in any long-ago radio drama, believing all you needed was grit, resourcefulness, exemption from hidebound cops' rules, to solve any great mystery."[15]

When Oedipa's husband tells her to hang up, her old boyfriend offers to pay him "a little visit from The Shadow" and hangs up himself, after which "Silence, positive and thorough, fell."[16] The absence of sound following the prank call is significant, since the mystery in which Oedipa becomes enmeshed seems to involve a secret history of silenced alternative discourse – a theme that the novel emphasizes with images of muted horns, a character's tongue torn out in a Jacobean drama, a delegation of deaf-mutes, and even a mute button that Oedipa's husband, a disc jockey, presses when he smiles on air. Whether this secret history actually exists, however, remains unresolved: the novel ends immediately before "the crying of Lot 49," the auction of a part of the estate related to the conspiracy, for which there is a mysterious bidder. Since publishing *The Crying of Lot 49*, Pynchon has continued to probe instances of resistance, both real and imagined, in American history. His latest, longest and most ambitious novel, *Against the Day*, even includes hard-boiled detection – featuring private eye Lew Basnight – among the genres of popular twentieth-century fiction it ventriloquizes.[17]

DeLillo also criticizes contemporary American culture, portraying it as so anesthetized and vacuous that citizens may long for the catharsis provided by moments of violent crime or terrorist attack. This theme appears in many of his novels, including *Libra*, which recounts Kennedy's assassination; *Underworld*, whose protagonist is convicted of murder in his teens; and *Falling Man*, which describes a family's reaction to the destruction of the World Trade Center on September 11, 2001.[18] DeLillo's fiction also influenced novels such as Chang-rae Lee's *Native Speaker*, in which a Korean-American's work as an undercover intelligence agent underscores his alienation from American culture and estrangement from his American wife.[19]

DeLillo's ninth novel, *White Noise*, is more satirical and less concerned with actual history, but reveals the same theme as his other works. It follows a year in the life of Jack Gladney, a professor who specializes in Hitler studies – although, to his shame, he cannot speak German, that "fleshy, warped, spit-spraying, purplish and cruel" tongue – and who gradually confronts his fear of death.[20] "White noise" refers to a random signal of all frequencies in the audio spectrum, used to mask sounds, test loudspeakers or provide synthesizer input: "a dull and unlocatable roar," as Jack describes it.[21] Although

DeLillo's title implies a pun on how whiteness dominates American culture, it also suggests speech that is blank and essentially meaningless. Throughout the novel, Jack is confronted with such sounds: "the human buzz" in a shopping mall, snatches of words in foreign tongues, warnings over loud-speakers, entreaties from the television, a smoke alarm that goes off "either to let us know the battery had just died or because the house was on fire."[22] On one occasion, his youngest son cries for almost seven hours without stopping, a "large," "pure," "wailing noise" that Jack finds "strangely soothing."[23] These sounds generally seem to indicate a kind of anonymous, amorphous, even unconscious collective panic. Jack shows his students footage of crowds in Nazi Germany, for example, uttering "chants, songs, arias, speeches, cries, cheers, accusations, shrieks."[24] Such noises also provide a soundtrack for violence throughout the novel: "insistent pressuring voices" that a sniper hears on TV, telling him to go down in history; "terrible and inarticulate sounds" from passengers on a plane that nearly crashes; an "amplified voice" made inaudible by distortion from a moving loudspeaker that orders Jack's family to evacuate because of a cloud of poisonous chemicals; and, finally, "sonic waves layering through the room" when Jack shoots someone, thinking that he has killed him, before the other man shoots him, too.[25] Both men survive, and Jack escapes punishment or even acknowledgment of his crime. Because of his exposure to the chemical cloud, however, he knows that he will die soon. And by the novel's end, he and his wife both imagine death, the ultimate experience of violence, as endless sound: "Electrical noise," "Sound all around," "Uniform, white."[26]

Sacred and profane

If the mystery in Pynchon's *Crying of Lot 49* begins with a prank call, then in Paul Auster's *City of Glass*, as the first sentence explains, "It was a wrong number that started it, the telephone ringing three times in the dead of night, and the voice on the other end asking for someone he was not."[27] Quinn, Auster's protagonist, is not a professional detective, although he pens mystery novels – featuring a "private-eye narrator" who "solved an elaborate series of crimes" and "suffered through a number of beatings and narrow escapes" – under the name "William Wilson."[28] When Quinn picks up the telephone receiver, he hears, "as if from a great distance, ... the sound of a voice unlike any he had ever heard. It was at once mechanical and filled with feeling, hardly more than a whisper and yet perfectly audible, and so even in tone that he was unable to tell if it belonged to a man or a woman."[29] The voice asks for Paul Auster, of the Auster Detective Agency, and Quinn explains that it must be a wrong number. The next night, the phone rings at midnight again, then hangs up. On the third night Quinn answers the phone, identifies himself as Auster, and agrees to meet a client the next day.

The client turns out to be Peter Stillman, a pale young man whose wife is his speech therapist and whose conversation is as odd as his voice: "This is what is called speaking. I believe that is the term. When words come out, fly into the air, live for a moment, and die. Strange, is it not? I myself have no opinion. No and no again. But still, there are words you will need to have."[30] Peter embarks on a soliloquy – comprising disjointed fragments, repeated phrases, assorted names for himself, and neologisms like "Wimble click crumblechaw beloo" – that lasts for nine pages, forcing readers to figure out his manner of speaking. The story that he tells explains both his strange speech and his need for Quinn's help. Peter's father, a religion professor at Columbia, locked him in a dark room for nine years, with no human contact except physical punishment if he spoke aloud, so that he might know God's language; now, years later, his father is being released from an institution for the criminally insane and Peter is afraid for his life. The mystery, then, concerns the nature of language, especially as a way to comprehend humanity's position in the world. It follows from Poe's "Murders in the Rue Morgue" and later metaphysical detective stories, such as Borges' "Death and the Compass" and Eco's *Name of the Rose*, that link earthly crime with attempts to pronounce God's name or speak God's language. Quinn tries to unravel this mystery by reading the father's scholarship, which argues that a new Tower of Babel will enable humanity to reverse the biblical Fall; by following the father through New York, along an itinerary that spells out "OWEROFBAB"; and by disguising himself as other people, including Peter, in order to talk with the father – but he begins to doubt his own perceptions and assumptions.

After Peter's father disappears and Quinn, becoming desperate, seeks advice from "Paul Auster" himself, he finds that he can no longer reach the Stillmans by telephone. There is always a busy signal, which becomes "a counterpoint to his steps, a metronome beating inside the random noises of the city. There was comfort in the thought that whenever he dialed the number, the sound would be there for him, never swerving in its denial, negating speech and the possibility of speech."[31] In a sense, Quinn experiences the kind of reversal that Peter's father sought. Unable to reach Peter, resolve the case, or return to his old life, he stakes out the Stillmans' apartment building in a vigil that lasts for weeks. After he discovers that Peter's father has committed suicide, the Stillmans' check for his retainer has bounced, and their telephone is disconnected, Quinn retreats to the Stillmans' empty apartment. There he experiences something akin to Peter's childhood trauma: lying alone in a dark room, eating food left by someone else, and recording words in a red notebook. Eventually, realizing that there are few pages left, Quinn wonders "if he could learn to speak instead, filling the darkness with his voice, speaking the words into the air," and then he disappears, too – leaving behind the notebook which is the source, the narrator explains, of the story we have read.[32] Peter, Quinn, and the red notebook do reappear, however, in different forms, in the other two novellas that comprise Auster's *New York Trilogy*.

Jack O'Connell's first novel, *Box Nine*, not only alludes to *The Maltese Falcon* and various tales by Poe, Borges and Cortazar, but also, like *City of Glass*, describes speech that raises metaphysical questions about language itself. The novel traces the parallel investigations of orphaned twins, who share a duplex but maintain separate lives in the imaginary New England city of Quinsigamond: Ike, a mild-mannered postman haunted by suspiciously damp, misshapen packages addressed to a post office box that no one owns; and Lenore, an intense undercover cop facing crimes associated with a new psychedelic street drug, including murders in which the victims' tongues are missing. Lenore learns about the drug at a meeting with the mayor, the police chief, and Dr. Frederick Woo, a linguistics professor who speaks six languages and is aiming for eight. Woo is identified by his distinctive speech: he "prepares to speak by making his hand into a fist, bringing it up in front of his mouth, and forcing himself to cough a few times," prompting Lenore to think that "he'll speak too softly and be a boring pain in the ass," but he turns out to have "a beautiful speaking voice, low, distinct, strong but rich with hints of emotion and emphasis."[33] The topic of Woo's discourse, in fact, is the drug's effect on areas of the brain involving speech and the comprehension of language. Woo plays a recording of an experiment in which a prisoner is fed Lingo, as the drug is called, and asked to read aloud a biblical account of the apostles speaking in tongues on Pentecost.[34] As it takes effect, the prisoner reads faster and faster until his "voice turns into something like the sound of a common summer insect recorded at a loud volume with a sensitive microphone."[35] Woo explains that Lingo not only enhances linguistic communication to a remarkable extent but also produces sexual arousal, paranoia and homicidal rage.

Box Nine develops those connections among language and other aspects of human behavior with scenes of eavesdropping, dictation, wiretapping, radio broadcasting, and even a recording of the word "dominance," uttered in different languages, that plays when Lenore and Woo make love. *Box Nine* also muses on the religious connotations of speaking in tongues: the novel's first words are "Talk to God," part of a talk radio host's rant, and the drug's producer is known only as "the Paraclete," or Holy Spirit.[36] Meanwhile, Lingo spreads through Quinsigamond, from the post office, where Ike's co-workers sample the drug, to a street corner, where a prostitute climbs up a telephone pole, "forming words faster than her tongue, lips, full mouth can handle," "until the bottom half of her face is a sickening, surreal blur," to downtown, where everywhere Ike looks he sees "someone's head and body in a jerking, spastic dance. And everywhere, hovering above him, is the noise. The buzzing. The clicking."[37] Like Quinn, Lenore becomes dangerously involved in the case under investigation, trying Lingo herself and falling in love with Woo – until the two storylines converge and she discovers, over a hidden microphone, the Paraclete's identity. Although she solves the Lingo case, acknowledges her own complicity, and reconnects with her twin, she is not unscathed: O'Connell's next novel, *Wireless*, reveals that she has been committed to a psychiatric institution. Throughout his Quinsigamond series, O'Connell blends bizarre crimes with meditations on cognition and consciousness. *Box Nine*, in particular, contributes to the development of postmodernist crime fiction by forging a link between investigations of divine language in earlier metaphysical detective stories, and cyberpunk's fantasies of neurological or cybernetic enhancement.

Auster's and O'Connell's detectives both find that their criminal investigations affect their ability to represent themselves in speech. Quinn becomes as silent and isolated as Peter Stillman; Lenore, after taking Lingo, hears her own speech "become slightly garbled, like she's enunciating too much, ... all harsh, chopping sounds," and in the last scene she cannot speak at all because her mouth is cut, swollen and stitched up.[38] In this sense, Quinn and Lenore lead to the narrator of Lethem's *Motherless Brooklyn*. As an orphan, Lionel Essrog was taken in and trained by Frank, a mobster who ran a shady limousine service and detective agency; Frank is killed, and Lionel sets out to solve his murder. The investigation is hindered, however, by Lionel's innocence, his inexperience and his neurological condition. He introduces himself, in the first paragraph, as

> a carnival barker, an auctioneer, a downtown performance artist, a speaker in tongues, a senator drunk on filibuster. *I've got Tourette's.* My mouth won't quit, though mostly I whisper or subvocalize like I'm reading aloud, my Adam's apple bobbing, jaw muscle beating like a miniature heart under my cheek.[39]

As this sentence shows, Lionel's condition gives his narration an associative and manic quality. The obsessive, pattern-seeking aspects of Tourette's syndrome seem ideal for a literary detective, although Lionel's stuttering, rhyming, cursing and other tics make it hard for him to work undercover or interrogate suspects. When confronting Frank's killer, for example, he can only mumble "Apocamouse ... Unplan-a-canal. Unpluggaphone."[40] Nevertheless, Lionel avenges Frank's death, takes over the detective agency, and comes to terms with his condition. *Motherless Brooklyn* does not link incoherent speech with crime – as *City of Glass* and *Box Nine* do – but with the detective's identity and methodology. At one point, Lionel remarks that he has "meta-Tourette's. Thinking about ticcing, my mind racing, thoughts reaching to touch every possible symptom. Touching touching. Counting counting. Thinking thinking. Mentioning mentioning Tourette's. It's sort of like talking about telephones over the telephone."[41] Such self-reflexivity makes *Motherless Brooklyn* another postmodernist novel that investigates speech itself.

Identity theft

Some postmodernist writers display gaudier patter in another sense, too. Like the cheap crook that Spade mocks in *The Maltese Falcon*, they imitate the tough, sardonic, glamorous style of their elders. Such authors are drawn to the gritty setting, corrupt atmosphere, world-weary stance and existential philosophy of hard-boiled detection; as Fredric Jameson suggests, nostalgia for a stylized but seemingly authentic earlier world – Chandler's world, in particular – makes imitation almost inevitable.[42] They are especially fascinated by the private eye's distinctive voice, with its wisecracks, underworld slang, and fresh, irreverent similes. Many postmodernist fictions impersonate that seductive voice, from William Hjortsberg's *Falling Angel* to Stephen King's *Umney's Last Case*.[43] Part of the pleasure of such impersonation, as in other forms of parody, is transforming the original by putting it in a new context. Consider Michael Chabon's *The Yiddish Policemen's Union*, which places "a Yiddish translation of Chandler" among a character's books while recounting, in the style of Hammett, Chandler and Macdonald, a mystery set in an imaginary Jewish settlement that was established in Alaska in 1941.[44] Chabon's novel is itself a Yiddish translation of the hard-boiled school – as well as an instance of alternate history, a science-fiction subgenre.

One of postmodernism's most intriguing aspects, in fact, is the influence of writers such as Chandler on cyberpunk and other subgenres of science fiction encapsulated by Paul Sammon's term "future noir."[45] That influence began with *Blade Runner*, a quintessentially postmodernist film featuring a jaded private eye in a grimy urban future.[46] A few years later, Gibson's novel *Neuromancer* helped to establish cyberpunk, a subgenre in which a solitary hacker or renegade – often wielding first-person narration that echoes Chandler's, or rather Marlowe's, voice – uncovers social corruption and corporate crime in some future dystopia. Lethem's *Gun with Occasional Music* is a recent example. Narrated by a "private inquisitor," and set in a near future when animals, thanks to evolution therapy, can talk and walk upright, it opens with an epigraph from Chandler's *Playback* in which Marlowe calls someone "as easy to spot as a kangaroo in a dinner jacket."[47]

Speaking with another's voice – due to literary parody, identity theft, or cybernetic modification – is also exemplified by *When Gravity Fails*, the first novel of George Effinger's Budayeen series, set in the Arab ghetto of an unnamed North African city. The novel begins with an epigraph from Chandler's "The Simple Art of Murder," praising Hammett's fictional detective as "the best man in his world and a good enough man for any world,"[48] and features a protagonist who not only meets that definition but reads Simenon, Fleming and Stout in his spare time. In the opening pages, private eye Marid Audran, waiting for his client in a bar, hears someone say, "My name is Bond ... *James* Bond."[49] Moments later, Bond shoots up the bar, killing Audran's client. He is not actually Bond, of course, but someone who thinks he is Fleming's character. In this world, people can temporarily alter their consciousness with "moddies," plug-in personality modules that "make you believe ... you are someone else," and they can gain "instant knowledge of any subject" with "daddies," or add-on software – but Audran himself disdains such neurological wiring.[50] Realizing that the killer transformed himself into Bond not for amusement, but to kill more efficiently, Audran pursues him by drawing on his own knowledge of Fleming's old-fashioned novels. Near one murder scene, for example, Audran finds cigarette butts encircled with three gold bands: "In the James Bond books, he smoked cigarettes made up specially for him of some particular mixture of tobaccos, and his blend was marked with the three gold bands. The assassin took his job seriously; he used a small-caliber pistol, probably a Walther PPK, like Bond's."[51] On another occasion, Audran overhears him ordering a drink: "Vodka martini, dry. Pre-war Wolfschmidt's if you've got it, shaken and not stirred. With a twist of lemon peel."[52]

As the plot thickens and corpses proliferate, the godfather of the Budayeen's underworld forces Audran to undergo neurological surgery, along with extra implants for moddies and a special set of add-ons, so that he can better confront the serial killer. Afterwards, Audran tries to improve his investigative ability by plugging in a moddy for Stout's hero, Nero Wolfe – "a detective out of some old books" – and persuades a friend to modify *his* personality to that of Wolfe's sidekick, Archie Goodwin.[53] With the moddy inserted, Audran's hard-boiled first-person narration even shifts to a formal third-person voice, reflecting his adoption of Wolfe's personality. Audran eventually eliminates Bond, but never determines his real identity; according to a police lieutenant with whom Audran enjoys the usual rivalry, he was a double agent whom the lieutenant himself had hired, sight unseen, to prevent a political assassination. Although Audran solves the case, he ends up alone and miserable: his friends and lover abandon him because he cooperated with the police and they do not want to acknowledge "the danger they'd been in, the danger they might be in again someday." In a passage that echoes Chandler's "Simple Art of Murder," Audran muses: "They wanted to pretend that the world was nice and healthy and worked according to a few simple rules that somebody had written down somewhere ... I was now a constant reminder that there *were* no rules."[54] Chandler's praise for a self-reliant hero seems especially poignant in Effinger's dystopia, where bodies, genders and identities are malleable and you can make anyone's voice your own.

Electronic Voice Phenomena

In the twenty-first century, crime in postmodernist novels includes not only homicide, assassination and serial murder but also terrorism, especially after September 11, 2001. Gibson's latest novel, *Pattern Recognition*, extends themes of paranoia and conspiracy from earlier works – such as Pynchon's and DeLillo's novels – to a world dominated by globalization, viral marketing, electronic communication and terrorist threats. While Pynchon's detective is a housewife returning "from a Tupperware party,"[55] Gibson's protagonist is a "coolhunter," able to identify fashions, trends or marketing campaigns that will be particularly successful. Cayce Pollard's talent is also a curse, however, because she is allergic to certain advertising logos, like the Michelin Man, and can control phobic reactions to them only by the "verbal tic" of repeating a particular sentence.[56]

Since her father's disappearance on September 11, Cayce has followed "the footage": enigmatic snippets of exquisite moviemaking that are released anonymously on to the internet and discussed by fans, including Cayce, on an electronic discussion board. Now a company, seeking to profit from the footage's popularity, has hired her to track down the artist. Cayce eventually finds her – an unknown Russian film-maker who stopped speaking when a bomb killed her parents, leaving a fragment embedded in her brain. To locate her, however, Cayce travels from New York to London to Tokyo to Moscow. She also navigates a global culture – reminiscent of DeLillo's *White Noise* – in which people rarely speak face to face but rely on electronic, digital, cellular and long-distance communication. Such disembodied exchanges affect their relationships with each other. Cayce notices, for example, how different someone you know through email "sounds" on a telephone.[57] She dreams of being mute, unable "to break this thing that so painfully shackles speech."[58] In another instance, an online friend, whom Cayce has never met, reads something posted by a stranger who knows how to identify the footage's digital watermark. Cayce's friend – a self-proclaimed middle-aged white guy – constructs an online persona as a Japanese schoolgirl in order to coax this stranger, through email correspondence, to determine where the footage was uploaded. And another friend, paid to promote products by praising them in conversation with strangers, finds that such viral marketing affects her social relationships: "I'll be out on my own with friends, say, not working, and I'll meet someone, and we'll be talking, and they'll mention something . . . And something in me stops."[59]

The novel's treatment of odd, ambiguous, indirect speech extends to Cayce's relationship with her parents. She never opens her mother's email because her mother, a believer in Electronic Voice Phenomena, claims that blank or unused audiotapes contain "the voices of the dead" – including her husband, assumed dead since his disappearance – and reports her findings in email. (Cayce's father attributed his wife's belief in EVP to apophenia, "the spontaneous perception of connections and meaningfulness in unrelated things.")[60] Cayce opens one email by accident, however, and learns that her mother now thinks his messages are warnings to Cayce. Remembering "the banal, inchoate, utterly baffling nature of the supposed messages" her mother has reported in the past, Cayce refuses to listen to the attached recordings.[61] And yet, even if she imagines it, her father's warnings seem to persist in more direct form. When someone poisons Cayce in a bar,

> from some deep and hidden eddy in the river of Sinatra's voice emerges a strange bright cartoonlike whirling snarl of sound, which executes the sonic equivalent of a back flip and becomes, as though compressed for transmission over unimaginable distances, her father's voice. "She's drugged the water. Scream." Which she does.[62]

And when Cayce escapes from a Russian sanatorium to wander, near death, in Siberia, she remains conscious by conversing with her father until he tells her to "Listen," and she hears the drone of the helicopter that rescues her.[63]

Ultimately, Cayce not only finds the orphaned artist behind the footage but learns her father's fate on September 11, as detective-story plot and mourning process conclude in a satisfying ending. *Pattern Recognition* also confirms the significance of excessive, incoherent speech in postmodernist fiction, where such gaudy patter takes various forms: allusions to prelapsarian language, the Tower of Babel and Pentecost; talking animals; painfully artificial soliloquies, drug-induced frenzies and a case of Tourette's; prank calls, wrong numbers, busy signals, disconnections; sirens, radios, loudspeakers and other equipment; emissions from outer space or beyond the grave; and the impersonation of other voices, including The Shadow, Philip Marlowe, James Bond and Nero Wolfe. Crime in postmodernist fiction, as a fictional talk show host remarks, is "beyond words."[64]

NOTES

1. Dashiell Hammett, *The Maltese Falcon* (1930; repr. New York: Vintage, 1990), p. 120.
2. For an overview of postmodernist fiction and its appropriation of other narrative forms, see Brian McHale, *Postmodernist Fiction* (New York: Methuen, 1987), and Linda Hutcheon, *A Poetics of Postmodernism: History, Theory, Fiction* (London: Routledge, 1988).
3. For definitions of these terms, see Patricia Merivale and Susan Elizabeth Sweeney, "The Game's Afoot: On the Trail of the Metaphysical Detective Story," in *Detecting Texts: The Metaphysical Detective Story from Poe to Postmodernism*, ed. Merivale and Sweeney (Philadelphia, PA: University of Pennsylvania Press, 1999), pp. 2–4.
4. William Hjortsberg, *Falling Angel* (New York: Harcourt, 1978); *Memento*, directed by Christopher Nolan (Columbia Tri-Star, 2000).
5. Edgar Allan Poe, "The Murders in the Rue Morgue" (1841), in *Edgar Allan Poe: Poetry, Tales, & Selected Essays*, ed. Patrick F. Quinn and G. R. Thompson (New York: Library of America, 1996), pp. 397–431.
6. See Michael Chabon, *The Final Solution* (New York: HarperCollins, 2004); Don DeLillo, *White Noise* (1985; repr. New York: Penguin, 1986) and *Ratner's Star* (1976; repr. New York: Vintage, 1992); and Thomas Pynchon, *Gravity's Rainbow* (1973; repr. New York: Penguin, 1995).
7. See Jack O'Connell, *Box Nine* (1992; repr. New York: No Exit Press, 2000); Jonathan Lethem, *Motherless Brooklyn* (New York: Vintage, 1999); and George Alec Effinger, *When Gravity Fails* (1986; repr. New York: Tom Doherty Associates, 2005).
8. William Gibson, *Pattern Recognition* (2003; repr. New York: Berkeley Books, 2005), p. 118.
9. Truman Capote, *In Cold Blood* (1965; repr. New York: Vintage, 1994); Norman Mailer, *The Executioner's Song* (1979; repr. New York: Vintage, 1998).
10. Ishmael Reed, *Mumbo Jumbo* (1972; repr. New York: Scribner, 1996).
11. See Vladimir Nabokov, *Despair* (1934), trans. Nabokov (1966; repr. New York: Vintage, 1989), *The Real Life of Sebastian Knight* (Meriden, CT: New Directions, 1941), and *Lolita* (1955; repr. New York: Vintage, 1989); and Jorge Luis Borges, "The Garden of Forking Paths" (1941), trans. Helen Temple and Ruthven Todd, and "Death and the Compass" (1942), trans. Anthony Kerrigan, in *Ficciones*, ed. Kerrigan (New York: Grove Press, 1962), pp. 89–101, 129–41. On Borges' influence, see John Barth, "The Literature of Exhaustion," *Atlantic Monthly* (August 1967): 29–34.
12. In *The Sign of Three: Dupin, Holmes, Pierce*, ed. Umberto Eco and Thomas A. Sebeok (Bloomington, IN: Indiana University Press, 1988), and Umberto Eco, *The Role of the Reader: Explorations in the Semiotics of Texts* (Bloomington, IN: Indiana University Press, 1979), Eco analyzes epistemological or narratological aspects of tales by Poe and Fleming, among others.
13. Umberto Eco, *The Name of the Rose* (1980), trans. William Weaver (New York: Warner, 1984), pp. 46, 48. Although not the murderer, Salvatore is arrested and tortured until his speech becomes "more Babelish than ever" and he regresses "to the state of a baboon" (p. 451).

14. Pynchon, *The Crying of Lot 49* (1965; repr. New York: Harper & Row, 1986), p. 11.
15. *Ibid.*, p. 124.
16. *Ibid.*, p. 11.
17. Pynchon, *Against the Day* (New York: Penguin, 2006).
18. Don DeLillo, *Libra* (1988; repr. New York: Penguin, 1991), *Underworld* (1997; repr. New York: Scribner's, 1998), and *Falling Man* (2007; repr. New York: Scribner's, 2008).
19. Chang-rae Lee, *Native Speaker* (New York: Penguin, 1995). As the title suggests, this novel also addresses tropes of linguistic understanding, but space limitations make it impossible to discuss it more fully.
20. DeLillo, *White Noise*, p. 31.
21. *Ibid.*, p. 36.
22. *Ibid.*, pp. 84, 8.
23. *Ibid.*, p. 78.
24. *Ibid.*, p. 26.
25. *Ibid.*, pp. 45, 92, 118, 312.
26. *Ibid.*, p. 198.
27. Paul Auster, *City of Glass* (1985), in *The New York Trilogy* (New York: Penguin, 1990), p. 3.
28. *Ibid.*, p. 6.
29. *Ibid.*, p. 7.
30. *Ibid.*, p. 19.
31. *Ibid.*, pp. 126–7.
32. *Ibid.*, pp. 156–7.
33. O'Connell, *Box Nine*, p. 38.
34. Acts 2.1–4.
35. O'Connell, *Box Nine*, p. 43.
36. *Ibid.*, p. 3.
37. *Ibid.*, pp. 132, 137, 262.
38. *Ibid.*, p. 271.
39. Lethem, *Motherless Brooklyn*, p. 1.
40. *Ibid.*, p. 204.
41. *Ibid.*, p. 192.
42. Fredric Jameson, "On Raymond Chandler," *Southern Review*, 6.3 (1970): 624–50.
43. William Hjortsberg, *Falling Angel* (New York: Harcourt, 1978); Stephen King, *Umney's Last Case* (1993; repr. New York: Penguin, 1995).
44. Michael Chabon, *The Yiddish Policemen's Union* (New York: HarperCollins, 2007), p. 305.
45. Paul Sammon, *Future Noir: The Making of* Blade Runner (New York: HarperCollins, 1996).
46. *Blade Runner*, directed by Ridley Scott (Warner Brothers, 1982).
47. Jonathan Lethem, *Gun with Occasional Music* (1994; repr. New York: Harcourt, 2003).
48. Raymond Chandler, "The Simple Art of Murder," *Atlantic Monthly* (December 1944): 53–9.
49. Effinger, *When Gravity Fails*, p. 12.
50. *Ibid.*, p. 171.
51. *Ibid.*, p. 96.

52. *Ibid.*, p. 144.
53. *Ibid.*, p. 196.
54. *Ibid.*, p. 283.
55. Pynchon, *The Crying of Lot 49*, p. 9.
56. Gibson, *Pattern Recognition*, p. 35.
57. *Ibid.*, pp. 148–9.
58. *Ibid.*, p. 121.
59. *Ibid.*, p. 87.
60. *Ibid.*, p. 117.
61. *Ibid.*, p. 192.
62. *Ibid.*, p. 326.
63. *Ibid.*, p. 335.
64. O'Connell, *Box Nine*, p. 326.

GUIDE TO READING

General

Cawelti, John. *Adventure, Mystery, and Romance*. University of Chicago Press, 1976.
  Mystery, Violence, and Popular Culture. Madison, WI: Popular Press 3, 2004.
Halttunen, Karen. *Murder Most Foul: The Killer and the American Gothic Imagination*. Cambridge, MA: Harvard University Press, 1998.
Haycraft, Howard. *Murder for Pleasure: The Life and Times of the Detective Story*. New York: Appleton-Century, 1941.
Klein, Kathleen Gregory (ed.). *Great Women Mystery Writers*. Westport, CT: Greenwood Press, 1994.
Knight, Stephen. *Form and Ideology in Crime Fiction*. Bloomington, IN: Indiana University Press, 1980.
Landrum, Larry. *American Mystery and Detective Novels: A Reference Guide*. Westport, CT: Greenwood Press, 1999.
Lehman, David. *The Perfect Murder*. New York: Macmillan, 1989.
Messent, Peter (ed.). *Criminal Proceedings: The Contemporary American Crime Novel*. London: Pluto Press, 1997.
Most, Glenn and William Stowe (eds.). *The Poetics of Murder: Detective Fiction and Literary Theory*. New York: Harcourt Brace Jovanovich, 1983.
Panek, LeRoy Lad. *The Origins of the American Detective Story*. Jefferson, NC: McFarland, 2006.
Porter, Dennis. *The Pursuit of Crime: Art and Ideology in Detective Fiction*. New Haven, CT: Yale University Press, 1981.
Scaggs, John. *Crime Fiction*. New York: Routledge, 2005.
Winks, Robin (ed.). *Detective Fiction: A Collection of Critical Essays*. Englewood Cliffs, NJ: Prentice-Hall, 1980.
  and Maureen Corrigan (eds.). *Mystery and Suspense Writers*, 2 vols. New York: Charles Scribner's Sons, 1998.

Early American crime writing

Cohen, Daniel. *Pillars of Salt, Monuments of Grace: New England Crime Literature and the Origins of American Popular Culture, 1674–1860*. New York: Oxford University Press, 1993.

Faller, Lincoln. *Turned to Account: The Forms and Functions of Criminal Biography in Late Seventeenth- and Early Eighteenth-Century England.* Cambridge University Press, 1987.

Reynolds, David. *Beneath the American Renaissance: The Subversive Imagination in the Age of Emerson and Melville.* Cambridge, MA: Harvard University Press, 1988.

Williams, Daniel. *Pillars of Salt: An Anthology of Early American Criminal Narratives.* Madison, WI: Madison House, 1993.

Poe and the origins of detective fiction

Hayes, Kevin (ed.). *The Cambridge Companion to Edgar Allan Poe.* Cambridge University Press, 2002.

Hoffman, Daniel. *Poe, Poe, Poe, Poe, Poe, Poe, Poe.* Baton Rouge, LA: Louisiana State University Press, 1998.

Irwin, John. *The Mystery to a Solution: Poe, Borges, and the Analytic Detective Story.* Baltimore, MD: Johns Hopkins University Press, 1994.

Peeples, Scott. *The Afterlife of Edgar Allan Poe.* Rochester, NY: Camden House, 2007.

Rosenheim, Shawn and Stephen Rachman (eds.). *The American Face of Edgar Allan Poe.* Baltimore, MD: Johns Hopkins University Press, 1995.

Women writers before 1960

Gilbert, Sandra and Susan Gubar. *The Madwoman in the Attic: The Woman Writer and the Nineteenth-Century Literary Imagination.* New Haven, CT: Yale University Press, 1979.

Goddu, Theresa. *Gothic America: Narrative, History and Nation.* New York: Columbia University Press, 1997.

Nickerson, Catherine Ross. *The Web of Iniquity: Early Detective Fiction by American Women.* Durham, NC: Duke University Press, 1998.

Slung, Michele (ed.). *Crime on Her Mind: Fifteen Stories of Female Sleuths from the Victorian Era to the Forties.* New York: Random House, 1975.

The hard-boiled novel

Breu, Christopher. *Hard-Boiled Masculinities.* Minneapolis, MN: University of Minnesota Press, 2005.

Cassuto, Leonard. *Hard-Boiled Sentimentality: The Secret History of American Crime Stories.* New York: Columbia University Press, 2008.

McCann, Sean. *Gumshoe America: Hardboiled Crime Fiction, and the Rise and Fall of New Deal Liberalism.* Durham, NC: Duke University Press, 2000.

O'Brien, Geoffrey. *Hardboiled America: Lurid Paperbacks and the Masters of Noir.* New York: Da Capo Press, 1997.

The American roman noir

Cochran, David. *American Noir: Underground Writers and Filmmakers of the Postwar Era.* Washington, DC: Smithsonian Institution Press, 1994.

Horsley, Lee. *The Noir Thriller.* Basingstoke: Palgrave Macmillan, 2001.

Marling, William. *The American Roman Noir: Hammett, Cain and Chandler*. Athens, GA: University of Georgia Press, 1995.

Polito, Robert (ed.). *Crime Novels: American Noir of the 1930s and 40s*. New York: Library of America, 1997.

(ed.). *Crime Novels: American Noir of the 1950s*. New York: Library of America, 1997.

Teenage detectives and teenage delinquents

Austin, Joe and Michael Nevin Willard. *Generations of Youth: Youth Cultures and History in Twentieth-Century America*. New York University Press, 1999.

Gilbert, James. *A Cycle of Outrage: America's Reaction to the Juvenile Delinquent in the 1950s*. New York: Oxford University Press, 1986.

Hine, Thomas. *The Rise and Fall of the American Teenager*. New York: Avon Books, 1999.

Nash, Ilana. *American Sweethearts: Teenage Girls in Twentieth-Century Popular Culture*. Bloomington, IN: Indiana University Press, 2006.

Rollin, Lucy. *Twentieth-Century Teen Culture by the Decades: A Reference Guide*. Westport, CT: Greenwood Press, 1999.

Schrum, Kelly. *Some Wore Bobby Sox: The Emergence of Teenage Girls' Culture, 1920–1945*. New York: Palgrave Macmillan, 2004.

American spy fiction

Britton, Wesley. *Beyond Bond: Spies in Fiction and Film*. Westport, CT: Praeger, 2005.

Furst, Alan (ed.). *The Book of Spies: An Anthology of Literary Espionage*. New York: Modern Library, 2004.

Hepburn, Allan. *Intrigue: Espionage and Culture*. New Haven, CT: Yale University Press, 2005.

Jeffreys-Jones, Rhodri and Andrew Lownie (eds.). *North American Spies: New Revisionist Essays*. Edinburgh University Press, 1991.

Wires, Richard. *John P. Marquand and Mr Moto: Spy Adventures and Detective Films*. Muncie, IN: Ball State University, 1990.

The police procedural in literature and on television

Hartsfield, Larry K. *The American Response to Professional Crime, 1870–1917*. Westport, CT: Greenwood Press, 1985.

Lovell, Jarret S. *Good Cop/Bad Cop: Mass Media and the Cycle of Police Reform*. Monsey, NY: Willow Tree Press, 2003.

Oggersby, Bill and Anna Gough-Yates (eds.). *Action TV: Tough Guys, Smooth Operators and Foxy Chicks*. London and New York: Routledge, 2001.

Wilson, Christopher P. *Cop Knowledge: Police Power and Cultural Narrative in Twentieth-Century America*. University of Chicago Press, 2000.

Mafia stories and the American gangster

Gardaphe, Fred. *From Wiseguys to Wise Men: The Gangster and Italian American Masculinities*. New York: Routledge, 2006.

Lavery, David. *Reading the Sopranos: Hit TV from HBO*. London: I. B. Tauris, 2006.

Messenger, Christian K. *The Godfather and American Culture: How the Corleones Became "Our Gang."* Albany, NY: State University of New York Press, 2002.

Munby, Jonathan. *Public Enemies, Public Heroes: Screening the Gangster from Little Caesar to Touch of Evil*. University of Chicago Press, 1999.

Pickering-Iazzi, Robin (trans.). *Mafia and Outlaw Stories from Italian Life and Literature*. University of Toronto Press, 2007.

True crime

Browder, Laura. "Dystopian Romance: True Crime and the Female Reader," *Journal of Popular Culture*, 39.6 (2006): 928–53.

Lambert, Alix. *Crime: A Series of Extraordinary Interviews Exposing the World of Crime – Real and Imagined*. London: Fuel/Thames & Hudson, 2008.

Schmid, David. *Natural Born Celebrities: Serial Killers in American Culture*. University of Chicago Press, 2006.

Seltzer, Mark. *True Crime: Observations on Violence and Modernity*. New York: Routledge, 2006.

Race and American crime fiction

Bailey, Frankie Y. *Out of the Woodpile: Black Characters in Crime and Detective Fiction*. Westport, CT: Greenwood Press, 1991.

Gosselin, Adrienne Johnson (ed.). *Multicultural Detective Fiction: Murder from the "Other" Side*. New York: Garland, 1999.

Knight, Stephen. *Crime Fiction 1800–2000: Detection, Death, Diversity*. Basingstoke: Palgrave Macmillan, 2004.

Reddy, Maureen T. *Traces, Codes, and Clues: Reading Race in Crime Fiction*. New Brunswick, NJ: Rutgers University Press, 2003.

Van DeBurg, William L. *Black Hoodlums: Black Villains and Social Bandits in American Life*. University of Chicago Press, 2004.

Feminist crime fiction

Clues: A Journal of Detection, 25.2 (Winter 2007). Theme issue: Sara Paretsky.

Cranny-Francis, Anne. *Feminist Fiction*. Cambridge, UK: Polity Press, 1990.

Klein, Kathleen Gregory. *The Woman Detective: Gender and Genre*. Chicago: University of Illinois Press, 1988.

Munt, Sally R. *Murder by the Book?: Feminism and the Crime Novel*. London: Routledge, 1994.

Pepper, Andrew. *The Contemporary American Crime Novel: Race, Ethnicity, Gender, Class*. Edinburgh University Press, 2000.

Reddy, Maureen T. *Sisters in Crime: Feminism and the Crime Novel*. New York: Continuum, 1988.

Crime in postmodernist fiction

Matzke, Christine, and Susanne Muehleisen (eds.). *Postcolonial Postmortems: Crime Fiction from a Transcultural Perspective*. Amsterdam and New York: Rodopi, 2006.

Merivale, Patricia and Susan Elizabeth Sweeney (eds.). *Detecting Texts: The Metaphysical Detective Story from Poe to Postmodernism*. Philadelphia, PA: University of Pennsylvania Press, 1999.

Tani, Stefano. *The Doomed Detective: The Contribution of the Detective Novel to Postmodern American and Italian Fiction*. Carbondale, IL: Southern Illinois University Press, 1984.

Thompson, Jon. *Fiction, Crime, and Empire: Clues to Modernity and Postmodernism*. Urbana, IL: University of Illinois Press, 1993.

Walker, Ronald G. and June M. Frazer (eds.). *The Cunning Craft: Original Essays on Detective Fiction and Contemporary Literary Theory*. Macomb, IL: Western Illinois University Press, 1990.

INDEX

Cambridge Companions to ...

AUTHORS

TOPICS

3 1170 00898 8770